The Best of Walter A. Maier

The Best of Walter A. Maier

Paul L. Maier

Publishing House
St. Louis

Library of Congress Cataloging in Publication Data

Maier, Walter Arthur, 1893-1950.
    The best of Walter A. Maier.

        1. Theology—Collected works—20th century.
    2. Lutheran Church—Collected works.   I. Maier,
    Paul L.   II. Title.
    BR50.M224   1981   230'.41322   80-23684
    ISBN 0-570-03823-5

For
HARRIET SCHWENK KLÜVER
and
EUGENE R. BERTERMANN
who helped W.A.M.
so admirably

CONTENTS

WITH VOICE AND PEN

By the time he died in 1950, Dr. Walter A. Maier had preached to more people than anyone in history. As founding speaker of *The Lutheran Hour,* he was also the first person ever to be heard around the world on a regular basis, the first to address some 20,000,000 listeners each week, and the first to receive nearly a half million letters each year from 120 nations and territories.

His place in American church history seems well established. He began broadcasting at a time when the nation was in both economic and spiritual depression, and his vigorous proclamation of a classic Christianity in the 1930s and '40s served both as antidote to the spiritual malaise of the times and as intellectual undergirding for all who opposed the sterile and blighting "Modernism" of the day. Many evangelical leaders today acknowledge their debt to Walter A. Maier and have, in the words of Billy Graham, tried to "pick up the torch where Dr. Maier left off."

11

His key role in the history of radio is acknowledged in one of the latest studies. In *The Electric Church* (Nelson, 1979) Ben Armstrong speaks of Maier as the "Miracle Worker" whose program became "the most popular regular broadcast—religious or secular—in the history of radio" (p. 39). His biography, *A Man Spoke, a World Listened,* was first published in 1963, and now 30 years have elapsed since his death. Many who heard his broadcasts are able to recall them today with an uncanny audio memory and seem astounded that a whole generation now separates them from the voice that became a Sunday institution in so many lives.

The broadcasting studio, however, formed only part of Walter A. Maier's ambience. Equally representative haunts included—

> *public mass meetings,* where he addressed crowds ranging up to 70,000;
>
> *the classroom,* where he taught Old Testament at Concordia Seminary, St. Louis;
>
> *his professor's office,* where he dictated 25 years' worth of editorials and articles for a Lutheran journal, the *Walther League Messenger;*
>
> *his study at home,* where he wrote 31 books as well as a voluminous amount of devotional material.

Quite probably Walter A. Maier was the first American churchman whose published works exceed 15,000 printed pages.

This anthology focuses on his literary production. Since it cannot hope to distill such a mass of material, this volume intends only a representative sampling of the Maier prose as it ranged across the aphorisms, editorials, articles, essays, addresses, sermons, and devotions that flowed from his pen. Friends and associates of Walter A. Maier who learned of this project have suggested so many different excerpts from his works that some must inevitably be disappointed that space precluded inclusion of them all.

So as to preserve the full flavor and authenticity of the original material, the editing in this volume has been strictly limited to excerpting and elision, together with consistent modernization of punctuation, hyphenation, capitalization, and the like. No words or phrases have been changed in the texts that appear, all of which are documented either immediately following the extracts or in the notes at the rear of this book. This sampling of his works, we hope, should at least demonstrate Walter A. Maier's versatility, at the same time accenting the most significant themes to which he dedicated his life.

P.L.M.

Western Michigan University
Pentecost 1980

1

EDITOR

Walter A. Maier and the Walther League, youth organization of The Lutheran Church—Missouri Synod, were born in the same year, 1893. He became first executive secretary of the League in October 1920 and served in this capacity until July 1922, when he accepted the chair of Old Testament Interpretation and History at Concordia Seminary, St. Louis. The League post had carried with it the editorship of the *Walther League Messenger,* and W.A.M. continued editing the monthly journal for the next quarter century, along with his seminary professorship.

The initials "W.A.M." are not inappropriate. He never signed any piece of writing he ever did for the *Messenger* with his full name, only the "W.A.M." Most magazine editors do just as the title implies: edit articles submitted by others, pen the editorials, and reply to letters to the editor. W.A.M. did all this and more. He personally wrote two or three (sometimes four) of the major articles in the journal each month, as well as a two-page series of observations on current events originally called "The Watchtower" until a reader wrote of the awful similarity of that term to the Jehovah's Witnesses journal.

From then on, W.A.M. styled it "Turret of the Times."

A survey of the nearly 300 issues for which he was responsible shows an editorial approach that was best summarized by W.A.M.'s successor as *Lutheran Hour* speaker, his former student Dr. Oswald Hoffmann:

> In the cultivated accents of Harvard, Walter A. Maier spoke of Christ to the common man. Whatever he touched leaped into life. . . . His breath was on the neck of the entire church, urging it forward in its mission for Christ.[1]

That breath was particularly hot in emphasizing the importance of Christian marriage and home life; the necessity of Christian education; a stress on the church's outreach in foreign missions and broadcasting; lessons from church history, especially the Lutheran Reformation; and on down to such practical matters as urging Lutheran unity, that pastors' and teachers' salaries be raised, or that Christians should run for public office.

Bottles of inked editorial wrath, on the other hand, were hurled at immoral movies, faculty atheists, evolutionists, religious claims of the lodge, Jesuit excesses, the Ku Klux Klan and other racial hatemongers, spiritualists and swamis, gambling, defeatism in the Depression, ultraliberal theologians, clerics in politics (like Father Coughlin), and the threat from international Communism. He was particularly irked when some misguided "authority" tried to roast Martin Luther for the subsequent ills of Europe, including Hitler and the Nazis, and W.A.M. founded what he called "The Lutheran Reply" in response: "truth-squad"-type materials made available to anyone.

Stylewise, W.A.M.'s freest forum was the *Messenger*, where he could craft phrases and express thoughts that would *read* better than they might sound in a public address or would not be confined by the demands of a sermon. Humor, in particular, could be indulged via the printed page. Accordingly, some of his best writing appears in the *Messenger*.

Aphorisms, Bons Mots, Epigrams, Witticisms

On Expanding the "Messenger" in 1921

15

The time is past when the Walther League must do big things in a little way. (*Walther League Messenger,* hereafter "*WLM,*" 29, 235)

On the Myth of the "Good Old Days"

When we hark back to the days of yore when everything was so much better than today, we do this more on the principle that distance lends enchantment than on the basis of facts. And when we look forward to a future golden age—when sin and worry shall have vanished from the earth, we are surely following a shadow image that has no substance. (*WLM,* 29, 164)

On the Fistfights and Disorder That Rocked the Democratic National Convention in 1924

The world is not quite safe for democracy in spite of the millions of lives which were offered, ostensibly for this purpose. But on the other hand, we sometimes feel that democracy has not been made safe for the world, either. (*WLM,* 33, 42)

On Prohibition

In the coming election [of 1928], we cannot . . . vote for certain individuals simply because they represent the wet elements of the country. We dare not sacrifice the great issues of the day because of our inclination to—or our own aversion for—a glass of beer. (*WLM,* 37, 49)

The Modern Home

The open Bible and the family altar seem as far from many homes as the present generation is from long skirts and long hair. The home of yesterday was a sanctuary; but the home of today is often hardly more than a human filling station. (*WLM,* 37, 521)

Does Education Instill Morality?

A college degree is not a certificate of morality. An uneducated thief will steal a ride on a train, but an educated thief will steal the whole railway system. (*WLM,* 37, 651)

The illiterate killer crushes his enemy's skull with a rock, but the laboratory murderer resorts to scientific refinement and subtle poisons. The coarse criminal attacks a helpless girl; but the cultured degenerate writes a novel of lust and debauch that helps to ruin the lives of millions. The lowbrowed burglar breaks into a house at midnight and steals the family jewels; but the highbrowed plunderer raids the nation's treasury and steals its millions in broad daylight, as Voltaire did, who cunningly cheated his country of a million francs. (*WLM,* 46, 487)

The Majority May Be Wrong

There is a certain magnificence in minority—provided such minority is built on the truth of God. God grant—at least—this magnificence!" (*WLM,* 36, 687)

Humor Is Humanizing

Laughter is the Rubicon, separating the brute and the human, across which no beast has ever crossed. (*WLM,* 41, 554)

Summer Vacation from God?

The claim is often made . . . that Christians "can worship God quite as well outdoors as inside." But it is the ideal of the New Testament that we are not to forsake the assemblies but follow the Savior's example in worshiping with His fellowman "as was His custom." When we sing:

> Fair are the meadows,
> Fair are the woodlands,

let us continue to believe

> Jesus is fairer,
> Jesus is purer,

and plan to make our summers seasons of spiritual growth. (*WLM,* 45, 685)

On Time

Americans must learn to invest, not spend, their time.[2]

On Chewing Gum in Public

While we readily concede to the chicle products the right of their elastic existence, gum should be chewed and not heard. In public, it serves only to make a conversation unintelligible and the words which the exponents of America's greatest movement—the jaw movement—try to utter, quite inarticulate. Let the chewing

17

gum industry boast that their product will save the teeth, sweeten the breath, cure the stomach, or, in general, present a panacea for the great ills of humanity, the fact of the matter is that when the gum chewers of the United States masticated $47,124,000 worth of their favorite product last year [1925], they sacrificed many millions of dollars to the twin idols of discourtesy and poor manners through their public emulation of the ruminant bovine. (*WLM*, 35, 73)

On Anti-Semitism

Instead of hating the Jew, let us show our love for this persecuted people. Those who work for the salvation of Israel can never be Jew-baiters. (*WLM*, 47, 406)

On the Eighth Commandment

"Think twice before you speak" is an old maxim. We would like to substitute in this day of talebearing, public and private defamation, blackmailing, perjury, and other related sins: "Think *thrice* before you say it!" (*WLM*, 47, 472)

On Modernism

Modernism is anything but modern. Modernism is ancient, as ancient as sin itself. (*WLM*, 35, 517)

W.A.M. delighted in giving tongue-in-cheek definitions for some of the rages and fads of his day. Thus the Charleston is styled "this new terpsichorean atrocity" (35, 103), while "Yes, We Have No Bananas" becomes "the musical atrocity which swept the country last summer [1923]." (32, 302) Yet he would not issue a blanket condemnation of popular music: "The Christian must refrain from putting sin into syncopation." (35, 166)

Clearly, W.A.M. loved to play with words, even when he had a serious purpose in mind. One of his favorite ploys was to redress and restyle a hackneyed or pedestrian phrase in bombastic English. Nothing, for example, could be more trite than the phrase "hauling coals to Newcastle." But when he reported organist Dr. Edward Rechlin's concert tour of Europe in 1931, W.A.M. wrote:

It may seem that bringing Bach to Germany quite parallels the transportation of carboniferous combustibles to the well-known

British anthracite center. But Rechlin has been hailed as a sensation in Germany. (*WLM,* 39, 559)

Again, when he wrote about the effect of cooking on romance:

I do not advocate materialistic philosophies of marriage which insist that the brute must be fed or that the avenue of easiest approach to the male cardiac region is by way of the alimentary canal.[3]

Still, good wives usually were good cooks:

What this country needs are calory-conscious wives who can prepare spinach so that the virtue of iron is not neutralized by the vice of sand.[4]

W.A.M. resorted to satire only when angered. The much-balleyhooed visit of Swami Yogablanda to St. Louis in 1932 sparked his ire because of the Hindu's pretentious claims. Reporting on his address in the Gold Room of the Hotel Jefferson, W.A.M.'s pen dripped both humor and acid:

They say that the intellectually great and near-great often belittle their magnitude of mind by their plain and sometimes repulsive appearance. But what a Titan our Swami turned out to be! ... Swami was fat—so fat that the disguise of flowing oriental robes could not successfully camouflage his unquestionably inelegant proportions. Swami was sensuous—so unmistakably leering that he completely belied the benign and beaming picture featured in the advertisements. Swami was oily, greasy, slippery. And—Swami sniffled with an unmistakable, audible and sometimes visible, sniffle; in fact his cold had developed into catarrh. Swami, who flamboyantly advertised "unique divine healing prayer vibrations: Bring your sick friends!"; Swami, who claimed to cure stomach ache by the concentrated chanting of "Thou art in my intestines"; Swami, who listed in his students' testimonials cures of fatigue, insomnia, deafness, heart and headache, nervousness and obesity—the same Swami suffered for several weeks from an ordinary, vulgar cold. Physician, heal thyself!" (*WLM,* 40, 419)

Some of W.A.M.'s most amusing comments came in response to the Letters-to-the-Editor column of the *Mes-*

senger, which he styled, quaintly, the "May I Have The Floor?" column. When a letter from Monrovia, California, suggested that churches ought to have dance floors and spooning nooks in their undercrofts for young people, he replied:

"Spooning" is as out of date as horsecars, and it is as out of place in a church as a saxophone in a celestial choir. The church is a place for worship, prayer, and praise, not an amusement park. (*WLM,* 38, 131)

Another note, from Sante Fe, New Mexico, enclosed a chain letter supposedly begun at Flanders in 1918, a so-called "Good Luck Flower" which the recipient was supposed to copy and send on to five others or risk the "bad luck" of breaking the chain. To which W.A.M. responded:

The whole matter is so puerile that it really deserves no comment. The patent absurdity of the scheme is exposed by the simple consideration that, if the chain had been started two weeks before the Armistice, allowing the generous average of one week for the transmission of each copy, by Washington's birthday, 1919, the "good luck flower" would have appeared in the appalling and altogether incomprehensible total of 105,453,311,625 copies, over fifty times as many as the estimated total of the human population—men, women, and children—of the whole globe. This particular "good luck flower" is now reposing in a bouquet of similar absurdities in one of the folders of our editorial files. Incidentally, the folder is labeled: "Superstition." (*WLM,* 38, 532)

Editorials

Because the following excerpts of editorials from the *Messenger* reflect the changing moods of life in America from the 1920s to the mid '40s, they are presented in chronological rather than thematic order. Unlike the previous headers, however, all subsequent titles are exactly as they appeared in the *Messenger* and as signed by "W.A.M."

Be Glad that You Are a Lutheran [1921]

Religion, what monstrosities are committed in thy name! Christianity, what absurdities are perpetrated under thy cover! Thus we are forced to exclaim, when, for example, we read some of the sermon subjects which . . . pastors have advertised in the newspapers as their Sunday themes: "Slip, Slips, Slippers," "Wobbling," "My Mother-in-Law," "The Ass Tied at the Door Without," "Three White Mice," "Psychometric Reading," "Street-car Ventilation," "The Dollmakers of Nuremberg," "A Man with His Nose Out of Joint," "Two Looks at Another Man's Wife."

As long as men who are supposed to feed their flock will fleece their sheep in this way, the ridicule and sarcasm which infidels and scoffers are only too willing to heap upon the Christian church will not be without a strong degree of justification. Admitting the weaknesses and inconsistencies of our Lutheran Church, we will never be able to be quite grateful enough for the fact that our pastors have never offered stones to hungry souls who have cried for the bread of life. (*WLM*, 30, 72)

5922 A.L.—2452 A.I.—804 A.O. [1922]

No, gentle reader, we are not calling the quarterback signals of the Rushem University varsity football eleven. Neither are we revealing the combination of the Treasury safe in Washington. Nor are we transmitting some cryptic message.

Guess again—and after you have given up, behold and marvel! 5922 A.L.—2452 A.I.—804 A.O. are just some of the ways in which the calendars of the Masonic orders, according to the *Masonic Voice Review,* designate our good new year 1922. Ordinary and uninitiated people are generally satisfied with calling this year by its usual name, 1922, and to reckon their time from the birth of the Savior; but not so the "Free and Accepted." Everything hinges upon the founding of their "eras," and the flights their imagination takes are absolutely beyond the comprehension of any sane and sensible man.

The Ancient Craft Masons, like the Odd Fellows, begin their era with the creation of the world, "in the year of the light," "*anno lucis*" (A.L.). 1922 thus becomes 5922 A.L. Royal Arch Masons commence their era with the beginning of the second temple by Zerubbabel, "in the year of the discovery," "*anno inventionis*" (A.I.). They write 1922 as 2452 A.I. The Templars date their era from the imaginary founding of their order, "in the year of the order," "*anno ordinis*" (A.O.).

But why go on with this tiresome nonsense with which Freemasonry tries to sustain the impression that it belongs to the oldest of all organizations, beginning with the very creation of the world itself? The whole thing is entirely false, absolutely ridiculous, and extremely childish. The Masons themselves know and admit that these figures are impossible and absurd. (*WLM,* 30, 201)

These Long Winter Evenings [January 1922]

There are vast possibilities for much good and for much evil in our evenings, especially in these long winter evenings. They constitute the only time during the day that most of our young men and women have at their own disposal, and whether given over to educational, social, business, or church activities, they must be employed in a responsible and profitable manner.

Make the three or four hours between supper and bedtime count in your program of self-development. Get acquainted with the treasures of your public library; go over the problems of your daily work with a view to attaining greater efficiency in the performance of your duties; put yourself in a position to speak authoritatively on the great political and social issues of the day; study music; take up art; develop your own particular talent. And with all this save some quiet moments of these long winter evenings for spiritual growth and development, keeping first things first, never forgetting the one thing that is supremely needful. (*WLM,* 30, 218)

New Predictions of the World's End [1923]

British "scientists" recently broadcast a cheery message to the world, stating that soon the oceans are to rise up and submerge the whole civilized world. Judge F. Rutherford, Pastor Russell's successor, is decidedly more optimistic, for he predicts that the year 1925 will inaugurate the beginning of Christ's visible rule for one thousand years over the nations of the earth. While it is true that we are hastening on to the collapse of all things, let us remember that the Savior expressly warned us that the day and hour of His coming is concealed to all human questions and speculation. (*WLM,* 32, 24)

Why We Need Student Pastors [1923]

"Attendance at the chapel exercise of the University of Pennsylvania has gradually dwindled until now there are just two students out of every 10,000 who attend services regularly." This statement, recently published in the newspapers, reveals a tragic situation. It shows the bankruptcy of the American college religion that is usually offered in such chapel exercises. Preaching that appeals to the intellect but that leaves the heart cold and untouched will never exert any lasting influence, even upon college students. And just because our Lutheran young men and young women who attend these higher institutions of learning as well as their unchurched friends need the warm and pulsating power of the Gospel that no church possesses as fully as our own, we must have a large corps of student pastors who will give these young people the message of true wisdom when they need it most.

Life on Other Planets? [1927]

The question of whether Mars and the other planets are inhabited was again considered by scientists, this time by Prof. Henry Norris Russell of Princeton. Prof. Russell takes the position that there may be thousands of habitable worlds in this universe but that the only one in our solar system that might sustain life is Mars. The Bible does not give us any definite information in this connection. It does tell us that our solar system is geocentric, that is, that it exists for the sake of the world. We know, too, that the redemptive activity of God was directed to our globe. But while these considerations have been taken to indicate that our world alone is inhabited by human beings, we must be careful not to press the statements of Scripture beyond their original import. If science can definitely show that the structure, temperature, air, density, position, and movements of other planets are such that they permit the existence of creatures similar in structure to human beings, we certainly are not interested in endeavoring to show that there are no other inhabited worlds. After all, the essential thing for every one of us is this, that we realize that we are living on this earth and that, as God's creatures, we have certain definite duties toward Him and toward our fellow-men. (*WLM,* 35, 295)

No Blue Laws! [1928]

The Christian religion is not a creed of morbid restrictions and dampening prohibitions. And the Lutheran Church believes that those teachers, reformers, and legislators who insist upon the Old Testament spirit and legislation for a day and age when "old things are passed away" are not only misrepresenting the evident intention of our Lord but are also guilty of the more serious sin of keeping men away from Christ. In denouncing all of the efforts which would restore the blight of puritanical Sabbath laws, the Lutheran Confessions point out that the Sabbath era has passed forever, being only a shadow of those things which were to come with Christ (Col. 2:16). (*WLM,* 36, 653)

A Sane Consideration of the Prohibition Question [1928]

At a time when our country is torn through dissension by the extreme positions in regard to the question of prohibition, the Lutheran Church reiterates the Scriptural position, which has often been disregarded or distorted in the heat of discussion. While the Bible in both the Old and New Testaments teaches quite directly that there is nothing reprehensible in the moderate use of alcoholic stimulants, it is equally decisive in warning against the power of such stimulants and in condemning the inordinate and intemperate consumption. Whether the restriction enacted by prohibition will make for the good of the nation is another question, which has been answered variously and which should be carefully considered. The Lutheran Church is, however, entirely opposed to the tactics of some religious organizations which have tried to give prohibition a Scriptural basis and make the whole question a religious issue, emphasized to the exclusion of the church's great message. This does not mean, however, that Lutheranism is the saloonkeeper's refuge or that this church stands behind the rumrunners and law evaders. On the contrary, the Lutheran Church teaches that the prohibition amendment is an integral and essential part of the law, the observance of which is incumbent upon all citizens of the United States, who, if dissatisfied with its provisions, have recourse to the ballot, the prerogative of all citizens of our republic. (*WLM, 36, 653)*

A Protest Against Pacifism [1928]

The Lutheran Church deplores war and the unspeakable sorrow which comes in the wake of such national catastrophes. The very thought of this brutal carnage must be repulsive to every sincere Christian who knows the admonition of his Lord and Savior, "Love one another." But any civil government is obligated to protect the lives and property of its citizens, and for this reason the Lutheran Church takes the position that war, as abhorrent as it is, may be justifiable and necessary, especially when it is defensive and the national safety of a country is involved. But why cry,

"Peace!" when there is no peace; and to do away entirely with national defenses and safety and to declare in an absolute manner: "No more war!" is a procedure which is contrary to the Scriptural admonition and national prudence. (*WLM*, 36, 687)

Sour-Minded Scrooges [1929]

There is a certain class of people, usually those who have met with reverses and disappointments, whose lives have taken a pessimistic tinge and who feel that because they have deprived themselves of happiness, all others must suffer similarly. Young people, especially, are made to feel the brunt of such bias. They are told that they should save all of their money and use as little as possible for pleasure and recreation. . . . Why give up an evening for a party when the time could be spent so much more profitably in work or in study? What's the use of spending time and money for Christmas decorations when one can do so much more good with the same energy and expenditure? All this is part of the varied onslaught that is being waged against the inherent right to be happy and to have a really good time.

We protest against such perverted conceptions, and we do this in direct harmony with the outspoken declaration of the highest of all authorities, which bids us: "Rejoice in thy youth." Youth is the joy season of life, the bridge that spans the years which separate the carefree days of childhood from the furrowed struggle of adult responsibilities. The precious years of youth come but once in a lifetime, and they are so full of life and action, so overflowing with energy and vitality, that young people cannot and should not stop to calculate coldly the cost of every action in energy, time, and money.

So let us enjoy—in an overflowing measure—the happiest days of the year which are to be brought to us in the Christmas season. Let us have parties and songs and dinners and games and rollicking hilarity in all of its happiness. Let us have brightly lighted homes with garnished tables and rooms that cheer with the red and green of Christmas. And especially, let us keep our Christmas trees with their tinsel and their riot of bright colors, for the Advent plea is: "Rejoice in the Lord" and the apostolic emphasis on this rings: "And again I say, Rejoice." (*WLM*, 38, 201, 251-2)

Just as these words were being written in the fall of 1929, however, the speculative bubble burst on Wall Street, with shattering impact on the American economy. The Depression thirties followed, smothering the mood of the country, and church life was not unaffected. Protesting against the defeatism he found all about him, W.A.M. unleased a string of editorials and articles in the *Messenger* to help lift the spirits of his readers. Excerpts from the most important ones follow.

Thanksgiving in Depression [1931]

It is inevitable that as we approach our annual day of thanksgiving, there are unnumbered homes in which the question has been asked, either in thought or in words, "Can we really give thanks this year?" There are doubtless many in the agricultural belts of the plague-ridden areas in the Dakotas who have found that the locusts left a harvest not even as large as the seed which was sowed in the spring; hundreds of thousands in our large cities who have vainly sought even part-time employment; millions throughout all sections of the nation who have experienced financial disappointment and reverses and many who, in addition, have felt the hand of affliction rest heavily upon them in sickness, family troubles, death or in the long list of other visitations by which adversity may express itself. At a time when native Christians in Cameroon, Africa, send a love offering of $3.77 "for starving America"; when our country faces the specter of one of the grimmest winters in our national history; and when the whole economic foundation of the world seems to be shaking, people are repeating with an insistence new and strange in prosperous America, "Can we give thanks this year?"

Now what does the Bible say? Here are the words of divine and heavenly wisdom: "*In everything give thanks*"; and this means that if we pause to take inventory of the blessings that have come down upon us, we must come to the unavoidable conclusion that this year, too, God's mercy and tender kindness are beyond the power of human computation and measurement.

Foreign visitors to our shores who have found the tranquility of the nation disturbed by the depression, tell us that the United States does not really know what hard times are and that the comforts and prosperity which we enjoy even in these darker days are so tremendous that they fairly overwhelm the poverty-stricken people of other nations. We speak of unemployment; but let us not forget postwar Europe and the countries that have not enjoyed a

26

year of real, normal industry since the conclusion of the World War; countries in which government doles, destructive labor troubles, and communistic agitation emphasize the striking contrast between the old world and the blessings which we enjoy here in the new. We exercise ourselves about bread lines and municipal soup kitchens; but witness the tragedies that have engulfed vast areas of China. For four years millions have suffered because of drought which, combined with civil war, has brought about the most disastrous period in the history of that unfortunate nation. And now, to add misery to misery, comes one of the greatest floods since Biblical times. In comparison with such supertragedies this present depression is a mere irritation. We still experience the fullness of blessings which makes us apply to our own country what the psalmist says of the Promised Land: O America, *the Lord hath dealt bountifully with thee!*"

Even though you are one of the vast army of the unemployed, even though you have been out of work for long and unproductive months, even though the financial reserve that you may have laid by to help you realize some higher hopes may now be exhausted—if you have the living assurance of Christ's faith in your life, you have overabundant reason to give thanks to your God. . . . Your life, as you live it in Christ, is the best possible existence, in which all things, even unemployment and financial stringencies, work together by divine arrangement for good.

Keep up your courage. Clouds will pass away. Business depression cannot last forever. Take your troubles to the Lord in prayer.

Hunt for work. A job may not "turn up" without your turning something over. Seek for a different sort of employment if your regular kind is not to be secured. A little income is better than being reduced to beggary or idleness.

Keep busy at something. There is work to be done around the home premises: repairing, painting, cleaning, gardening. Make the place shine. When other work is found, then you will have a nice home in which to live.

Study and read along your chosen line. Books can be borrowed from public libraries or from friends. Be determined that when you go back to your old job you will be better equipped for service.

Leave off all luxuries. They may be all right as long as the money keeps coming in, but when the pay envelope ceases to make the rounds, these items must be clipped off from the budget.

Borrow, if you must, from one source. Pay cash to all others. Maintain your general credit by meeting bills promptly.

But as the one source of comfort and encouragement, we ask you to live thankfully, hopefully, and confidently in Christ with the implicit confidence that God's promises to you cannot tarry long in their fulfillment. (*WLM*, 40, 142)

The Spending Spree [1935]

The Christian's ideals in financial matters are uncompromising in their indictment of nonchalance in money matters which complacently disregards the necessity of balancing the individual budget. We have little sympathy with the policy which would seek to have us spend our way out of financial embarrassment. We have no great hopes of coaxing prosperity from around its elusive corner by a change in monetary standards or by any artificial stimulation. The path to individual as well as national stability, under God, lies in earnest, productive labor, coupled with thrift and a rigid sense of economy in money matters.

The homely virtues of economy, budgeted expenditures, and systematic saving cry out for emphasis in the present world of useless, senseless expenditure. We can compute the loss which the American homes sustain through burglary and theft, as well as through fraudulent investments and blue-sky stocks; but we shudder when we think of the cumulative loss incurred by thoughtless, needless spending. If all the evidence of senseless expenditure could be extracted from our American homes—all the Elbert Hubbard Scrap Books, all the electric belts and quasi-scientific medical apparatus, all the plaster of Paris monstrosities in the form of highly colored kewpies, shameless Venuses, and livid Hiawathas; all the dust-catching paper flowers and the pajama dolls with knotted limbs; all the millions-now-living-will-never-die literature; all the correspondence courses on Coconut Painting, Oratory Overnight, Chopin in Ten Lessons; in short, if all the numberless items in America's senseless spending orgy could be redeemed for the original purchase price, the funds restored to our family treasuries would be more than enough to offset the results of a depression. Statistical sleuths would be able to tell us that if every dollar thus saved were placed side by side, this financial belt would encircle a portion of our country as formidable in area as the territory from Poverty Flats, Ohio, to Wealthy, Michigan. (*WLM,* 43, 329)

By the later '30s, however, the rigors of the Depression were surmounted, and W.A.M. could return to other editorial themes of more normal character. The following was to inspire the senior set, and the next to warn against spiritualism.

Life Begins at Twice Forty [1937]

Between the ages of seventy and eighty-three, Commodore Vanderbilt is said to have added about a hundred millions to his fortune.

Verdi at eighty produced *Falstaff* and at eighty-five the famous *Ave Maria, Stabat Mater,* and *Te Deum.*

Goethe at eighty-two completed *Faust.*

Tennyson at eighty-three wrote "Crossing the Bar."

Titian at ninety-three painted his historic picture of the *Battle of Lepanto.*

"Old" George Bernard Shaw, who will be eighty-one in July, can still outwrite his juniors. Only last year his latest works—three plays—were published.

Victor Hugo wrote a great novel when he was eighty.

Chauncey Depew was very active at ninety-two.

Thomas Edison was active in his laboratory working on a process for manufacturing synthetic rubber when he was past eighty.

Sir William Herschel at the age of eighty-two was contributing regularly important papers on double stars to the Royal Society, and notwithstanding his advanced age, was elected the first president of the Royal Astronomical Society. (*WLM,* 35, 345)

"No Manifestation!" [1940]

Casual visitors to Chicago's Jackson Park recently beheld an interesting spectacle. On a blustering March afternoon a Detroit magician, surrounded by a few witnesses and a group of newspaper reporters, stood poised on a lagoon bridge. After a few preliminary remarks the magician, Claude Noble, asked the assembly to bow their heads and join him in the Lord's Prayer. He then paused

29

dramatically, grasped a hymnal, and called out: "Clarence Darrow, I am here in fulfillment of the pact we made with each other. If you can manifest your spirit to me, do so now!" For a full minute he stood in rigid silence. The wind blew, a bird twittered on a nearby limb, the subdued drone of the city's traffic played a monotone background, one of the reporters coughed apologetically. Suddenly Noble relaxed, turned to the witnesses, and replied, "No manifestation!"

He had previously explained that this attempt to establish contact with the spirit of the departed agnostic attorney was prearranged. Noble had met Darrow in a Detroit hotel three years ago. There, together with Howard Thurston, another magician, the three agreed that after death they would try to manifest their spirits. Darrow promised that his spirit would try to shake the hymnbook so that it would drop from Noble's hand. Last year Noble tried to establish contact through a seance in the hotel room where the agreement had been made, but the result was "No manifestation!" This year he selected the park bridge where Darrow's ashes had been strewn to the four winds; but the book remained rigidly clutched in his hand.

For three quarters of a century "No manifestation!" has been the consistent verdict of such prearranged tests. In our own country Herman the Great declared that he would try to return; he never came back. Houdini, foe of spiritists, told his wife and his friends that after death he would make every effort to return if that were possible; but repeated tests have not produced any response from his spirit. . . .

It is well that we remind ourselves that spiritism is an ugly, dangerous fraud, even though prominent people often endorse its claims. It is the rule of God that when men die, they face judgment, and thereafter heaven or hell. They do not come back. The claims made by spiritists who assert that their seances have called forth the shades of the departed are false and fraudulent. All their impressive tactics can be exposed and reproduced by sleight-of-hand experts.

Spiritism, however, is more than a fraud; it is a soul-destroying delusion. In the Old Testament God commanded that spiritist mediums should not be permitted to live in Israel (Exodus 22:18). In the New Testament spiritism (witchcraft) is one of the works of the flesh which involve banishment from God's kingdom (Galatians 5:19 ff.). (*WLM,* 48, 440 f.)

America, however, could enjoy her "normalcy" only a few scant years, because 1939 brought war to Europe, and the Japanese attack at Pearl Harbor plunged America into hostilities in December 1941. W.A.M.'s startling predictions about the world conflict will be dealt with in a later chapter, and the next editorial reveals only his general policy toward war.

Youth in a World at War [1942]

Since the United States has been for us the most generous and God-blessed nation on the face of the earth, with liberties, privileges, and opportunities such as no other country has ever granted its citizens; if we have enjoyed peace up till this time while other nations have already had more than two years of strife; if God has granted us the free worship and the blessings of His full Gospel while the exercise of religion has been curtailed in other countries, we must be ready to defend our shores and take part in the all-out effort made to defeat our enemies. Whatever our previous opinions may have been in regard to war, now that the nation has been attacked we must wholeheartedly rise to its defense. Increasing demands will be made on our time, our money, and our willingness to sacrifice. Out of sheer gratitude for our past blessings, for the guarantee of our future benedictions, and for compliance with God's Word we must be ready to cooperate, not grudgingly and with protest but with glad, wholehearted willingness.

Even if you are drafted for military or naval service, you must not think of time spent in defense of the government as wasted. It may be a period of inner strengthening and character building. With new fervency our prayer must be raised in behalf of the country, the men of the armed forces, and our leaders. . . . Every Christian, with his regenerated being and his determination to follow Christ as far as humanly possible, adds to the country's moral strength, increases the righteousness which can exalt a nation, and battles against the reproach of sin.

Those will serve our country best in this crisis who earnestly speak—and live—this double declaration of loyalty: "I pledge allegiance to the flag of the United States of America and to the republic for which it stands, one nation indivisible, with liberty and justice for all." "I also pledge allegiance to the Cross and to the faith for which it stands, one Savior eternal, Jesus Christ, with grace and mercy for all. So help me God!" (*WLM,* 50, 262)

31

And of the various sacrifices required by war, one of the most inevitable was raised taxes. W.A.M. had an editorial for that too.

Pay Taxes—and Like It! [1943]

During this year our country will reach a new high in tax assessments. Increased income levies, which include many of our families for the first time, several war taxes, and specifically the 5-percent victory tax will combine to make our people contribute the largest amount this country has ever paid the government in a single year.

As an antidote to any feeling of dissatisfaction, Christians should remember Luther's attitude. When the Turks threatened to overrun Western Europe, the Elector of Saxony sought to exempt the great Reformer from paying war taxes. But in a remarkable letter Luther, while thanking the Elector for his interest, nevertheless pledged himself to pay his assessment, a total of 610 florins (about $337) for his garden property. He explained his insistence on assuming his financial share in the cost of national defense by declaring, "I am anxious to be in the army against the Turk with a few pennies of mine, in company with others who are likewise contributing of their own free will." In the same spirit we certainly ought to admit that if several million young men are risking their very lives in the nation's cause, the least we can do is to contribute of our material blessings.

For some church members this increase in taxes will suggest a decrease in church contributions. It would be most dangerous if Christians, in a country that has not suffered from bombing or invasion, should reduce their gifts to the Kingdom in such a time as this. . . . Here too the great Luther is our example. Although his salary never was large, he, in the words of Dr. Mackinnon, "gave always out of his slender resources with his left hand as well as his right." The poor were often liberally remembered, and he received and accepted nothing for many of his services.

We have the Scriptural promise, "The Lord loveth a cheerful giver." (*WLM,* 51, 321)

This was Walter A. Maier at his best: ever-so-Lutheran, patriotic, quarrying apt illustrations out of history, concerned about the church, and rooting his appeal in Scripture.

2
AUTHOR

Since W.A.M. wrote an average of two or three major articles himself for each issue of the *Messenger* in addition to the editorials—except in 1928, when he was studying for his doctorate at Harvard University—it becomes impossible to provide even a representative cross-section of his articles within the confines of this chapter. Still, a somewhat arbitrary selection of his main themes follows, again in chronological order. The Luther and Lutheran emphasis in these articles was *much* more pronounced than in his radio sermons, since the former were aimed at a predominantly Lutheran readership whereas the latter were broadcast to a much wider audience.

To commemorate the quadricentennial of Martin Luther's famous stand at Worms in April of 1521, the following article appeared in the April 1921 *Messenger* as some of W.A.M.'s earliest writing.

Luther at Worms—The Victory of Truth and Light over Error and Darkness

On the twenty-fourth of March, 1521, the imperial summons directing Luther to appear before the Diet or royal convention, at

Worms was placed in the Reformer's hands at Wittenberg. Papal intrigue had left no stone unturned in the effort to prevent Emperor Charles from issuing this summons; for the pope had already condemned and anathematized the heretic German monk, and then what possible good could result from his appearance before emperor and princes? This feeling of resentment was flamed into burning indignation when the emperor addressed the letter of safe-conduct: "To the honorable, our dear and pious Dr. Martin Luther," and simply stated:

> We, and the states of the Holy Roman Empire, having resolved to make an inquest touching the doctrine and the books which you have published for some time past, have given you . . . our safe conduct. Have no apprehension of either injustice or violence.

But the friends of the excommunicated monk did have apprehension—of both injustice and violence. They remembered John Hus and felt that, unless divine power interfered, history certainly would repeat itself. Luther, however, was animated by a heaven-inspired resolution and determination. He told his friends:

> Before my blood is cold, thousands throughout the world will be called to answer for having shed it. The most holy adversary of Christ, the father, master, and generalissimo of homicides, insists on having my life. Amen—let the will of the Lord be done. Christ will give me His spirit to vanquish these ministers of error. I despise them during my life and will triumph over them by my death. They are doing all they can at Worms to compel me to retract. Here, then, will be my retraction: I once said that the pope was the vicar of Christ; now I say that he is the enemy of Christ and the apostle of the devil.

On the second day of April Luther left Wittenberg, accompanied by his ardent friend Amsdorf, by a professor of law, and by an adventurous Danish student, who later helped to spread the light of the Reformation in Pomerania and Denmark. Having told Melanchthon: "If I do not return and my enemies put me to death, O my brother, cease not to teach and remain firm in the truth. . . . If you live, it matters little, though I perish," Luther and his companions set out in a carriage provided by the city council, the imperial herald with the insignia of his office prancing proudly ahead.

The Journey to Worms

His entry to Leipzig passed without notice. At Naumburg a priest held up to Luther a picture of Savonarola, the Italian martyr, in ominous but well-understood silence. At Weimar, however, the journey began to assume the characteristics of a triumphal tour. An eyewitness states: "Whenever Luther entered a city, the people ran out to meet him, wishing to see the wonder man who was brave enough to stand up against the pope and the whole world." When some expressed their fear that because there were so many cardinals and bishops at the diet they would burn him to powder, Luther simply declared: "And if they should make a fire from Wittenberg to Worms that would reach up into the heavens, because I have been summoned, I shall appear in the name of the Lord and step in between the great teeth in the jaws of Behemoth and confess Christ and let Him rule." To his friend Spalatin he wrote that he was determined to enter Worms even though there were as many devils there as tiles on the roofs.

On the Sunday after Easter Luther preached in the university city Erfurt. While he was sounding the keynote of justification, one of the galleries seemed to crack, as though it had collapsed under the pressure of the throng. For a few moments it seemed that panic would reign, but the speaker paused and cried out: "Fear nothing. The devil is seeking in this way to prevent me from proclaiming the Gospel; but he shall not succeed." Luther's calmness was effective, and soon order and quiet were restored.

At Eisenach, his "dear city," Luther became ill, but when he entered Frankfurt, he was in much higher spirits. Here he ate and drank in the public inn and later in the evening played and sang in such a carefree and buoyant manner that the dismay of his adversaries bordered on consternation.

It was on the morning of April sixteenth that Luther finally entered Worms. Thousands of curious spectators ran out to meet him, more even than when the emperor made his entry into the city. Suddenly, relates a historian, "a man clad in a singular dress and carrying a large cross before him, as is usual at funerals, breaks off from the crowd, advances towards Luther, and then, in a loud voice and with the plaintive cadence which is used in saying mass for the repose of the souls of the dead, chants the following stanzas, as if he had been determined that the very dead should hear them:

Adventisti, O desiderabilis!
Quem expectabimus in tenebris.

'Thou hast arrived, thou, whom we longed and waited for in darkness.' Luther's arrival is celebrated by a requiem. If the story is true, it was the court fool of one of the dukes of Bavaria."

April 17, 1521

It was four o'clock on the afternoon of April seventeenth when Luther was led into the town hall at Worms where the diet was in session. Passing up the crowded stairs, George of Freundsberg, a veteran of many campaigns, placed his hand on Luther's shoulder and said: "Poor monk, poor monk, you have before you a march the like of which I nor a great many captains have ever seen in the bloodiest of our battles. But if your cause is just and you have full confidence in it, advance in the name of God and fear nothing. God will not forsake you."

It is estimated that more than five thousand people surrounded the building and crowded every inch of available space in the antechambers. In the diet hall there were gathered: Emperor Charles V, his brother, Archduke Ferdinand, six electors of the empire, twenty-four powerful dukes, eight margraves, seven ambassadors from France, England, and other countries, princes, counts, barons, archbishops, and prelates—more than two hundred representatives of the powers that controlled the civilized world.

When Luther entered the diet hall, he advanced slowly and apparently overawed by the august assembly, until he stood before the throne of the young emperor. After the marshall of the empire had warned him not to speak unless spoken to, John of Eck (not the well-known Dr. Eck) addressed Luther as follows: "Martin Luther, his sacred and imperial majesty has cited you before his throne . . . to call upon you to answer two questions. First: Do you admit that these books were composed by you," pointing to some twenty books lying on the table before him; "secondly: Do you mean to retract these books and their contents, or do you persist in the things advanced in them?"

Before Luther could reply, his counsel, Jerome Schurff, demanded: "Read the titles of the books." After the list of books had been read, Luther acknowledged them as his writings, but as for retracting what he had written, he added: "I should act imprudently if I should answer without reflection. . . . Wherefore I pray your imperial majesty, with all submission, to give me time that I may answer without offense to the Word of God."

This had been spoken so meekly and respectfully that the papal party began to hope anew. It seemed that Luther was hesitating and therefore lost. But they entirely misunderstood the diplomacy which the counselors of Frederick the Wise had devised much to Luther's chagrin, who in his characteristic impetuosity was only too determined to give a clear and uncompromising testimony. Who knows what might have happened if the Reformer had left Worms that same night?

Luther's request was granted, but the time was measured very closely: on the morrow Luther was to appear before the diet once more, and this time he was to give his unequivocal answer.

The night of April seventeenth brought hours of high tension, fraught with excitement and uncertainty. Politicians offered plans for compromise; the papists predicted certain defeat for Luther; the Spanish soldiers pillaged in the city; the streets were thronged with people of all classes, speculating on the probabilities of the morrow.

The calmest man in the whole city was probably Luther himself. Returning from the diet he sat down and wrote to a friend:

> I write you from the midst of tumult. I have within this hour appeared before the emperor and his brother. I have acknowledged the authorship and declared that tomorrow I will give my answer concerning retraction. By the help of Jesus Christ not one iota of all my works will I retract.

We pause to wonder what thoughts, what doubts and misgivings must have surged beneath this calm surface. Luther was too human not to experience the overwhelming importance of this crisis, and his courage was sustained only by strengthening from above and by the Spirit of the Lord supreme, in whose name and for whose truth he was called to testify.

April 18, 1521

At four o'clock on the afternoon of April 18th Luther was again led to the diet. The assembly being engaged, he was obliged to wait without, in the midst of a crushing throng of friends, enemies, and curious spectators, until six o'clock, when the doors swung wide to receive him. The lighted lamps lent a somber aspect to the whole assembly hall. The chancellor immediately addressed Luther and concluded: "Do you mean to defend your books out and out, or do you mean to retract some part of them?" Luther's calmness in answering is best described by the *Acts of Worms:* "He did not raise his voice; he spoke not with violence, but with meekness, candor, suitableness, and modesty and yet with great joy and Christian firmness." In a long address he stated that he could retract neither the books on articles of faith nor the books against the pope nor the books directed against other individuals. He qualified all this by stating that he would retract whatever the Word of God would prove to be erroneous. When he had concluded these remarks in German, he repeated the whole clear testimony in Latin for the benefit of the emperor, a task of no little exertion, as Luther later recalled, saying: "I was covered by perspiration, heated by the crowd, standing the midst of the princes."

His answer was still too indirect for the papal followers, since it opened up the possibility of disputation and debates, a prospect by no means pleasing or promising. So the chancellor sprang to his feet and asked, after denying the permissibility of even considering heresies which had already been condemned: "You are asked to give a clear and definite reply. Will you—or will you not—retract?"

The Immortal Testimony

Then Luther replied in the classic and inspired words that every Lutheran young man and young woman should memorize: "Since your most serene majesty and your mighty highness call upon me for a simple, clear, and definite answer, I will give it, and it is this: I cannot submit my faith either to the pope or to the councils, because it is as clear as day that they have often fallen into error and even into great self-contradiction. If, then, I am not disproved by passages of Scripture or by clear arguments; if I am not convinced by the very passages which I have quoted, and so bound in conscience to submit to the Word of God, I neither can nor will retract anything, for it is not safe for a Christian to speak against his conscience." And then, as if placing his cause with God, he concluded: "Here I stand. I cannot do otherwise. God help me. Amen."

[*Note:* In recent years there has been some doubt as to whether Luther actually spoke these oft-quoted words. The most recent authority, however, states that while the earliest record reports Luther as saying simply: "God help me. Amen," there was so much tumult in the hall at the time that the speaker could not be heard. At least one record of the year 1521 brings the full quotation, and anyone who knows Luther's spirit will appreciate how characteristic these words are. See Gustav Wolf, *Quellenkunde der deutschen Reformationsgeschichte,* vol. II, p. 269 (Gotha, 1916).]

Admiration, dismay, and hatred were written on the faces of the assembly. As a final threat the chancellor declared: "If you do not retract, the emperor and the states of the empire will consider what course they must adopt towards an obstinate heretic"—to which Luther replied: "God help me, for I can retract nothing." Then, leaving the building and entering the vast throng that now regarded him as a national hero, he lifted up his hands in token of victory and cried out: "I have come through! I have come through!"

And indeed he had come through—and with him millions of grateful hearts have come through from darkness to light and thank God for His mighty minister, who broke the fetters of error and deceit and so unselfishly dedicated himself and his all to the confession of Jesus Christ as the world Savior. (*WLM,* 29, 260 ff.)

This was representative of the many quadricentennial articles commemorating various prime dates in the Lutheran Reformation. Could W.A.M. drag Lutheranism even into the celebration of Christmas? Easily! As witness the following article from December 1923.

The Lesson of the Christmas Tree

Did you ever stop to think that the world at large owes our Lutheran Church an overwhelming vote of thanks for making Christmas the day of happiness and rejoicing which we all cherish so dearly? As we hasten through these crowded holiday weeks and the spirit of Christmas becomes so contagious that even Jew, unbeliever, and skeptic seem to be warmed by the outward and material happiness of the season, we usually take it for granted that Christmas has always been the greatest joy day of the whole year.

But history teaches us a different lesson. We are surprised to learn that in the early days of our own country the most stringent laws were enacted to prevent the observance of Christmas. A statute of the Colonial Laws of Massachusetts, for example, dated in 1646, states very emphatically:

Whosoever shall be found observing any such day as Christmas or the like, either by forbearing labor, feasting, or any other way upon any such account as aforesaid, every such person so offending shall pay for every such offense five shillings as a fine to the county.

And on the very first Christmas which the Pilgrims celebrated at Plymouth there was a sensation in the colony when Governor Bradford publicly rebuked a number of young men for taking a holiday on Christmas Day!

Contrast this with the first Lutheran Christmas which was held in America, two years previous to the landing of the Pilgrim Fathers, when the Danish sailors wintering at Nova Dania, on the shore of the inhospitable Hudson Bay, record:

The Holy Christmas day we celebrated jointly in a Christian manner. We had preaching and the Lord's Supper.

This reverent and yet joy-filled observance of the Savior's birthday has always characterized our church. The *New York American* last year declared that Luther's wife Katherine was the originator of the well-nigh universal custom of the Christmas tree. And while it might be difficult to prove this point, yet it is a matter of indisputable fact that the spirit which pervaded Luther's home and the wholesome, radiant happiness which marked the celebration of the Christmas season introduced a new Christmas spirit.

This spirit was continued in our own country. It is a fact that deserves to be recognized and to be published that the first Christmas tree which was ever placed inside of a church was set up in 1851 in the congregation of the Rev. Henry C. Schwan, who was then pastor of one of our Cleveland churches and before his death was President of the Missouri Synod for many years. We would miss the Christmas trees in our churches today, but what happened when this first church Christmas tree made its appearance? We are told:

The feeling over this first tree in the community ran high among other denominations. It was styled idolatrous and sacrilegious, and it would bring down the wrath of God. Others laughed at the tree as absurd. Members of the church in which the Christmas tree had been inaugurated were even boycotted for a time in their business and in other ways were made to suffer, their accusers claiming that they groveled before a hemlock tree with lighted candles and cheap pictures. One or two of the members, it is said, were even threatened with discharge by their employers if they ever again participated in arranging for another Christmas tree.

Today practically all churches have adopted our Lutheran custom, and the Christmas tree is accepted as almost a necessary part of the holiday celebration. Yet while Lutheran common sense and reverence of the day has kept the observance of Christmas within the limits which Scripture sets, other churches which once denounced that first Christmas tree as superstitious and idolatrous have in many instances so completely lost their sense of judgment that they have permitted some of the most objectionable features to mar the spirit of real Christmas devotion. It is the old trouble of going from one extreme to the other. The former straight-laced churches have done their share towards encouraging the paganizing of this day by elevating the red-nosed and wide-girthed Santa Claus and by making the reindeer, holly, mistletoe, jingling bells, plum pudding, and other harmless by-products of Christmas often more important then the divine and reassuring message of the day.

There is a strong lesson which the history of the Christmas tree teaches us. This is not the only instance where our church has carefully followed the golden middle way while others have swung from one extreme to its opposite. History teaches some very strange lessons in which the opponents of our church have not only adopted the position which they once ridiculed but have also gone far beyond the limits of that which is right and proper.

The Congregational Church of our country in its early days was a blue-law church that was decidedly somber and puritanic. We read, for example, of the fact that in the early history of Massachusetts a man was placed in stocks for kissing his wife on Sunday and that others were fined for partaking in forbidden amusements on other days. We skip over two centuries and find the Congregational Church at Lawrence, Massachusetts, gaining newspaper publicity by conducting a dance and charging admission at the rate of one cent per inch of the waistline of each dancer.

The Presbyterian Church in the early days of its existence refused to sing anything else but psalms in its services. That a congregation should sing "Rock of Ages" or "Nearer, My God, to Thee" was considered little short of sacrilegious. A few weeks ago

41

the Second Presbyterian Church of Chicago advertised a sacred cantata rendered by Chicago's leading musicians.

The Methodist Church was originally motivated by the desire to have its houses of worship as void of all decorations as possible. It followed the spirit of the iconoclasts of Luther's times who denounced Luther because he refused to join them in destroying priceless works of art and in declaring that churches should be bare and barren to an absolute degree. But today Methodism has changed. As we have recently seen, it has spent many millions of dollars in erecting its Loop skyscraper church in Chicago that is noted for its lavish beauty.

All this teaches us that our church need not hesitate when its policies and practices disagree with those of other churches. The common-sense and Scripturally correct position of our church may yet be vindicated by the endorsement of those who oppose us at present. If our parochial school system is attacked and branded as un-American, we sit back quietly and see that representative men of practically all churches are beginning to recognize that America's greatest peril lies in its unchurched youth and that the surety for the future lies in Christian education. If we witness the great agitation which is being upheld by many churches in favor of prohibition, let us not be disturbed by the fact that our church refuses to treat prohibition primarily as a religious issue. The future may witness a change of opinion which will make the attitude of our church more popular. When self-styled Christian pastors lend their pulpits to air and endorse the monkey claim of evolution, we may rest reassured; for while scientific research can never discover anything that will disprove the record of the creation in the image of God, really scientific study may add other and convincing reasons for the impossibility of Darwinism.

There are not a few members of our church who feel that Lutheranism is behind the times, that it is too narrow, and that it must learn from others, especially from the different denominations that surround us. Young people especially may only too easily be attracted by the display and flashy methods of many American churches. But if Lutheran young men and young women think that their church must follow where such churches lead, let them look back to the story of the Christmas tree, and let them thank their God for the privilege of membership in a safe and sane church. (*WLM,* 32, 200 ff.)

Earlier in this century the one great problem afflicting the church body to which W.A.M. belonged was its insularity and heavily German flavoring, a phenomenon common to many immigrant and ethnic Christian bodies. The next article, published in July 1926, shows the author trying to burn through this insulation.

Americanism—Lutheranism: Each Needs the Other

Did you ever pause to realize what an intensely American attitude the Lutheran Church takes on the great issues of the day that are engrossing the attention of the American people? Take pacifism, for example, and you will be reminded of the fact that while the Lutheran Church deplores war as an abhorrent result of sin, nevertheless it entirely rejects the pacifist propaganda to the effect that all war is wrong and that no steps should be taken to secure adequate military and naval preparedness. Take secretism— and again when our church condemns any and all attempts to set up oath-bound organizations that often claim greater power than the government and that are based on undemocratic principles, it is acting in the spirit of real, genuine Americanism. Likewise, in the matter of education, when our church insists that our parents have the privilege of sending their children to any school which they may choose and that they are not bound to the public school system, it is simply emphasizing one of the fundamental principles laid down in the constitution of our country. In the relation of church and state, too, there is evidence of this same constructive and highly American attitude, according to which we insist that these two institutions must be kept separated and that while the government may not control religious belief and practice, it is similarly un-American for churches to attempt to sway the government and to assume its functions. And thus the Lutheran position in many other matters— for example, prohibition, Bible-reading in public schools, the blue laws—is essentially the attitude which is demanded by the principles of sound Americanism.

Yet is it not strange and deplorable that in spite of this emphasis on real American principles, the position of our church is so often misunderstood and that there is so much inaccuracy and incorrect information in regard to the history and work of American Lutheranism? Not long ago a prominent Pacific Coast churchman made repeated and eloquent reference to Luther's "ninety-nine" theses, and his numerical inaccuracy has been typical of much foggy and hazy thinking on the part of American church leaders in regard to our church. We can excuse the schoolboy whose composition on Luther was reprinted in *The Nation* and who said, in effect, that Luther wanted to get married but that the pope would not permit this and sent a bull to intimidate Luther. But the Reformer managed to kill the bull and so found himself free to marry and establish Protestantism. It becomes somewhat alarming when a Bostonian telephones to our Martin Luther Orphanage in West Roxbury and asks the superintendent to call Mr. Luther to the phone. But it becomes a veritable challenge to all young people of our church when a New York newspaper classifies the Missouri Synod with the Mormons, Swedenborgians, and other outlandish bodies; or when an Eastern Presbyterian publication, in listing the numerical strength of the Protestant churches, entirely omits the Lutheran Church; or when, at a religious gathering at Winona Lake, the leaders of a certain religious conference, unable to explain just what the Missouri Synod was, conjectured that this body might be and probably was an association of Reformed Jews.

It follows therefore that one of the great tasks which confronts the young men and young women of our church today, who will be the leaders and the guardians of Lutheranism tomorrow, is this, that they emphasize here in our country the highly American character of their church and demonstrate that our country needs more of the sound, constructive thought and action for which Lutheranism so emphatically stands. And they will be the better able to do all this if they realize that as our country needs the support of our church, so our church needs to adapt itself, as far as it conscientiously can, to the American attitude and frame of mind. For if it is true that Americanism needs Lutheranism, it is similarly evident that Lutheranism in our country needs Americanism to this extent that we have a broader vision of the possibilities of our church in this country, a deeper appreciation of the fact that we must continue to adopt American methods and policies, and finally that we show a more pronounced readiness to make a direct appeal to the American mind.

First of all, then, we must realize that our church needs a wider horizon in this country. With two states of the Union without a single Lutheran worker, with several states that have only one or two missionaries and pastors, with hundreds of cities of over five and ten thousand population altogether untouched by the Lutheran message, we must be ready to give more and to pray with greater earnestness, so that workers may be sent into the vast unoccupied fields of our own nation. And these workers should be sent not only to such places where there are German-speaking people and people of German descent but to all places, irrespective of nationality and language, where there are immortal souls that may still be saved. And remember, in that degree that our church adds to its membership such names as Jones, Smith, Williams, MacCarthy, O'Brien, Kelley, and similar American or non-German names, the insinuations that Lutheranism is foreign will dwindle away and disappear.

Then, in our own congregational work, young people should assist in making the adoption of American methods and policies possible. For example, if there is a German sign on a church or German lettering in conspicuous places, this will certainly not tend to attract people who cannot read or speak German, any more than the reader would feel drawn to a church that had an Italian sign on its walls. And in such cases young people can readily offer the financial support required to make the necessary changes. Similarly young people can assist in maintaining regular English sermons in their churches. During the last ten years the number of those congregations that have no such regular services in the language of the land has been drastically reduced. But often in the relatively few congregations where there is no English service every Sunday and there actually is room and reason for such a service, the young people can again assist financially and morally in making the English work possible. . . .

But a positive policy of publicity is necessary in addition. Advertising is one of the great American characteristics, a fact which can be appreciated the more when we read that during the year 1925, according to a recent statement made before the Federal Trades Council, the newspapers of our country alone carried more than $720,000,000 worth of advertising. And there is a legitimate reason for careful and systematic publicity in behalf of our church. Many who have heard the radio messages of our church, have read our tracts, or studied our advertisements have of their own accord written in to tell us that their conception of the Lutheran Church has been changed and that they understand why the Lutheran Church takes the position that it does in many issues. Here, too, young people can assist their congregations and help in the cause of establishing a greater Lutheranism by distributing tracts, helping in securing the proper newspaper publicity, providing for signboards before their churches, and in many other ways bringing their church and its message to the attention of the community in which they are situated.

Again, there is a lesson which we can learn from the spirit of our country and that is the truth that there is strength in unity. A characteristic of the German mind that has brought much and deplorable sorrow is the tendency to avoid unity and concerted action and to follow one's own individual inclinations. Historians have repeatedly commented on the fact that as long as the Teutonic peoples were united they could not be defeated; and correspondingly, that their reverses came only when they refused to participate in concerted action. Perhaps many of us have inherited a similar independence of thought—a trait which is certainly not without many commendable considerations but which is entirely out of place in the constructive program for the extension of the Savior's kingdom. There we must have a wholehearted, churchwide, united cooperation which unfortunately has been missing in some of the great projects of our church.

Let us then realize the high and holy relation which exists between our church and our country. Let us avoid the "*Deutschland, Deutschland, ueber Alles*" spirit while we pay ready tribute to the debt which our country owes to Germany. . . . Let us, in short, not with the waving of flags or with showy spectacles or with loud-mouthed and blatant assertions of Lutheran patriotism but with the quiet, yet determined and energetic policy, work for the upbuilding and the strengthening of the two greatest institutions in the world, the American government and the Lutheran Church. (*WLM,* 34, 672 ff.)

W.A.M.'s strictures were not limited to his own church body. He looked about with a prophetic eye and found other Christian churches of his day wanting as well. *Time* magazine reported the following address, first delivered at Ocean Grove in New Jersey and then published as an article in the *Messenger* in September 1931. The Letters to the Seven Churches of Asia Minor in Revelation 2 and 3 gave W.A.M. the germinal idea for a 20th-century parallel.

Seven Fatal Follies

If the seer of Patmos was driven by the Spirit in his day to write his letters of warning to the seven congregations of Asia Minor, God alone knows how sorely modern American Christianity needs the rebuke of stern disapproval for the seven follies of present-day church life and its adamant indifference to the fundamental work of the church, that of saving souls. Here we have, first of all, *the political church,* that feels itself divinely constituted as a power in American political life, that does not hesitate to ride ruthlessly over the Savior's pronouncement: "My kingdom is not of this world"; that surrenders the constitutional principle of the separation of church and state and either follows the dictates of an ecclesiastical head who is regarded as higher than the highest voice of our nation or tries to mold the influence of American legislators by professional lobbyism and foists upon the free and sovereign people of our nation a program of selfish and sectarian ambitions. To all of those who today would perpetuate on the shores of this tolerant nation the spirit of the Inquisition, the brutality of St. Bartholomew's Night, the ruthless rule and rote of Puritanism, or the establishment of a Christian nation by a legislative and judicial force—to all such the Savior declares: "Put up again thy sword in its place, for all they that take the sword shall perish with the sword."

Then there is *the sensational church,* that uses the springboard of publicity to hurl itself into the attention of the American people by a long list of novelties and innovations: children in the pulpit and dogs in the pew; jazz bands to accompany the hymns of prayer and praise and picked beauties as ushers to attract otherwise indifferent men; an endless list of catchy phrases and an inexhaustible catalog of bizarre attractions. To all those who thus play while people perish, the Lord of Love declares: "My house is a house of prayer." Let them stop this theatrical drivel and go out into the highways and byways and compel men to come in, for all things are now ready.

Again there is *the church with a financial complex,* that lives and moves and has its being in the pursuit of the allegedly almighty dollar, that makes the end justify the means and institutes raffles, gambling devices, and roulette wheels, resorting even to the most flagrant violations of the law of the land in their frenzied financing; the churches that wheedle unwilling contributions from unbelievers and coerce the indifferent into giving grudging support to the cause of Christ. To all such the Savior, who made a scourge of small ropes with which he lashed the temple merchants of His day and who speaks so disdainfully of money for its own sake, repeats His declaration of righteous indignation: "Make not my Father's house a house of merchandise." Let them go out and learn the full import of His words: "Seek ye first the kingdom of God."

The fourth folly is found in *the epileptic church,* which disregards the Scriptural admonition that everything be done decently and in order and works in convulsive jerks and fitful gyrations, the church that institutes Bible-reading marathons or applauds the preacher who wins the endurance prize for preaching the longest sermon in history; churches that froth and kick and scream—while the serene Prince of Peace looks on in wounded wonder and says: "The kingdom of God cometh not with outward observation." Let them be still and know that Christ is the Lord.

Then there is *the social church,* which maintains that the church's field of first duty is to solve race relations, to fight against industrialism and capitalism, to investigate the coal mines and the steel strike, and in general to present a panacea to the evils of the day by social service in its varied ramifications, by working for the body instead of for the soul, for the here in preference to the hereafter, churches that have the glitter but lack the gold—"tinkling cymbals" and "sounding brass." To them the Savior, who first forgave sins and then removed the consequences of sin, raises his voice in reproach and says, "Clean ye first the inside of the cup." Let them stop this diet of stone and learn that the hungry multitudes will perish spiritually without Christ, the veritable Bread of Life.

But more calamitous than all of these is the inactive church, *the smugly self-sufficient church* that takes its talents—the time and the money and the prayer that should be employed in rescuing perishing souls for eternity—and wraps them in the napkin of stolid indifference and buries them in the cemetery of neglect. To those who live on without raising their gaze from the four walls of their narrow environment to look out compassionately into the world that cries for its deliverance, the Lord says, "Ye are unprofitable servants." Let them learn that the church today must offer its best and widest energies in limitless self-giving, even as its Savior gave all.

But the last is the worst. The seventh sin of contemporaneous churches is *the craving for a modernistic creed,* the passion for creating a new Christianity that is "up-to-the-minute." There you have the starkest tragedy in modern American church life, this widespread endorsement of a "modernism" that is so ancient and hoary that every anti-Christian delusion preached from liberalistic pulpits today can be traced back to the heresies of the first and second centuries of the Christian era. There you have the subtle and sinister poison that is paralyzing the spiritual hopes of the nation, the brazen pretense creeping over churches built and paid for by believing fathers and mothers only to be desecrated by the leaders of their children who claim that the essence of religion is not God's great and free gift to man but man's intelligent and repeated gifts to God; not divine atonement but human attainment. There, in this infidelity of modern pulpiteers, in the cutthroat preaching of these pulpit pirates, who have boarded the ship of the church, thrown overboard every one of its sacred doctrines, and are now (and not altogether unsuccessfully) trying to seize its helm and make those who refuse to join with them walk the plank of church politics into the depths of discard, there you have the great issue and challenge that confronts all virile, red-blooded Christians who by the grace of God have refused to bow their knees before the Baal of modern skepticism. I repeat, when students at modern divinity schools can label the Soviet debauch as an enterprise embracing some high and noble ideals; when preachers can publicly and boisterously reject the inspiration of Scripture, the deity of our blessed Lord Jesus Christ, the reality of sin and the blessed redemption, the resurrection of the dead, and the second coming of Christ . . . when American churches have finally attained to the unbelief which flooded Europe a generation or two ago, we who still maintain these two basic principles of faith, "only the Scriptures" and "holy by grace," are confronted by a challenging conflict.

Remember, it is a bitter conflict, for it is a battle against the mobilized resources of some of the wealthiest families in America and against the prestige and facilities of publicity that they commandeer. It is a battle against power, specifically against forces such as the National Broadcasting Company, that generously bestow hundreds of thousands of dollars' worth of radio time to some of the leaders in the descent of American churches but wilfully refuse to sell, even at the regular rates and the regular terms, a moment of radio time to a church that would tell America's millions (deluded to ennui by blaring jazz bands, fraudulent fortune tellers,

49

and lying "true stories") the truth of God in Jesus Christ. It is a battle against organization, because it is a protest to the bitter end against the spirit of such powerful (but happily diminishing) organizations as the Federated Council of Churches of Christ in America that have abused the strength of organization by working to the detriment of the Cross, and that means to the damage of human souls and the retardation of our national welfare.

Thus the church stands at the crossroads, confronted by tremendous alternatives. On the one hand there is the broad and rolling boulevard flanked by those who raise their voices in applause every time a church takes a step away from Christ—the easy avenue called "Rationalism," that offers little resistance to the foibles and frailties to which self-absorbed humanity clings so tightly. And on the other side is the rough, uphill road that leads away from all the glamour of our modern life, to the highest that life holds and the best that the hereafter promises. No shouts of applause reach the ears of those who take the pilgrimage of this path, no revelry and show of pomp guide those who travel on its courses, for it is the same path along which the Savior wearily dragged His cross; it is the road to Calvary, the path that leads to the cross as Heaven's holiest symbol.

Along which of these two ways can the church at the crossroads find its highest hope and happiness? Two thousand five hundred years ago Jeremiah the prophet answered this question with his solemn and reverent: "Thus saith the Lord: Stand ye in the way and see and ask for the old path, where is the good way, and walk therein, and ye shall find rest for your souls." And if the church is to be roused from the lethargy into which it is sunk; if it is to be the salt of our spiritual lives and the leaven in our daily existence; if it is to be what Christ wants it to be, His holy, precious, spotless Bride, then it must come back to the old path where the saints of God trod—to the old path blazed by the apostles and evangelists, marked by the blood of the martyrs, and restored by the spiritual heroism of Martin Luther. (*WLM,* 40, 50 f.)

Finally, a remarkable story directly out of World War II gave W.A.M. the key illustration for an Easter article in the *Messenger* in 1942:

We Who Are Christ's Shall Live Again!

On the Sunday afternoon of December 7 Mr. and Mrs. Max Mueller, members of the First Lutheran Church in Omaha,

Nebraska, were listening to the University of Chicago Round Table broadcast when they heard the first radio news of the attack on Pearl Harbor. With a sudden premonition Mrs. Mueller turned to her husband and said, "Daddy, our boys are dead!" She referred to the two older sons in the Mueller family: Erwin, seventeen, and Henry, nineteen, who had enlisted in the Navy at the beginning of the year.

The parents had permitted the boys to volunteer not only because they felt that one could help the other but because Mr. and Mrs. Mueller were true Americans, even though German born. At the time the two sons left Omaha, their mother told them, "If any nation like Japan jumps on this country, you defend it with your last drop of blood!" When news of the Pearl Harbor attack was released, Mrs. Mueller felt some strange foreboding that her Erwin and Henry had fulfilled these instructions to the letter.

Her fears were soon confirmed. Nine days later this telegram came to the Mueller home: "The Navy Department deeply regrets to inform you that your sons, Erwin and Henry Mueller of the United States Navy, were killed in action in the performance of duty and service of country. . . . The department extends to you its sincerest sympathy. . . ." Stunned over the loss of both sons, Mrs. Mueller could only say, "I am proud that they died in serving our country."

Because the boys had been active members of our First Lutheran Church in Omaha, special memorial services were held on December 22. It was an impressive occasion, both for the parents and for the overflowing congregation. A lieutenant commander of the Navy laid a memorial wreath at the foot of the flag. Many, unable to attend the service, sent letters and telegrams of condolence.

Another nine days later, however, Mr. and Mrs. Mueller received from the boys two of the regulation military post cards dated December 11. The forms were checked to read, "I am well. Letter follows at first opportunity." Since the Navy death notification was dated five days later than the card, it seemed that the official government notification gave a more recent report and contained the sad truth. However, Mrs. Mueller began to hope that both her premonitions and the Navy telegrams had been wrong. Can you imagine the joy in the parents' hearts when late on the night of January 2 two telegrams came from Rear Admiral Randall Jacobs, Chief of the Bureau of Navigation? The one read: "The

Navy Department is glad to inform you that your son, Henry Max Mueller, seaman second class, United States Navy, previously reported missing following action in the performance of his duty, is now reported to be a survivor. He will doubtless communicate direct with you at an early date informing you as to his whereabouts. The anxiety caused you by the previous message is deeply regretted." The second telegram concerned Erwin, the other son, and was otherwise worded in the same manner. "It is certainly a happy New Year!" Mrs. Mueller cried. "No one can be happier than I am," she said with tears in her eyes. How completely heart-deep rejoicing must have replaced the sorrow of double mourning!

While few people have ever known a surge of happiness as great as this, yet every one of us through faith in Christ's resurrection can have the far greater joy of knowing that whenever unbelief tells us our dear ones, asleep in Jesus, can never live again, this report is even more false than the first telegram to the Muellers announcing the death of their sons. While it is only exceptional that the Navy sends out incorrect death notices and while it is tragically true that many hundreds of our American soldiers and sailors lie buried in distant graves or are drowned in deep oceans, there is no exception to the promise that Christ Himself proclaimed: "If any man keep My saying, he shall never see death," in the eternal death, the wages of unforgiven sin. Our Lord never makes a mistake. He never issues a misleading promise. When He says, "I am the Resurrection and the Life, He that believeth in Me, though he were dead, yet shall he live," that is the highest truth of Heaven itself. It can never be broken.

Jesus told His disciples in the upper room a few hours before He set His face toward Gethsemane and its agony, "In My Father's house there are many mansions. I go to prepare a place for you." He was going, first of all, to the cross, but beyond all the shame and agony of Calvary He was directed to heaven. How overfilled are these words with personal comfort! He speaks intimately of His "Father's house" and assures those who believe that there is a blessed existence for them beyond the grave. Cling closely to each word of this promise, especially during these days of doubt when the concluding statements of the Apostles' Creed, "I believe . . . in the resurrection of the body and the life everlasting," are assailed with new, destructive hatred, laughed away in ridicule! We need a ban on the allegedly humorous references to heaven. Public or private slurs on Bible teachings concerning the life to come are always objectionable but doubly so in a period of emergency like the present, when masses of American youth defending our country may be close to death on land and sea. Men, we are told, are only high-grade animals. Millions of them are killed in world conflict, laid into hastily dug graves, their bodies drowned in the deep sea or exposed to the devastating elements; and that, unbelief sneeringly claims, is the end. How bitter and cruel life would be if death were the end! Instead we ought to find constant, reverent comfort in the fact that through Christ death is only the beginning of glory incomparable, immeasurable, unutterable!

The Easter triumph is the seal and assurance of our own victory over the grave. "Where I am, there shall also My servant be," Jesus pledges. He is now in heaven. We are to be God's house-guests to live where our Lord lives. What unspeakable glory! To worship the Creator, who gave us our existence; to sing our praises to the Savior, who redeemed us by His own life-giving death; to exalt the Holy Spirit, who gave us the new birth in holiness and righteousness—can any earthly privilege even approach that dwelling with the Almighty, the Lord of heaven?

Perfection, sinlessness, absolute holiness always dwell with God. Besides, the Scriptures want us to believe that in the celestial, eternal city there will be no sorrow, no grief, no pain, no broken hopes, no partings, no tears. There in a radiance we cannot describe or understand, all the frantic, unrewarded toils of life; all the aching anguish of broken hearts; all the sorrow of sin will utterly vanish as we realize that "the sufferings of this present time are not worthy to be compared with the glory which shall be revealed in us." Though we can never faintly picture the celestial beauty and its dazzling splendor, let us rest with the assurance that if this world, despite all sin, contains marvels of beauty and breath-taking scenes—the towering mountains etched against the flaming sky, the amethyst-green surf, the rainbow raising its arch of color across the land—what must be the magnificence of the celestial city!

Why then, with heaven as our real home, should our hearts be troubled? Why should we weep at funerals as those who have no hope? In the second century a Greek named Aristides wrote to his friend concerning the early followers of our Lord: "If any among these Christians passes from this world, they rejoice and give thanks to God. And they escort his body with songs and thanksgiving, as if he were setting out from one place to another nearby." God grant you the same resolute faith, so that when death finally takes a beloved one or comes to summon you, you may be able to rejoice in spirit even through tears of human sorrow! Clinging to the resurrected Christ, may you look forward joyfully to the Savior's presence, the celestial glory, the reunion with all the children of God, and particularly to our own personal prepared place, where we shall see Jesus "as He is." O God, bring us all together for that glory! (*WLM*, 50, 435 ff.)

3
PROPHET

A prophet, in the Biblical sense, was more a spokesman for God in denouncing sin and proclaiming His will than a foreteller of future events. W.A.M.'s article on "Seven Fatal Follies" is an example of prophecy in the primary Old Testament definition, and many of his *Lutheran Hour* sermons would also strike a prophetic note in this understanding.

Still, the great prophets of the Bible also foretold the future under divine inspiration. Without in any sense claiming similar inspiration for himself—in fact, he specifically denied having the gift of prophecy—Walter A. Maier nevertheless was so keen an observer of the times that he had an uncanny knack of predicting future events with astonishing accuracy. He never scatter-shot his "prophecies"—unlike contemporary practitioners who are "saved" by the sheer varieties of their predictions and the law of averages. Indeed, the listing here is nearly the sum total of his forecasts.

For the present mania of trying to date the Second Coming of Christ by misuse of apocalyptic literature in Ezekiel, Daniel, and the Book of Revelation, he would have shown disdain. In 1941, for example, he wrote:

Too often men seek the fulfillment of an Old Testament forecast in some contemporaneous event of history, and they are guided in their selection neither by Scripture nor history but by their own personal and preconceived political opinions. Frequently such speculative prophecy assumes more importance than the preaching of the Gospel itself, and many Christians who attend church to find the way to forgiveness, comfort, and heaven are entertained by an amateurish presentation of the role that Russia, Turkey, Hitler, or Stalin "play" on the Old Testament pages. (*WLM,* 49, 561)

For prophecies of fortune tellers and psychics he had contempt and scorn, and one of his favorite ploys in the "Turret" column was to hold spoiled predictions under the noses of the predictors, as in this piece from 1943:

The war will end before Christmas. At the International Fortune Tellers Convention at New York City various members among the 300 in attendance asserted, among other things, that General MacArthur will be our next president; that President Roosevelt will not run again; that Hitler will die a slow, torturing, mental death. These predictions were based on tea leaves, playing cards, crystal balls, palms of hands, bumps on the head, beer suds, and dunked doughnuts. . . .

Nostradamus, the Jewish medieval mystic and astrologer, foretold that when Easter would fall on its latest date, April 25, the end of the world would come. This year Easter has come on this latest possible date—and gone, but the world still continues. Despite these and other failures by Nostradamus, he continues to receive widespread study and acceptance by people who would be far better off if they turned to Christ for assurance for the future. (*WLM,* 51, 612)

Dr. Maier's own batting average for accurate prediction was far more impressive. The following citations, again, are in chronological order.

As early as 1921 he predicted World War II:

The late and lamented World War was brutal and inhuman in the extreme, but in the next war wholesale massacre will be more scientific and therefore even more brutal and inhuman. (*WLM,* 30, 179)

56

In 1923 an elaboration:

When the next war comes, as it certainly must come, perhaps in the generation of which we are part, history will witness the futility of a world peace that has no place for the world's Prince of Peace. Even the horrors of the World War will pale into insignificance when civilization is torn by the next great conflict, for then, in diabolic mockery of all peace projects, there will be newer and more terrific instruments of wholesale human destruction . . . large aeroplanes will carry newly discovered explosives which will wipe out entire cities . . . more powertul tanks, new methods of warfare on land and sea will institute a crimson carnage absolutely indescribable. (*WLM*, 32, 55)

In 1934 a reiteration:

There is nothing more certain on the horizon of international affairs than this, that there will be a Second World War, which in some respects will definitely be more horrible than the first. May God in His mercy and power postpone that war of extinction! (*WLM*, 43, 230)

In 1937 he nearly had the date:

Today it is not a question of whether there will be a war in Europe. The question is whether war—either declared or undeclared—will break out tomorrow, next year, or at the turn of the fortics. (*WLM*, 46, 212)

On Ghandi

Mahatma Ghandi, India's nationalist leader, is waging war against England without arms and ammunition. . . . Perhaps passive resistance will accomplish more in India than any military uprising. (*WLM*, 30, 179)
Prediction in 1921; fulfillment in 1947.

The King of Spain

Alfonso's throne is tottering. Even the easy going Spaniards are taking a noticeable offense at the somewhat loose and unkingly conduct of their unkingly monarch. . . . Most of us will not be very much surprised if we wake up some fine morning and read that the ruling Spanish dynasty has been overthrown. (*WLM*, 32, 238)
Prediction in 1923; fulfillment in 1931.

The King of Rumania

King Carol is again under fire. This time he is assailed for his lavish program of spending. . . . We claim no gift of prophecy, but we have the feeling that Carol, of notorious past, will eventually go the modern way of most kings. (*WLM,* 41, 364)
Prediction in 1933; fulfillment in 1940.

America Would Not Go Communist

"America is ready for Communism," says Lincoln Steffens, biographer and lecturer. Indeed, he describes our country as "a hundred more times ready than Russia ever was." These scare lines exaggerate. Our entire social structure and the expressions of American life are so different from those of Russia that even at present [i.e., depths of the Depression] a successful Communistic revolt seems impossible. (*WLM,* 41, 454)
Prediction in 1933; fulfillment to date.

Danger from the Japanese Navy:

Japan's navy is on the increase . . . and will have 140 underage cruisers, destroyers, and submarines by 1936 to 100 of these craft in the American navy. Figures of this kind do not impress one with the conviction that peace is at hand or that American precautions in the way of armament and preparation can be swept aside according to the program of the radical pacifist. (*WLM,* 42, 429)
Statement in 1934; confirmation in 1941.

Atomic Energy

At times the prophetic insight came eerily close to material W.A.M. could not have known was classified information, as in the following excerpt.

What do you suppose is the most remarkable discovery in our age? Ask American scientists, and many will agree that "one of the greatest, if not the greatest, discovery in modern" times is U-235, a chemical twin to uranium. . . . Scientists on both shores of the Atlantic are feverishly at work behind closed laboratory doors in the attempt to secure large quantities of U-235—an achievement which could bring victory in the present war to whichever side first completes the process.[4]
Prediction in 1941; fulfillment in 1945.

58

Infantile Paralysis

Restless human genius, under divine guidance and blessing, will not be satisfied until an effective antidote to the deforming disease can be found. (*WLM,* 44, 298)

Prediction in 1936; fulfillment in 1953.

TV Will Blanket the Country

Television sets will soon be on the market. . . . Their field of dependable usefulness will be limited to an area of within a hundred miles' radius of New York and Philadelphia.—Doubtless this limitation will soon be removed, and before many years pass, television instruments, reduced in price but advanced in effectiveness, will be in use throughout the land. (*WLM,* 46, 246)

Prediction in 1937; fulfillment in 1951.

A similar prediction for FM broadcasts in 1939 (*WLM,* 47, 458).

Russia Would Abridge Religious Freedom

If Russia becomes the dominant figure in continental Europe and remains atheistic, the postwar world will witness a chaos such as we have never known. The freedom of religion which we have promised to extend to all the world would be impossible under Communistic regime. (*WLM,* 51, 437)

Prediction in 1943; fulfillment in 1947.

The Shroud of Turin

The Holy Shroud has been secretly moved from the Cathedral of Turin . . . in consequence of aerial bombardment. . . . The genuineness of this relic has been repeatedly contested, but it is asserted that its authenticity was established scientifically twelve years ago.—Claims like this mean nothing to us. We submit that it is usually impossible to prove that an article of this kind is genuine. (*WLM,* 51, 500)

Statement in 1943; confirmation to date.

The Communist Takeover of Eastern Europe

With Russia victorious and dominant, the radical elements in . . . the Baltic countries, the Balkan nations, and the several states into which defeated Germany itself is to be divided would need little inducement and would find little difficulty in becoming affiliated with the Soviet sister republics. In the east several large and influential Chinese provinces could be easily drawn into the same alliance. (*WLM,* 52, 289)

Prediction in 1944; fulfillment in 1948.

Postwar Gains for Labor

Labor will constantly assume new importance; politicians will bid for the workingman's support; trade unions will grow stronger; and on the other hand, clashes between management and labor will be more frequent and more severe. (*WLM,* 53, 9)

Prediction in 1944; fulfillment to date.

Communist Takeover of China

Six years ago the *Messenger* predicted, "Whoever else triumphs in this war, godless Communism will certainly win." That forecast is being fulfilled to a startling extent. . . . Largely, it seems, through the instrumentality of American-British intercession, Chinese Communists are now to work directly in the conduct of the war. To us this means that before long they will control China's 400,000,000. (*WLM,* 53, 190 f.)

Prediction in 1945; fulfillment in 1949.

Not that W.A.M. was right with *every* prediction. Still this researcher found only two glaring miscues in a quarter-century's worth of *Messengers.* They are:

State of Israel and the Temple

Scripture offers no warrant for the belief in the restoration of the Temple which is held in some branches of the Christian church. . . . Our Savior prophesied that the Temple of His day would be reduced so that not one stone would be left standing on the other. But He offered no hope or promise of its rebuilding. And a temple on the original site and with even a shadow of its original splendor, like the whole notion of a restoration of the Jewish state in Palestine, will never be much more than the fond reverie of visionary rabbis. (*WLM,* 32, 39 f.)

Prediction in 1923; half of the prediction regarding a Jewish state was proven wrong in 1948; the other half regarding the Temple still stands.

Hitler

Adolf Hitler's repudiation of communistic atheism and his unqualified insistence upon a return of the German nation to the God of its fathers is one of the most hopeful signs in the reconstruction of Germany. . . . It seems to us that here, at least, we have the expression of a spirit that may show Germany the way. (*WLM*, 41, 461)

Prediction in 1933; disproven shortly thereafter.
When further details about Hitler emerged from Germany, W.A.M. did a 180° turnabout in his opinions of the German dictator, whose deceptions proved a bitter disappointment. Many others in the early thirties were also taken in by Hitler's original promises.

But for these exceptions, W.A.M.'s predictions proved startlingly accurate. Unlike others, however, he rarely prided himself on his hunches and regularly tried to cut the ground away from pretentious contemporary "prophets." At one point in 1937 he even identified their secrets:

Occasionally, prophetic utterances do seem to have an uncanny clutch on the future. They are to be explained as coincidences. They strike the truth on the same principle that the mere result of chance makes the dice fall in certain calculable ways. (*WLM*, 45, 271)

The prophecies that pleased him most came from his beloved Old Testament, as this excerpt demonstrates:

In all human experience there is only one form of accurate prophecy and exact fulfillment—the prophetic record on the pages of Scripture. In the ruins of Nineveh, Ashur, Babylon, Jerusalem, Tyre, Sidon, and a score of other places specifically mentioned in the Scripture, we have abundant and compelling instances of fulfilled prophecy which ask us to rise up and defend the truth of the Old Testament. (*WLM*, 45, 326)

In 1943 he put it even more succinctly: "No man can ever unlock the future. Only God can foretell accurately, and as a matter of record only His Bible has forecast the truth." (*WLM*, 52, 147)

4
ESSAYIST

When W.A.M. wrote scholarly articles and reviews for the *Concordia Theological Monthly* or read papers at seminaries and universities, another form of writing was appropriate. One of his most important essays was delivered at the University of Virginia in Charlottesville on August 9, 1930. Because its theme concerns that ever-debated relationship of church and state and its conclusions still have much relevance, the essay is presented in its entirety. The address is a good index both to W.A.M.'s political thought and to his critique of American church life in the early thirties. It was also reported widely in the nation's press. But readers less interested in this theme should move ahead to the next chapter.

The Jeffersonian Ideals of Religious Liberty

In 1768 three Baptist ministers were arrested in Virginia, charged with disturbing the peace, and denounced by a prosecutor, who bellowed out this indictment: "They cannot meet a man upon the road but they must ram a text of Scripture down his throat." Their arrest and trial on what appears to us to be only a flimsy pretext for ill-disguised bigotry was, however, in the strictest accord with both the letter and the spirit of the law, by which the statute books of Virginia were constituted mentors of things religious. According to their provisions, civil service and political privileges were denied to those who held doctrinal positions contrary to the dogmas of the Established Church; according to their definite specifications, children of Unitarian parents could be legally removed from their homes and entrusted to any Trinitarian, quite regardless of his moral and mental qualifications for assuming this responsibility. To deny the doctrine of the Trinity was a major crime, punishable with imprisonment of three years. A penal sentence awaited those parents who refused to have their children baptized, and those who lived in open and unrestricted heresy could be burned alive.

But the Dominion State was not isolated in its religious prejudices and in its opposition to religious freedom as we enjoy it today. Nowhere in America was there a comprehensive provision by which any colony granted unqualified freedom of religion to all its subjects. In Massachusetts the law demanded compulsory attendance at church and civil support for ministers. Dissenting Christians were exiled, and that heresy was regarded as a civil crime may be seen from the fact that Rev. Henry Dunster, first president of Harvard College, "was indicted by the grand jury, . . . because he had preached against infant baptism." It was not until 1833 in Massachusetts, that eminently progressive state, that Church and State were completely separated. The attitude of the other colonies differed only in degree but hardly in principle. The second constitution of South Carolina declared Protestantism to be the established religion of the state and insisted that its chief officers believe in a future state of rewards and punishments. North Carolina and Pennsylvania made the acceptance of the inspiration of the Old and the New Testament a qualification for office. Even in Maryland religious liberty was granted only to those who believed in the deity of Christ.

And beyond the confines of this country, in France, for example, the Huguenots were still some decades away from the edict that permitted them to beget legal children and to die with equal legality but did not give them permission to think, speak, or worship with that freedom which today is an inherent right of every American.

In England the denial of the divine inspiration of the Bible could be punished by the boring of a red-hot poker through the tongue of the skeptic!

Now, those three Baptist ministers, three representatives of a long line of protest that was beginning to assert itself with indomitable persistence, were defended by that ardent apostle of human liberty Patrick Henry. In his speech in their behalf the forensic Virginian stood up before the court and said:

> If I have rightly understood, these three inoffensive persons have been arraigned for a crime of great magnitude—as disturbers of the peace. May it please the court, what did I hear read? Did I hear it distinctly, or was it a mistake of my own? Did I hear that these men whom your Worships are about to try for misdemeanor are charged with—with—with—what? . . . With preaching the Gospel of the Son of God.

The conclusion of Patrick Henry's appeal is equally classic:

> From that period when our fathers left the land of their nativity for these American wilds,—from that moment despotism was crushed, the fetters of darkness were broken, and Heaven decreed that man should be free, free to worship God according to the Bible.

But even if the oratory of Patrick Henry could help to sway the decision in this case, it required something more definite to remove such preposterous provisions forever from the legislation of Virginia and to make the America that was soon to enter its battle for civil liberty safe for religious liberty. To have accomplished this herculean task, to have defeated the organized opposition fostered by the clergy of the Established Church in Virginia, and to have inspired the framers of the Constitution with the courage and determination required to have them embody in this document the principle that *"Congress shall make no law respecting an establishment of religion or prohibiting the free exercise thereof"*—all this is the imperishable distinction of him whose cherished memory is being commemorated this evening. As his self-chosen epitaph immortalizes, Jefferson regarded as one of the greatest accomplishments of his great career and as an achievement which he ranked parallel to his authorship of the Declaration of Independence and the founding of the University of Virginia—his authorship of the Statute of Virginia for Religious Freedom.

64

We pause to remind ourselves that Thomas Jefferson's was not the first voice in history to be raised for the proper evaluation of the respective spheres of Church and State. As far back as 1656 in England Sir Henry Vane, the voice of one crying in an unsympathetic wilderness, had insisted that—

> Every one might give an account of himself in all matters of God's worship unto God and Christ alone, . . . not in these things to be oppressed or brought before the judgment-seats of men.

And two long centuries and a half before Jefferson's time a group of princes, assembled in historic Augsburg in the effort to establish a unified church, laid down this fundamental proposition, unique in its clarity and surprising in its modernity:

> Seeing, then, that ecclesiastical power concerneth things eternal and is exercised only by the means of the Word, it hindereth not the political government any more than the art of singing hinders political government; for the political government is occupied about other matters than is the Gospel. The magistracy defends not the minds, but the bodies and bodily things against manifest intruders and coerces men by the sword and corporal punishment that it may uphold civil justice and peace. Wherefore the ecclesiastical and civil powers are not to be confounded.

Small wonder that an enlightened world in which these principles have found application pauses after four long and eventful centuries to pay its tribute to the spirit of Augsburg by sending representatives there in grateful memory of the events of June 25, 1530, when men again hearkened to the injunction of the lowly Nazarene: "Render unto Caesar the things which are Caesar's and unto God the things that are God's." It is therefore not without intense significance to note that "the idea of legally establishing unalienable, inherent, and sacred rites of the individual is not of political, but religious origin,—in reality the fruit of the Reformation and its struggle." (Jellinek, 75)

But it was Jefferson's task to give the first practical and systematic demonstration of these principles. This he did, first of all, through his Bill for Religious Freedom, which after nine years of bitter struggle was finally passed as the first detailed law in all human ordinances giving perfect freedom of conscience. This he did in the larger activities of the national policies by his unintermittent avowal of a program of religious liberty.

We are not assembled this evening to investigate Jefferson's religious convictions; nor would he countenance any such investigation. To him—and I interrupt to eradicate the picture of Jefferson as an atheist or agnostic—religion was a matter of personal conviction, a sacred concordat existing between the individual and his Maker, and as such infinitely above the possibility of prying investigation and carping criticism on the part of others. We may not share his religious convictions. I certainly do not. But, I repeat, we are concerned about Jefferson the American rather than Jefferson the religionist; Jefferson the statesman rather than Jefferson the sectarian.

Viewed in this way, his one consuming ideal of religious liberty is the fundamental thesis that there can be no tyranny over the conscience of men. He swore, as he himself emphatically avowed, "upon the altar of God eternal hostility against every form of tyranny over the mind of men." He elaborated upon this principle frequently and at considerable length, and in his *Notes on Religion* he gives a homely and practical illustration of this position:

> No man complains of his neighbor for ill management of his affairs, for an error in sowing his land or marrying his daughter, for consuming his substance in taverns, pulling down, building, etc. In all these he has his liberty; but if he do not frequent the church or there conform to ceremonies, there is an immediate uproar. The care of every man's soul belongs to himself. But what if he neglect the care of it? Well, what if he neglect the care of his health or estate, which more nearly relate to the State? Will the magistrate make a law that he shall not be poor or sick? Laws provide against injury from others, but not from ourselves.

Jefferson was opposed in principle to every act of intermeddling—or even any suggestion of it—according to which the State would regulate the affairs of the Church, a logic based on the fundamental premise which he expressed in one of his letters:

> I have considered religion as a matter between every man and his Maker, in which no other, and far less the public, has a right to intermeddle.

Jefferson's adherence to this principle was so rigid and

inflexible that he not only steadfastly refused to discuss his religious convictions with others, telling one of the professional biographers of his day: *"Say nothing of my religion. It is known to my God and myself alone. Its evidence before the world is to be sought in my life";* but he also did not shrink from the logical consequence of refusing to follow the practice of Washington and Adams in issuing presidential proclamations for thanksgiving festivals and days of fasting and repentance, a custom which, especially in reference to Thanksgiving, has been perpetuated until today, although in the strictest analysis we must unhesitatingly concede that Jefferson's position is eminently the more consequent.

With consistency in such details, we may well anticipate that the broader principles of complete separation of the State from the functions of the Church are expressed with unequivocal precision. Jefferson demands, as a corollary of the right of every individual to worship God according to the dictates of his conscience, that the State shall not compel anyone to attend a church, that no one shall be forced to contribute to the maintenance of any religious organization or institution, and that there shall be no official preference according to which the civil rights of the individual are to be restricted or increased because of his religious belief. Public safety and convenience may, of course, under the stress of abnormal circumstances, suspend the application of some of these principles, as Jefferson admits in his *Notes on Religion,* where he says:

> It is ordinarily lawful to kill calves or lambs; they may therefore be religiously sacrificed. But if the good of the state required a temporary suspension of killing lambs, as during a siege, sacrifices of them may then be rightfully suspended also.

He admits, too, that governmental separation from religious affairs may never become a mantle of lawlessness. He states:

> Whatsoever is lawful in the commonwealth or permitted to the subject in the ordinary way cannot be forbidden to him for religious uses; and whatsoever is prejudicial to the commonwealth in their ordinary uses and therefore prohibited by the law ought not to be permitted to churches in their sacred rites.

But beyond such natural and self-implied limitations he admits of no restriction of personal liberties of the individual in his religious life, no interference on the part of the government, local,

State, or Federal, in the exercise of religious functions. He did not believe, as he himself summarized the situation, that it was *"for the interest of religion to invite the civil magistrate to direct its exercises, its disciplines, or its doctrines."*

His emancipation of the Church from the dominion of the State was so radical and revolutionary that it met with the most vehement opposition on the part of the state-supported clergy, whose complacency and social security it certainly disturbed. It was so defiant and destructive to the traditions of the Old World that the ideals of Jeffersonian religious freedom as they were perpetuated in our national Constitution could find a European reflex only in the establishment of isolated free churches and dissenter movements of various types, although Jefferson's writings on religion were translated into French and Italian and read at many courts. It was in fact throwing the gauntlet down to the age-old delusion expressed in emperor worship, to which the excavations in the cradle lands of humanity lend their graphic testimony. It was a fiery protest against the pagan cults that clutter the pages of ancient history, with depraved rulers functioning as high priests before human sacrifices. But it was especially an unsparing indictment of every bloody act of persecution committed by the punitive arm of the state in the name of the Lord of Love. It was a stinging rebuke of every form of man's inhumanity to men, of every tyrannical usurpation of power by which the sword of the government has been unsheathed to persecute nonconformists and heretics. With the groans of ten thousands of martyrs in France on St. Bartholomew's night and in the ensuing massacres ringing out piteously into the hopeless night of religious intolerance; with the hideous massacres of the Spanish Inquisition, cataloguing more than 18,000 unfortunates burned alive in only the beginning of the bloody chapter of its history; with the smoke of these autos-da-fé rising as a challenge to the heroic genius who would deliver humanity from the most unsparing tyranny that history knows, Jefferson vindicated the cause of racked bodies and tortured souls when he summarized his conviction:

> I consider the Government of the United States as interdicted by the Constitution from intermeddling with religious institutions, their doctrines, discipline, or exercises.

The heritage of this freedom, one of the foundation stones of national happiness and American prosperity, has been bequeathed to us, as to a generation in which religious liberty is so well understood and therefore accepted with such indifference that the titanic character of Jefferson and the gigantic struggle which he waged for humanity is not fully estimated and adequately appreciated. Indeed, such organized movements as crystallized in the Oregon School Bill a few years ago, which would permit the State to interfere in a most drastic manner in the educational policies of certain churches, showed—in the powerful propaganda that was recruited for this movement—that there are masses in our country that may be mobilized for the destruction of the very fundamental ideals of noninterference by the State for which Jefferson contended so incessantly. With several states using part of their tax money for the support of religious institutions; with the quiet but determined policy that exists in some of our larger cities according to which the administration extends a very attractive patronage to favored denominations; with weighty elections sometimes decided by our citizenry on the basis of denominational preference, it hardly need be remarked that even today the Jeffersonian policy of absolute governmental neutrality in religious matters has not been fully assimilated and needs emphatic restatement in this otherwise enlightened age.

But if the State was not to exercise any form of control over the Church beyond such as is dictated by the plain expedients of harmonious communal life, then certainly, according to the Jeffersonian platform of reconstruction, the churches too were not to exercise any form of control over the affairs of the State. In thus emphasizing the spiritual realm of the Church and insisting upon its clean-cut aloofness from political issues, Jefferson unhesitatingly and unsparingly denounced all political sermons. In one of his letters he states his position with this unreserved frankness:

> On one question I differ—the right of discussing public affairs in the pulpit. . . . But I suppose there is not a single instance of a single congregation which has employed their preacher for the mixed purposes of lecturing them from the pulpit in chemistry, in medicine, in law, in science, and the principles of government, or in anything but religion exclusively. Whenever, therefore, preachers, instead of a lesson in religion, put them off with a discourse on the Copernican system, on chemical affinities, on the construction of government, or the characters or conduct of

those administering it, it is a breach of contract, depriving their audience of the kind of service for which they are salaried, and giving them instead what they did not want. . . . In choosing our pastor, we look to his religious qualifications, without entering into his physical or political dogmas, with which we mean to have nothing to do.

Yet with all this Jefferson would not emasculate the clergy and make the minister of religion a voiceless, spineless, complacent person. The toga of the sovereign rights of citizenship was not removed when a young man became a clergyman; and in the same letter from which I have quoted to you, Jefferson insists:

The preacher has the right, equally with other citizens, to express his sentiments, in speaking or writing, on the subjects of medicine, law, politics, etc., his leisure time being his own and his congregation not being obliged to listen to his conversation or to read his writings.

A glance at the church advertisements in almost any one of our metropolitan dailies will quickly reveal that this conception of a clergyman's office is frequently honored more by the breach than by the observance. When American churches feature sermons on such topics as: "Is Mussolini the Man of Destiny?" "The Meaning of Dimension," "The London Naval Treaty—What It Means," "The Message of the Visting Nurse," "Streetcar Ventilation," or "Psychometric Reading," we are confronted with conditions which a few years ago prompted a layman to complain that we now go to church to hear sermons on the minimum wage, adequate housing of the poor, the regulation of moving pictures and the dance halls, how to vote, and the latest vice-investigation report. He tells that a child returning home from Sunday school was asked by its mother the subject of the lesson. It was how to keep the streets clean. On another Sunday kindness to dumb animals furnished the subject of the lesson. A woman who had suffered greatly because of a recent sorrow brought herself to go to church, longing for some comforting word. She heard a sermon on the Charity Organization Society and the Visiting Nurse.—It is the tragedy of modern American church life that it has too frequently permitted its purely spiritual functions to be obliterated by patent bids for notoriety in political, quasi-scientific, and industrial subjects. Too many crusading pastors are political impostors; too many Scriptural texts are mere partisan pretexts; too many militant clergymen are really virulent policemen.

But the political sermon is only an incidental indictment in Jefferson's condemnation of church interference in governmental affairs. He hurls devastating invectives against the inequity of religious preference or sectarian favoritism, which would give any particular denomination political or social ascendency over others. He invokes the warnings of history to show how tragic consequences are when the spiritual privileges are abused to satisfy political ambitions. He rises up against the spiritual arrogance which boasted: "God left to Peter not only the Church Universal, but also the whole world, to govern" and which so disrupted the course of political administration that a great churchman could interdict Henry IV [of Germany] and declare: "I absolve all Christians from the oaths which they have sworn or may swear to him and forbid all obedience to him as king." Against this old system, that both "the spiritual sword and the temporal" are in the power of the Church, Jefferson thunders out his protest of civil independence from ecclesiastical tyranny, without which even his declaration of national independence would have degenerated into a mere caricature of human liberty. Against the sullen background of depressing history, where arrogant pontiffs moved their puppet kings with the string of ecclesiastical tyranny and where they wielded the naked sword of persecution over the lives and destinies of uncounted millions and where no prince was too exalted in the splendor of his palace and no peasant too lowly in the obscurity of his hovel to escape the vengeance of the church that had forgotten the injunction of its Founder: "Put up thy sword"—against all this Jefferson's emancipation of the State from the Church looms up as the light which is to usher in a new and promising day in the history of human affairs.

Need I say that the world has not kept pace with the high standard which these Jeffersonian ideals have set; that our own country has not so thoroughly assimilated these principles that it *avoids* even today grave inconsistencies and flagrant intrusions by church bodies into the realms of pure politics? We think almost instinctively of the hostile incursions into the political life of the nation that are being led by paid reformers operating under church sanction and with church salary; of the maintenance of political lobbies by religious groups in the national capital and in the political centers of our states; of the conscious and defiant utterances of churchmen who still maintain, in spite of all the tragedies to which this principle has given expression, that the Church must direct the affairs of the American nation, of the national Constitution, which would mean the drafting of the governmental sword for the propagation of Christ's faith; of the well-meant yet nevertheless un-American tendency to make Bible reading a compulsory part of our public-school curriculum; of the less commendable campaigns designed to make the American Sunday a replica of the Jewish Sabbath through the passage of dismal blue laws—we think of all this, and the conviction that forces itself upon us is this, that we need a deeper appreciation of the Jeffersonian spirit, a more sincere application of the Jeffersonian ideals.

In order to give our discussion a direct and practical bearing, how can we view the treatment which certain church bodies are according the prohibition amendment in the light of these Jeffersonian principles? The spirit of his writings leaves, it seems to me, no doubt as to the attitude which this great liberalist would assume if he were among us today. He would first of all establish the fact that the constitutional amendment for prohibition is part and parcel of our civil legislation. He would insist then that as such it should not be assailed or championed by any church and denominational group, just as little as any tariff provision, traffic ordinance, or game regulation should be accorded ecclesiastical approval and disapproval. He would add that, while it is the duty of the churches to emphasize to their followers the virtue of temperance and the vice of drunkenness, yet such indoctrination under no circumstances is to assume a definite political coloring or to express itself in the maintenance of political intimidation campaigns or legislative lobbies or similar modified forms of force. He would tell us, in short, that, while every citizen is entrusted with the privilege and responsibility of exercising the sovereign function of his ballot either for or against the repeal of the amendment, denominational bodies as spiritual organizations have no call to enter into legislative agitations, whatever their tendencies may be.

His voice of warning would also be raised, we may well believe, against those aggressive interferences in the industrial life of the nation on the part of authorized federal church organizations which have gone beyond the scope of the Church's province in busying themselves with economic issues, financial problems, and purely sociological questions. He would not countenance the campaigns conducted by church organizations to mold popular opinion in regard to such purely political issues as the entrance of our country into the League of Nations or the adoption or modification of international treaties. He would disavow the outspoken pacifist tendencies of certain religious groups, the ironfisted control which some churches wield in the petty circles of ward and city politics, the customary procedure of church bodies passing political resolutions or endorsing political candidates at their annual conventions, and the whole unholy relation by which the spiritual power of the Church is prostituted, its appeal to the soul materialized, and its inner effectiveness hopelessly paralyzed.

Bigotry and national misunderstanding would be minimized by the Jeffersonian conception of Church and State. Who is there that knows and believes in the complete restoration of those eminently American ideals who does not yearn with profound sincerity for the reincarnation of the spirit of Jefferson rising majestically over the intolerance of a materialistic age and crying out as it cried once before: "I have sworn upon the altar of God eternal hostility against every form of tyranny over the minds of men"?[5]

5

COUNSELOR

Whether because of his work with young people or in response to editorial and broadcast mail, Walter A. Maier had a lifelong sensitivity to problems of courtship, marriage, children, and home life. But for his other responsibilities, he could easily have functioned as marriage and family counselor and in fact did so via the printed word. Marital and family themes show up in his earliest *Messenger* articles as in his final *Lutheran Hour* sermons.

In 1934, in the interim between the first and resumed *Lutheran Hour* series, he completed his best-seller on Christian marriage, *For Better, Not for Worse.* At 598 pages it was less a typical manual on matrimony and more an epic on the clash between Christian and secular morality, as these paragraphs from the Preface demonstrate.

When Vera Brittain, in her *Testament of Youth* (a volume which stirred at least one university campus "as no other book in recent years"), admits that, while fifteen years ago she would have turned to a prayer-book for solace in the bereavement of her *fiancé,* today she would find comfort in Bertrand Russell's philosophies, her confession typifies the wide revolt against the morality of our Christian faith.

The following pages have been written to record a protest against this growing disparagement of Scriptural ethics and to help stem the onrushing tide which champions the pagan, despiritualized interpretation of courtship, marriage, and family relations.

We find a host of counselors today who "look at marriage." The doctor, the psychologist, the psychiatrist, the psychoanalyst, the biologist, the anthropologist, the sociologist, the Communist, the radical novelist, the Hollywood strategist—all have beheld marriage with a professional scrutiny; but they have given no trustworthy direction for the attainment of genuine and permanent marital happiness. Too often their overemphasis of the physical, their bias, skepticism, or venom have remained utterly undisguised.

More than ever before, then, the church must look at marriage and in the spirit of its Lord and Savior offer as the basis for all family felicity the truths of divine revelation found within the covers of the Bible. The application of these Biblical principles is not only concordant with the best results of sociological research but has been demonstrated in unnumbered homes; for our Christian faith, with its eminently practical endowments, bestows these definite helps for the attainment of the higher happiness in married life: the presence of the redeeming Christ and His renewing Spirit, the strength of His purifying Word, the power of His sustaining sacrament, and His pledge of answered prayer.

This volume is essentially a code of Christian marriage, drawn from the Scriptures, which would help to make marriage "for better, not for worse." For fifteen years it has been my privilege to edit the *Walther League Messenger,* the young people's organ of my church. And many of the questions that have been repeatedly voiced in the extended editorial correspondence of this decade and a half have not only suggested this volume but have also helped to formulate its presentation. From contact with youth groups throughout the land, from private consultation with students, and from personal inquiries that have been submitted in connection with chain [i.e., network] broadcasts I believe that the problems discussed in these chapters are among the major perplexities which confront our young people, and I have endeavored to give the church's answer in a nontechnical, practical manner.

I am convinced that in the broad educational outlines for

young people there should be adequate room for the constructive study of marriage blessings and problems. For what is a young woman profited if she can speak authoritatively on Byzantine art yet has no definite understanding of the high principles of Christian home life? Or what advantage does a young man enjoy who can quote Homer and Vergil in the original and still is woefully unprepared for the personal issues of the family? The increasing frequency with which courses on marriage appear in the curricula of American colleges shows that even worldly wisdom has been aroused to the necessity of premarital preparation. But since the church offers more than academic information when it presents the divine will and the help of Heaven, its guidance along the pathway to domestic happiness is doubly imperative. The future of our church and of our country depends, under God, upon stalwart, Christian homes, consecrated Christian families, the exaltation of the Christian doctrines concerning marriage, parenthood, and home.[6]

After submitting a Christian marriage code, the author shows his Germanic thoroughness in immediately testing it against a classical background:

This code is practicable. Its provisions are no pious platitudes or hazy generalities, incapable of application. The history of matrimony offers successive demonstrations by which the power of Christ-inspired ideals may be measured. Particularly convincing were the radical readjustments of marital standards in the transition from paganism to Christianity during the cradle days of the church. Roman historians have left sordid pictures of the degeneracy into which domestic relations dropped during the luxury of the empire. The perversions openly practiced were so revolting that St. Paul, in his letter to the congregation at Rome, can speak only broadly of these unnatural lusts.

Yet it is possible to measure that wantonness by other standards which permit discussion. Divorce steadily became more frequent and was granted on trivial claims, while the satires of contemporaneous writers exhausted themselves in the futility of protest. Seneca's soliloquy is frequently quoted: "Does any woman now blush on account of divorce, since the time when certain distinguished women of noble family reckoned their years not by the number of the [annual] consuls, but by that of their husbands?"

(*De benef.*, III, 16). Juvenal, flinging his barbed sarcasm against a woman who habitually remarried before the previous nuptial garlands were faded, concludes: "So eight husbands have become hers in five autumns, a worthy fact for the inscription on her tomb" (*Satires,* VI, 227 ff.). Martial recorded the almost unbelievable experience of one Thelesina, who married her tenth husband within less than a month (*Epigrams,* VI, 7).

The zest for licentiousness was accentuated by the sneering avoidance of marriage ties. Augustus placed heavy taxes upon those who refused to enter matrimony; but legislation could not check debauchery. Wives were interchanged. The austere Cato honored his friend Hortensius by giving him his wife and then marrying her again after Hortensius died. Wives were borrowed or lent for stipulated periods. Daughters of proud, patrician lineage became professional devotees of lust and in such numbers that the Senate passed resolutions disenfranchsing them. Sanctuaries dedicated to the worship of the gods, particularly of Isis, were transformed into dens of unrestricted vice. A contemporary observer declares that the temple officials of his day saw more debauchery than those who made their livelihood from immorality.

The curse placed on childhood was one of the most frightful barbarities of this haughty decadence. Cicero indicts those who assert that the death of a child "is to be borne with an undisturbed mind; that, if indeed an infant in the cradle dies, there is to be no complaint whatever" (*Tusc. disp.,* I, 39). The hideous brutality practiced against unwanted children was exposure or murder, which either left newborn infants victims of wild beasts and vultures or crushed and strangled them to death.

Here, then, in this morass, was a testing ground where the marriage morality of Christianity could be gauged. With no social prestige, no political influence, no popular support in their behalf, Christian standards achieved the most radical revolution in morals that history has ever seen. Women were torn out of the clutches of sensuality. "What women these Christians have!" exclaimed Libanius, the pagan teacher of Chrysostom. And in the ennobling influences exerted by Anthusa on Chrysostom, Monica on Augustine, as well as by lesser-known Christian mothers on their families a new womanhood and a glorified motherhood arose.

Matrimony itself was dignified by the Christian doctrine of its holiness, its blessing, its permanence; before the approach of this new appraisal of connubial life the pollutions of paganism retreated. Children, exalted by the precepts and examples of Jesus, could no longer be exposed or murdered; they were welcomed with a new love and guarded as divine heritages. "Christians," admits an early writer whose identity has been lost, "marry and have children like every one else, but they do not expose their children. They have meals in common, but not wives. They are in the flesh, but they do not live after the flesh" (*Auctor ad Diognetum,* 5 f.).

In short, out of the disintegration of a brilliant society, steeped in its own vice and calloused by its own carousals, came a Christian code of marital ethics by which all subsequent progress has been regulated. While imperial legislation, framed to curb licentiousness, failed to extricate an empire from this chaos of crime; while the barbs of the satirists dropped wide of their mark and the sallies of moralists fell on heedless ears, the impulses radiated by an unobtrusive and persecuted Christianity brought about the dawn of a happier day in the morals of marriage.[7]

The role of Scripture as an impulse to purity was portrayed in a later chapter through one of W.A.M.'s favorite illustrations:

In the year 1789 mutineers from the English government ship *Bounty,* together with a group of Polynesian men and women, settled on lonely Pitcairn Island in the South Pacific. A ten-year orgy of drunkenness and debauchery, supplemented by continued bloodshed, decimated the colony and left only one white man. Isolated on that tiny speck in the vast Pacific, his thoughts turned to the Bible which had been salvaged from the wreck of the *Bounty,* and in the study of this book both the sins of the past and the promise of the future were vividly impressed on his disquieted mind. That was the beginning of a remarkable transformation. Nineteen years later, when a whaling ship accidentally reached Pitcairn Island, its astonished sailors found a community of thirty-five English-speaking people with a high morality. Marriage vows had been introduced, and faithfulness to these vows was rigidly observed. Where lust had reigned unbridled, virtue was now triumphantly enthroned. The power of the Book had once more prevailed.[8]

Toward the close of the book the author emphasizes that wives should be full partners in family finance. This, he wrote, was certainly the case in Wittenberg.

Martin Luther, after twelve years of married life, wrote: "God be thanked, I have a pious and true wife, in whom the heart of a husband may trust. I count her dearer than the kingdom of France and the dukedom of Venice." As the great Reformer explained in his last will and testament, her devotion to him extended also to the varied affairs of his unusual household. Luther's salary as professor at the University was two hundred gulden. He had no other professional income, for he refused special fees for preaching, lecturing, and translation and could say: "God be thanked that I have kept the reputation of not taking money." To offset this, it is true, gifts of provisions, corn, malt, beer, wine, meat, and other necessities, including clothing and money, were frequently sent to him. Yet the open door to his hospitable home led many monks and nuns who had escaped from monastic restrictions, persecuted preachers, indigent students, poor relatives to go in and out of his house as though it were a public inn. When the Prince of Anhalt planned a visit to Wittenberg so as to enjoy a closer acquaintance with Luther, a friend wrote him that he should by no means plan to stay with Luther, because his house was stuffed with an overflow of students, maidens, widows, and romping children. At the end of his third married year his generosity had forced him to incur debts to a total of one hundred gulden, and he was compelled to pawn three expensive chalices that had come to him as gifts. When his salary was raised to three hundred gulden, his hospitality increased proportionately; and in all this it was his wife Katherine who superintended the little farm, raised flowers, fruit trees, grape vines, managed the meals, and kept the domestic books balanced and, with all, memorized Scripture-passages.[9]

A few years later, in 1941, Walter A. Maier prepared an epitome of *For Better, Not for Worse* in the form of a 72-page booklet, *The Happiest Home.* He defined that institution as follows:

The happiest home is the one that lives closest to Christ. It need not be large, architecturally attractive, nor must those who dwell within its walls be blessed with money, social position, university training. Christ to guide the family, to lead the children, to avert the dangers of too much prosperity and sustain the household in days of need, sorrow, and sickness, will bring a joy that neither money, culture, nor position can ever bestow.

The happiest home, we repeat, is the dwelling place, be it ever so small, unnoticed, humble, in which Christ enters to say, "This day is salvation come to this house" (Luke 19:9) and remains daily to bless all the family. Let pessimists point to the number of broken homes and unhappy marriages; through the Savior ours can be an inner joy that neither sickness, disaster, nor death can remove. Let modern social scientists urge their special theories for building the happy home—family budgets, child psychology, parent training, sex information, domestic preparation—we gladly accept whatever is not contrary to God's Word; but we insist that home happiness requires soul happiness and that above everything else we need the purifying presence of Christ, who promises, "Behold, I make all things new" (Revelation 21:5).

No matter how sad your home has been in the past; no matter how problematical and question-marked your hopes for a future household may be, Christ can give you the pledge of assurance, hope, and happiness; and if it be His will, that is, if it be for your best, He can remove seemingly insurmountable obstacles, solve the most complex problems—if only you will follow the instructions in His infallible Bible!

First of all, you must understand that marriage is a gift of God and the family one of the Creator's greatest human blessings, since He instituted wedded life and continues to sustain the home.

This truth is, however, widely attacked today. Increasing numbers of unbelievers assert that home life started millions of years ago with the beasts. From animal mating, by process of improvement and development, came human mating, and finally, they claim, after many other changes, marriage emerged as we have it today.

As opposed to all this we see from Genesis 2:24 that, coming from God, marriage in itself must be holy. Only man's sin has brought unholiness into wedded life. In the beginning God, who created male and female, made sex a blessing; and it is only human transgression which mars this magnificent divine endowment.

Since it was our Lord who made the first husband and wife and brought them together, the Scriptures firmly teach, "Marriage is

80

honorable in all" (Hebrews 13:4); "Whosoever findeth a wife findeth a good thing and obtaineth favor of the Lord" (Proverbs 18:22). Even those engaged in the highest human activity, the service of Christ and the church, the clergy in the early Christian centuries, including Peter, were married, and the holy apostle Paul writes, "A bishop . . . must be blameless, the husband of one wife" (1 Timothy 3:2). Only in later centuries did the idea develop, entirely outside the Scriptures, that the clergy should be unmarried, and from that time on, as history proves, this human exaltation of celibacy over Christian marriage provoked many problems and was attended with much evil.

The fact that marriage when based on divine principles is God's gift shows itself by its blessings. Thus, married people live longer on the average than the unmarried. Carefully compiled statistics indicate that the single are more liable to suicide than the married.

Marriage is helpful in building morals. A study of arrests in one of our large cities reveals that unmarried men were seized from two to eleven times more frequently for various classes of crimes.

Marriage helps mental development. Insanity rates in some instances are twice as high among the unmarried as among the married.

Christian marriage can be a definite aid to spiritual life. Not only is it true that Christian wives often win unbelieving husbands (see 1 Peter 3:1-2), but the home support for the church's cause has been one of the most helpful factors in the spread of the Kingdom.

Marriage can be a stimulus to success. The encouragement Christian husbands and wives give to each other as they face unemployment are strong factors in human achievement. This has been unreservedly acknowledged by thousands of leaders in various walks of life.

Marriage is an undeniable help to the joy of life. Despite the frequent attacks from within as well as from without, the home still remains our shelter and refuge, the haven of the highest happiness we can know on earth.

Because marriage comes from God and is thus endowed with holy blessings, our heavenly Father can give those who are His some of earth's highest joys in their home. It is necessary, however, that we keep our homes in contact with God and that through Christian faith we follow the apostolic injunction: "Whatsoever ye do in word or deed, do all in the name of the Lord Jesus" (Colossians 3:17).

This appeal becomes the more urgent because of the widespread attack on Christian marriage raised in the filthy magazines, the debauched books, the sex-mad motion pictures, the radio broadcasts of triangle plots, the whole loose and lustful spirit of our age. Even more destructive than this is the sinfulness in our hearts, the fleshly lusts that seek to turn us from God's truth and purity, the unholy desires and longings that would make us slaves to our own vices.

These questions, therefore, are of the utmost importance for all Christians: "How are we to keep Christ in our homes? How are we to check our unholy desires? How can we defeat sin and follow God's instruction for home happiness?" When they are answered clearly and unhesitatingly, we have the promise of the happiest home.

Money can build a beautiful house, intelligence can design an efficient dwelling place; but only the defeat of sin and selfishness can erect a happy home (*The Happiest Home,* hereafter *THH,* pp. 36).

After discussing the importance of purity before and after marriage, W.A.M. moves on to the eminently practical questions about the optimum age for marriage and the criteria for selecting the best mate.

The question, "Whom shall I marry?" is often regarded as difficult and complex. Many books and treatises have been written in answer; yet we believe that the principles laid down in the Bible, plus an application of sound, Christian common sense, will prove the most helpful guide.

Is it necessary to emphasize, first of all, that *love* is the prime, absolutely essential requisite for a happy home? Marriages entered simply to please parents, spite marriages, marriages on the rebound, marriages as avenues of economic escape that provide a home for old age are far from the highest ideals. Often, of course, by God's pure grace some of these marriages turn out satisfactorily; but it is unwarranted to demand happiness when deep-rooted, genuine love is missing.

But love must not be blind. To many young people *beauty and physical attractiveness* have become the chief requisites in the choice of a life partner. Now let nothing that we write give the impression that beauty is not a gift of God. If even the Scriptures take pains to point out that some of the notable women in the Kingdom have been distinguished for their personal attractiveness, we certainly should show no resentment toward beauty. However, when a girl's endowment is only her physical attractiveness, when she lacks inner qualities that must outlast physical beauty, or when she is unlovely socially and spiritually, we think of Solomon's warning, "As a jewel of gold in a swine's snout, so is a fair woman which is without discretion" (Proverbs 11:22). We remember that the greatest catastrophe ever to overtake this world was ushered in when God-fearing men took as their wives women whose only distinction was their good looks (Genesis 6:2).

We have already pointed out that *health* is a notable asset in marriage; but we cannot endorse the claims of radical eugenics, which would breed human beings by principles that produce blue-ribbon horses. At the same time we must be mindful of the Old Testament attitude: "None of you shall approach in marriage to any that is near of kin to him" (Leviticus 18:6) and understand clearly the teaching of the Scriptures concerning *the prohibited degrees of relationship.* The detailed answers to the questions that may be asked in connection with this subject would more than fill all the pages at our disposal, and we refer any of our readers for whom this may be a personal, pressing problem to their pastors. Frequently we receive letters dealing with the marriage of first cousins. No Scriptural prohibition bans this union, although many states do. However, before planning marriage in those communities where this is permitted, young people so related should understand the dangers that may lurk in certain cousin marriages. They should study this question carefully on the basis of standard reference material.

A happy marriage ordinarily requires a general *mental and intellectual agreement.* Husband and wife are to be partners, to enjoy the same pleasures, share mutual confidences, meet adversities together—and for this common interests and a similar outlook on life are normally required. A college education is not necessary for family felicity. Trouble may arise, however, when either spouse is highly intellectual and the other of far inferior mentality. Often, of course, the ennobling power of Christian faith can exert a blessed influence in the family where the husband is a genius and the wife a simple but consecrated homemaker.

One of the most frequent of all requirements young people set for their helpmates lies in the field of *finances*. High money rating is repeatedly regarded as an essential prerequisite. We do not encourage shoestring weddings, in which young people give no real thought to income or delude themselves by believing that two can live as cheaply as one. With all the uncertainty before us, prospective brides and grooms should have definite and adequate financial prospects before they marry. When the inevitable question is put, "How much must we have before we can marry?" it is difficult to establish a schedule of salaries and savings accounts which can be regarded as a safe minimum. The minimum should be large enough to provide not only for bare existence but also for emergencies, the growth of the family, some cultural and recreational advantages, participation in the work of the church, and a financial reserve.

On the other hand we must remember these Scriptural injunctions: "Better is a dry morsel and quietness therewith than an house full of sacrifices with strife" (Proverbs 17:1). "Better is a dinner of herbs where love is than a stalled ox and hatred therewith" (Proverbs 15:17). All human experience supports this Old Testament verdict and its implied denunciation of marriage for money. When young people marry at a reasonable minimum income, live frugally and with self-denial, without fur coats, large diamonds, fancy furniture, and enjoy the cooperation of striving, they are often welded more closely together than if everything came to them without effort.

Most important of all, however, in the choice of a helpmate for life is the question of *religion* and unity in Christ's faith. The happiest marriage, experience shows, is the union of two young people who have the same faith and belong to the same true Christian church. No factor is more important in selecting a helpmate than this common faith. Yet too often no serious thought is given to spiritual like-mindedness. Christian young people often believe that, if the person they marry is not interested in any church, their prayers and example can effect a change; and the apostle reminds us in 1 Peter 3:1-2 that sometimes "if any [husband] obey not the Word, they also may without the Word be won by the behavior of their wives while they behold your reverent and chaste behavior."

Often, however, marriages in which faith is coupled with unbelief turn out unhappily. Complete understanding and permanent harmony cannot always be promoted if the specter of eternal separation arises or an unchurched partner continually rejects Christian faith. Especially when the waves of sorrow break over the family is there urgent need for mutual spiritual encouragement and complete dedication on the part of husband and wife to the one Lord, who "doeth all things well."

Marriage with an unbeliever is indeed an acid test of faith; and the lamentable fact that this test is usually too strong is evident from the repeated instances in which the Christian husband or wife is at first gradually and imperceptibly but at last openly estranged from the church. I have seen the evidence of this blight in so many letters that I have not hesitated to state this as my definite opinion. If young men and young women are contemplating giving their hearts to those who disregard the Savior, they should stop, look, and listen to the counsel contained in Holy Scripture, to the many wrecks of matrimonial bliss, and to the claims of unborn children before they enter a union that has no common ground for prayer, no mutual hope for reunion in eternity (*THH,* pp. 17-20).

Courtship Takes Time!

One of the axioms which needs emphasis today is the warning: Don't marry in haste! Take your time in courtship! Learn definitely to understand your own feelings! Be sure to know the young man or young woman to whom you pledge yourself for the rest of your days!

True, whirlwind courtships are often regarded as romantic, even fashionable and decidedly modern, by the twisted standards of our age; but the very newspapers which offer generous headlines to the overrapid romances of some society leaders are often honest enough to print the frequent sequel—a disrupted marriage. Recently a Hollywood dispatch reported that an actress was divorced from her husband after only fourteen months of wedded life. With an interest that divorce judges do not often show, the presiding magistrate asked the actress how long she had known her husband before marriage. Candidly the four-star headline performer replied, "Only about four weeks." "I think that's the answer," the judge commented. "You had better take more than three or four weeks next time."

But Christian young people, who can never think of a "next time" as just another affair or publicity event, will normally need more than even three or four months before they become engaged.

Even social experts and psychologists warn against streamlined courtship. A Chicago University authority, examining the "happiness prospect" of 1,000 engaged couples, declares, "Hasty marriages, for whatever reason they are made, have less chance of success than those in which the couple have known each other for at least a year." Those who elope, he believes, have the least prospect of happiness.

If even worldly wisdom raises its voice in such pointed warning, how much greater care should Christian young people exercise, since they understand even more fully the importance of engagement and marriage! They will realize that the months before the marriage can be divided into two parts, the courtship, during which two young people should spend much time together to learn whether they are suited to each other, have compatible habits and ideals, and what in general their individual characteristics, inclinations, and personalities are. Only when young people have arrived at certainty regarding the qualifications of their life's partner, after every vestige of doubt has been removed, and both the young man and young woman are convinced (after an acquaintance long enough to make this conviction intelligent) that they love each other and that they want to live together, for better or for worse, until death parts them, only then, after having brought the whole issue to God in earnest prayer, should they take the first step toward the second premarriage state, engagement. This is the mutual, voluntary, unconditional, definite promise of marriage given by two young people who can enter a valid marriage and who have their parents' consent. Engagement is not the secret or tentative promise. It involves the public announcement or recognition of the marriage pledge.

The time of engagement, after the announcement, should not be long. Betrothal is not for the purpose of making further tests as to whether the couple will really marry. The period is to be a definite time of preparation for marriage itself and should therefore be short.

If all young people would take plenty of time in arriving at this, the most important decision in their lives; if they would really know the qualifications of the one with whom they plan to share their home and the responsibility of rearing a family, the unhappiness ratio in modern marriages would be drastically reduced (*THH,* pp. 25-27).

6
FOUNDER

It was the joining of voice to pen, however, that would soon elevate Walter A. Maier to national prominence. His radio ministry began long before he served as founding speaker of *The Lutheran Hour* in the fall of 1930. He had stepped before his first microphone in 1921 at Louisville, Kentucky, when an address he delivered for a Walther League convention in that city was aired. Instantly intrigued by radio's potential for the Gospel, W.A.M. fired off a salvo of *Messenger* articles to alert the church to this new medium. His editorial "Why Not a Lutheran Broadcasting Station?" in the March 1923 *Messenger* was rewarded the following year with the birth of Station KFUO on the campus of Concordia Seminary, in St. Louis.

To exceed the limited range of one station, however, a network program was necessary. When the CBS radio network agreed to sell time for such a broadcast, W.A.M. turned to the resources of the Lutheran Laymen's League, the very active men's organization of his church body. The league resolved to sponsor the radio series, and the premiere broadcast of *The Lutheran Hour* was set for 10 p.m. on

Thursday evening, October 2, 1930, over Station WHK in Cleveland.

Thursday? Evening? Cleveland? Incredibly, a midweek night was chosen because there had been much concern—not shared by W.A.M.—that the program might be deemed a substitute for Sunday church services! And the Ohio metropolis was selected so that the famed Cleveland Bach Chorus might supply Lutheranism's finest music for the occasion.

The Lutheran Hour, however, almost died a-borning. Shortly before air time, CBS suddenly worried that a sermon-oriented program inserted into its prime-time "amusement hours" would court disaster with its radio audience, so they insisted that the speaker abridge his 20-minute address to 16. W.A.M. complied, but with one hour until air time, CBS demanded further cuts down to only 10 minutes of sermon. This W.A.M. regarded as intolerable. Rather than comply, he categorically refused to broadcast. Minutes passed. The entire effort seemed doomed. But finally, mindful of a possible breach of contract suit, CBS softened its stand and agreed to a compromise by which W.A.M. trimmed away comparatively little of his address.

The following—the first *Lutheran Hour* sermon ever aired—is from the actual broadcast script, not as this was later edited in *The Lutheran Hour* sermon book. Words and segments in brackets denote W.A.M.'s compromise cuts just minutes before air time. The "I.N.J." at the middle top of the script, typical of all his sermon manuscripts, is the abbreviation for *In Nomine Jesu,* "In the Name of Jesus."

I.N.J.

Radio Address #1   October 2, 1930

There Is a God

[In accepting the unique privilege of establishing one of the most extensive radio broadcasting chains ever supported by one church—a chain that embraces thirty-six stations and that extends from coast to coast—the Lutheran Laymen's League is conscious of but one purpose, actuated by but one impulse: the consuming desire to hold up the cross of Jesus Christ to the 120,000,000 people of our nation as the only but all-sufficient source of salvation, both spiritual and temporal. Every Thursday night at this time, over almost 60,000 miles of wire, over a network of stations with a total power aggregating about one-sixth of a million watts, over frequencies that will reach not only into every nook and corner of this country but through two auxiliary shortwave stations also to the very outposts of civilization throughout the world, a constructive message will come which, please God, will bring into uncounted myriads of homes a positive statement of Christian faith and with it the God-given solution to the problems and issues of our day.

These Thursday evening messages, sent out by the oldest Protestant Church (very appropriately in the year in which the world pauses to observe the four-hundredth anniversary of the first Protestant statement of faith, the Augsburg Confession) are not to be speculations which misguided men like to call modern, not a series of pessimistic lamentations on the sordid and sensual materialism of our mechanical age, not a program in which blatant bigotry and narrow sectarianism can raise a selfish voice, but a succession of uncompromising and unhesitating messages which without fear or favor will offer an unshaken acknowledgment of a changeless Christ for a changing world.]

This evening we are to dedicate the message of our first broadcast to the fundamental conviction that there is a God, that the great and infinite Father of the entire human race, who has revealed Himself in many and remarkable ways, is no fantastic formation of superstition, no creature of childish tradition, no will-o'-the-wisp of religious delusion, but that atheism, materialism, agnosticism, [skepticism,] and all the many other similar theories which deny or question the existence of God are not only irrational, [deficient,] and disappointing, but also anti-Scriptural and therefore thoroughly destructive from every point of consideration.

In completing the demonstration of the existence of our God, there are convincing reasons which emphasize the truth to which the psalmist gave expression when twice he asserted that only a fool could say in his heart, *"There is no God."* There is, first of all, the universal belief in God [and the universal religious instinct.] In the census of India taken in 1911, when the religious affiliations of the 300,000,000-plus children of Mother India were tabulated, it was found that only seventeen persons described themselves as atheists, that less than five-millionths of one per cent of that nation of ancient and profound philosophies denied the existence of a Supreme Being. Cicero's question still awaits an answer: "What people is there, or what race of men has not, even without traditional teaching, some presentiment of the existence of God?" 1,500,000,000 people cannot be wrong, we say, adopting the advertising phraseology of our day, particularly when the Scriptures assure us that there is a natural knowledge of the existence of God inborn in every human being (Romans 1:16-18).

But God has not left us without witnesses to His power and His existence. St. Paul tells us (Romans 1:20) that the created world, [God's second Book,] nature, is an eloquent testimony to the divine existence and omnipotence. Who is there who can gaze upward to the mysterious heights of the heavens with the 7,000,000 charted stars and the uncounted hosts of other heavenly bodies beyond the searching reach of the most penetrating telescope without being overcome by the conviction that behind the immensity of these overpowering reaches there is the master mind of One whose glory the heavens declare and of whose greatness, even in their immensity, these starry heights are but weak reflections? Or, [to descend to the microcosm, who is there, again,] who can hear that modern physiology shows that the human eye has 800 complementary parts of the most exquisite fineness, arrangement, and combination without coming to the natural and instinctive conclusion that the temples of our bodies have been fearfully and wonderfully made by a superhuman and divine Architect?

Even cold and calculating human reason assures us that the stupendous marvels of nature in and about us cannot be the result of mere chance. You can take ten keys on your piano, and mathematicians will assure you that you can play more than 3,628,000 combinations of notes. But how much probability is there of these piano keys ever playing the national anthem by mere chance? [Surely no rational person with the average quota of ordinary common sense will shrink from the inevitable conclusion that this universe with its system, its order, its superhuman complexities, has been called into existence not by mere mechanical chance but that it is the evidence of a superior design and superhuman arrangement.] Small wonder that scientists in every branch of human learning who have delved into the deep and hidden mysteries of the natural world have emerged with a definite conviction that there must be a superior and supreme Being responsible for all the intricate, complicated, and inconceivably numerous processes of nature. [Louis Pasteur, one of the greatest scientists of recent generations, gave expression to the scientific denunciation of atheism when he wrote: "Posterity will one day laugh at the foolishness of modern materialistic philosophy. The more I study nature, the more I am amazed at the Creator."]

Human experience and the annals of human history likewise lend a decisive voice not only to the existence of God but also to the folly and immorality of atheism. Not only has there never been a great atheist, but there have been few, if any, consistent atheists. [John Quincy Adams saw the failure of unbelief in his day, and sent to Thomas Jefferson this review of the freethinkers of that period:

> [Bolingbroke says his philosophy was not sufficient to support him in his last hours. D'Alembert said, "Happy are they who have courage, but I have none." Voltaire, the greatest genius of them all, behaved like the greatest coward of them all at his death.]

And this failure of the atheistic philosophy is beheld today in the moral breakdown that inevitably follows wherever the attempt has been made to put it into consistent practice. The terrors of the French Revolution, which symbolized its victory over revealed religion by enthroning a Parisian actress on the high altar of Notre Dame Cathedral, are being repeated today, when organized atheism, sitting in the high places of whatever government is left in that chaos which we used to call Russia, has supported with official fanaticism the world's greatest away-from-the-Bible and away-from-God movement, only to produce the supertragedy of history. We may well pause to look to our own country at a time in which atheist organizations, legally chartered to carry out their destructive principles, boast of allegedly tremendous conquests, in which Societies of Damned Souls and similar godless groups have been organized at our colleges and universities and in which the number of those who have dedicated themselves to the task of dethroning the almighty God is legion times legion. In this day we may well harken to the words of Daniel Webster when he declared:

> If we abide by the principles taught in the Bible, our ocuntry will go on prospering and continue to prosper; but if we and our posterity neglect its instruction and authority, no man can tell how sudden a catastrophe may overwhelm us, and bury all our glory in profound obscurity.

But more conclusive than all this is the incontrovertible testimony of the infallible Word of God. In the Old Testament alone in more than 9,000 passages the existence of God is definitely assumed when God is directly mentioned in His relations to humanity. In more than 2,500 instances we read the announcement, *"Thus saith the Lord."* And who is there who would venture the brazen assertion that in all these thousands of instances the Bible is guilty of the most pernicious sort of dishonesty, when the whole regenerative, ennobling, and redeeming power of this Word has been operative in uncounted millions of lives? Men may not understand the philosophical, scientific, and moral arguments for the existence of God which profound thinkers of all Christian ages have advanced; but here is the proof positive, lifted up above all possibility of error, no mere personal conviction that you and I may entertain and that others may contradict—but above all this, the absolute Truth of Truth.

And as a victorious climax to the revelation of God in His Word comes the revelation of God in the Person of Jesus Christ. Here is this Immanuel, this *"God with us,"* *"in whom all the fullness of the Godhead dwelleth bodily,"* who assures us that *"he that hath seen Me hath seen the Father,"* of whom St. John testifies that *"this is the true God,"* whom St. Paul calls *"God, over all, blessed forever,"* whom St. Thomas acknowledges as *"my Lord and my God."* In Him as He walked the paths of His earthly life, as He fulfilled His mission of unfathomable love and immeasurable mercy, giving His own holy body, shedding His own precious blood, raising up the downtrodden masses of sin-sick humanity, and ushering in the happy existence of the new age that dawned upon the earth when He came—in Him the world saw God. Because Jesus Christ [is in every sense and implication of the term a historical Figure, as Caesar or Napoleon or Washington or Lincoln, and because this same Christ] before a host of unimpeachable witnesses demonstrated His divine and superhuman power in His wonders and miracles, climaxed by His victorious resurrection from the dead, we repeat: The world saw God in Christ. Yes, it still sees God in the exhibition of His divine power in the lives of those who can call Him Father through the Sonship of Christ, who, kneeling down before the glory-crowned cross, with the fire of divine Truth enflaming even the depths of their souls with the conviction that the blood of Jesus Christ, the Son of God, cleanseth us from all sins, hear His invitation of grace: *"Come unto Me, all ye that labor and are heavy laden, and I will give you rest,"* and answer:

Just as I am, without one plea,
But that Thy blood was shed for me,
And that Thou bidd'st me come to Thee,
O Lamb of God, I come, I come.

Men can live without money, without fame, without erudition; they can eke out an existence without friends, without health, or without personal liberty and the possibility of the pursuit of happiness; but they cannot live in the fullness of a life that lives beyond the grave without God. Let them repeat their age-old challenge of blasphemy, let them stand up before large audiences to deny the existence of God and condescend to grant Him five minutes to strike them down dead; [let them speak glibly and boastfully of the freedom from restraint which the denial of God has brought them. He who is in the heavens still laughs, and when the echo of His laughter transforms itself into a sterner demand, what sorry spectacles these self-sufficient, self-existent deniers of God present!] But in the crises of life and the pivotal hours of our existence, only the Christian, having God and with Him the assurance that no one can successfully prevail against him, is able to carry the pressing burdens of sickness, death, financial reverses, family troubles, and misfortunes of almost innumerable kinds and degrees, and yet bear all this with the undaunted optimistic faith and Christian confidence that alone make life worth living and death worth dying.

(The original conclusion, following the word "undaunted" in the last sentence, read:

"undaunted optimism which enables him to join in the conviction, victorious even over death, and cry out in exultation:

I am persuaded that neither death nor life nor angels nor principalities nor powers nor things present nor things to come nor height nor depth nor any other creature shall be able to separate us from the love of God, which is in Christ Jesus our Lord. Romans 8:38 f.")[10]

And so *The Lutheran Hour* was born. CBS need not have worried about the sermon segment of the broadcast, because soon Walter A. Maier was receiving more audience response mail than any other religious program in the nation, more even than such top secular shows as *Amos 'n' Andy.* Quietly CBS withdrew its restriction on sermon length! But far more serious than such technical restrictions were the economics of the venture. America had just plunged into its worst depression, and with network costs still fearfully high in the earliest '30s, the listening audience was unable to contribute enough funds to keep the Hour on the air. In June 1931, therefore, the series was suspended, only to be reborn again in February 1935, and it has been on the air ever since.

At the beginning of the third *Lutheran Hour* season in the fall of 1935, Dr. Maier sounded the keynote for the resumed series in the following address.

Nothing "Save Jesus Christ, and Him Crucified!"

I determined not to know anything among you save Jesus Christ and Him crucified!–1 Cor. 2:2.

The mighty apostle St. Paul, who could have earned popular acclaim by his impassioned oratory, his literary brilliance, his astonishing endowments; the man of red-blooded courage who fearlessly rode Mediterranean hurricanes, resolutely faced shrieking mobs and cynical tyrants; that towering genius who pulled the props from decaying heathendom and mightily helped to shape the upward course of human history; greatest of Christ's ambassadors that he was, when he summarizes his one, all-absorbing life task, he directs his Christians not to the academic halls of Athens or the imperial palaces on the banks of the Tiber but to an unmarked hill of desolate death near Jerusalem. His thoughts perpetually envision the rough-hewn cross upon Calvary, where Jesus Christ, suffering as only God could suffer, paid with His blood the appalling price of human sin. What though his loyalty to this cross meant becoming a fool for Christ? What though his allegiance to the Crucified put a price upon his head? What though he could still feel the cut of forty lashes less one as their leaded thongs ripped open his quivering flesh? Above rack and torture, prison and dungeon, starvation and blistering thirst his determination *"not to know anything . . . save Jesus Christ and Him crucified"* rings out in eternal triumph.

As we inaugurate today the third season of this radio mission over a special network from Minnesota to the Atlantic seaboard, you may ask in challenge: "What is the message of this broadcast?" With many and conflicting voices on the air, some that appeal to reason and intellect, some that would inflame passions and prejudices, we promise that these weekly broadcasts have no political aims. This microphone will not be employed to fan the fires of class hatred, bigotry, and intolerance, to flood the American nation and our Canadian neighbors with economic theories, financial strategies, and social speculations. Rather do we acknowledge as our own the apostle's determination *"not to know anything... save Jesus Christ and Him crucified."* Addressing you from the campus of a divinity school that for almost a century has dedicated its resources to the Christ of the Scriptures, I offer you in the name of the triune God not the Christ of present-day compromise and concession, not the Christ of twentieth-century indifference and indecision, not the Christ of modern doubt and denial, who has been exalted in His humanity only to be robbed of His deity, but the Christ of the cross. With my hand on the Bible I dedicate this radio mission to the preaching of that cross, the cruel gibbet on which the Savior died the blackest death of all history. That crucified Christ, Son of God yet Son of Man, the all-sufficient Savior, and Him alone, we offer with the pledge:

"Nothing . . . Save Jesus Christ and Him Crucified

in every message, every prayer, every hymn broadcast over this Gospel network.

Our Distracted Age Needs the Crucified

Is not this the resolution that our scarred and bewildered age needs with alarming urgency as blind, willful men clench their fists against the Almighty and sneer: "Anything *but* Christ and Him crucified"? The battalions of organized atheism in Russia, still mobilized to tear down every church of Christ; wily Communism, which lifts its serpent head with leering insolence as it inaugurates in our own country a cutthroat campaign against the Christ of God; that vicious philosophy of life, glorified in lecherous novels, sanctioned even on the campuses of tax-supported universities, championed by sensualists, who, dropping down to the gutter of lust, gloat, "Animals we are, and animals we remain!"—these are the glaring evidences of worldwide uprising against Christ prophesied three thousand years ago by the inspired author of the Second

95

Psalm: *"Why do the heathen rage and the people imagine a vain thing? The kings of the earth set themselves, and the rulers take counsel together against the Lord and against His Anointed."*

Even where Christ is not thus brutally attacked, His high and holy teachings are often neglected, His love and mercy cast into contemptuous discard. In spite of the catastrophes of this generation, men are forgetting their royal Redeemer. Instead of witnessing the merciful Christ in control of human affairs and His love hallowing the relation of individual to individual and nation to nation, we are staggered by the present spectacle of two Christian countries [Italy and Ethiopia] engaged in the bloody business of war, seeking to destroy each other by poison gas, whistling shrapnel, and hellish aerial bombs.

There is nothing of the Savior's love in all this nor in any other conflict that rages in the class hatred, the endless friction between the laborer and the capitalist, the systematic exploitation of American masses that have made some of the rich richer and millions of the poor poorer.

Among American churches too the reverence for Christ has not increased in favor or in fervor. If it were possible to approach individually the quarter of a million men in our country who are called ministers of God and ask for their endorsement of St. Paul's determination *"not to know anything . . . save Jesus Christ and Him crucified"*—not hundreds but thousands would deliberately refuse to make Christ the heart of their preaching and their praying. Unfortunately a class of clergymen is abroad in the land who, ill informed as they may be, insist upon knowing a hundred things in preference to the Crucified. They must speak on banking systems, presidential policies, inflated currency, and allied subjects, which exclude the Savior of men from His own sanctuary. Long ago have they banished from their sermons the high-priestly Christ, who declared with blessed finality, *"It is finished!"* They want to finish the task of saving men—if indeed we must be saved, and they can only plunge desperate souls into deeper dismay, only offer new versions of age-old delusions that place men before the impossible task of earning heaven.

American homes, in far too many instances, have spurned the abiding presence of the Crucified, who, as the death fever raced through His torn body, looked down upon His mother and provided for her support. "Anything but that Christ and His code for domestic happiness," brazen unbelief protests as millions laugh at the Christian's "until death do you part" loyalty, sneer at that first of all divine commands: *"Be fruitful and multiply,"* lampoon Christ's ideals of personal purity, marital faithfulness, filial piety, and parental responsibility, proclaiming instead the reign of unbridled lust and of jungle morality.

No wonder that millions in America are trying to live without Christ and have willfully rejected the grace of the Crucified. Too many want a bread-and-butter paradise here on earth. Too many are ready to welcome the Christ of the loaves and the fishes but spurn the Christ of the thorns and nails; for His cross, an imperishable monument to God's hatred of sin but to His greater love for the sinner, makes no appeal to selfish affections and self-indulgent ambitions. "Anything but Christ and Him crucified!" the cry that rises from the lives of misguided multitudes, deprives the souls, minds, and bodies of men and women of all permanent benedictions and happiness.

We Need the Crucified for Grace and Strength

How blessed, by contrast, is the joy of peace, the patience of hope, the strength of spirit which comes to those who commit themselves to the Redeemer's care! Once you regard Jesus as the apostle did, in that intensive focus which beholds only *"Christ and Him crucified,"* you need nothing else to help you discover a cheering, sustaining answer to every problem of life. When your soul is cleansed, your conscience stilled, your heavenly Father reconciled, then are you prepared to meet the best or the worst that life may hold for you. Let the avalanche of human miseries sweep over you; if you know the Crucified, you will hear His sustaining *"Let not your heart be troubled."* Let whirlwinds of disaster blow the high towers of your hopes into shapeless ruins; over the wreckage Christ's voice will ring clear: *"Behold, I make all things new."* Let the ravages of incurable disease, the feebleness of old age, the terrors of approaching death shake the foundation upon which life itself rests; your Savior's stabilizing pledge declares: *"Thou shalt be steadfast and not fear."* Let sin and hell raise their charges against you; if you have Christ as your *"Advocate before the Father,"* you need nothing else to assure you of God's pardon.

Because Christ freely offers all contrite hearts the full release from sin; because with Christ we can move mountains and without Christ, as He Himself warns us, we *"can do nothing,"* the direct appeal that would now wing its way into every destitute, Christless soul is to receive Him, to believe Him, and to crown Him Lord of lords. Our message to the 60,000,000 unchurched in America is not: "Up, for the day of class conflict has come!" but: *"Repent ye, for the kingdom of God is at hand!"* We have no pretentious organization for which we seek your membership; but we do pray that your name may be enrolled in the Book of Life and in the church of Christ. We have none of the pomp and acclaim of widely heralded endeavors that clamor for your support; but we have Christ, and we can promise you that, if you seek Him and His kingdom first, everything that you need for this life will be added unto you. *"Come . . . with us,"* we beseech you, as in Christ's name and by His command we promise, *"We will do thee good."*

To you who are enrolled in Christ's marching army and with the apostle know that Christ must be all in all, let me say that this ignorance of everything *"save Christ and Him crucified"* must be no empty slogan. Because it is either reformation with Christ or ruin without Christ, we need a twentieth-century revival and a nation-wide protest against pulpit infidelity. The call of the crisis is for spiritual before social security, a return of American preaching to the Christ of the Bible. American churches must disavow secular ambitions, eliminate worldliness and commercialism, and go back to the program of their charter, the saving and ennobling of souls through Christ as the basis of every abiding personal or national benediction.

Will you not rally to the cause of the Crucified in word and in deed, in faith and in life, in testimony and in protest? Will you not support through your prayers, your letters, your gifts the radio crusade that we have today inaugurated for the glory of the Crucified? May God's Holy Spirit grant that from East and West, from Canada and our nation, from the mountains and the high seas, from the silent forests and our teeming cities, from the hovels of the impoverished and the comfortable homes of the richly blessed a mighty chorus may ascend to God's heavens with the never-changing refrain: *"Nothing . . . save Jesus Christ and Him Crucified!"* Amen.[11]

In all, Walter A. Maier delivered 509 sermons over *The*

Lutheran Hour, which presents the anthologist a hopeless task should he try merely to cull out the most representative addresses for a volume of this size. The next two chapters venture the attempt nevertheless. Another solution, however, is to extract sample lines or paragraphs from the sermons, which show W.A.M. using the same linguistic tools he employed as wordsmith for the *Messenger.* It was all part of his great aim: to clothe the Gospel in fresh, communicative language that would snare the ear of any listener who chanced to tune in. The following selections are arranged thematically to mirror W.A.M.'s theology, which began with God and creation and led, through Christ, to humanity and its needs.

Citations from Sermons

God or Materialism?

If you and I are only creatures of chance that crawl helplessly on the crust of this accidental planet called earth; if all existence on our sphere owes its beginning to a collision with a wandering star; if the impulses of life are only chemical reactions; if our emotions and personalities are controlled by glands and glandocrats; if mother love may be expressed in a chemical formula embracing manganese, calcium, and prolactin—there can be no sustaining, strengthening hope, no comfort for our multiplied problems; then life is a fluke, our destiny a tossup.[12]

Creation Reflects the Creator

Think of the startling design in the architecture of the globe: land, water, air, in their good proportion and relation; the miracle of the calendar, with day and night, summer and winter, moisture and dryness; the ninety-six known elements found in the quantities and combinations required to meet the needs of the race, with perverted man, not God, splitting the atom for mass murder and devilish destruction; the number of babies almost equally divided between boys and girls, and often, after severe loss of men in war, a slight preponderance of male infants! Picture the innumerable marvels of planning and system evident not only in the mighty forces of nature around us but in a blade of grass, a swallow of water, a breath of air, a ray of sunlight! Then ask yourself how, in an age when unbelievers demand scientific proof for every Bible statement, almost in the same breath they claim there is no God, no Designer for this stupendous universe of order, no Architect for the magnificent aggregate of nature's symmetry and system. It takes only seven separate pieces to make a pair of wooden-handled pruning shears. No infidel dare assert that these pieces created themselves, that the steel and the lumber automatically shaped themselves; yet some people do maintain that the tree which the shears prune and which in its beauty and growth represents a long series of divine miracles actually is the result of accident.

No atheist would stultify himself by declaring that the Panama Canal is the product of mere chance; but many of them do say that the mighty Mississippi, many times larger and more marvelous than the Central American waterway, created itself without divine supervision. What infidel, beholding a swift streamliner, would say: "This train, the Diesel locomotives and the coaches, built itself. No designer, no blueprints, no factories were required to form and fix its thousand parts; no workmen, no craftsmen and laborers were employed to put them together. They just jumped into their places"? "No one," you answer, "would be silly enough to utter such nonsensical drivel." Yet men with many university degrees are guilty of far worse folly. They actually claim that no God made the sunlight which speeds five and a half million times more rapidly than the fastest train; no God made the wind which has greater power than all the Diesel engines in the world; no God made you, who in your own body count mightier miracles of divine power than in the most advanced locomotive. The Bible warns atheists that *"His eternal power and Godhead" "are clearly seen,"* and pointedly Scripture tells all unbelievers that *"they are without excuse."* The Almighty has given them the proof of His existence; but they reject it.[13]

Providence

Have you ever wondered how Joseph and Mary supported themselves in a foreign country? The Bible does not tell us, but it seems to me God timed the arrival of the Magi so that, laying their gold, frankincense, and myrrh at the Savior's feet, they could give Him the means of providing the necessities for the stay in Egypt. God will likewise help you in Christ.[14]

Sin

Sin, the everlasting millstone around humanity's neck, tries to drown men and women in the sea of selfishness and in the riptides of their own passions.[15]

Concealing Sin

In our current vocabulary, a man who uses profanity and abuses the high and holy name of God is said to show "bad taste." A racketeer whose ruthless machine gun sweeps down an innocent pedestrian "suffers under a series of complexes." A child that refuses to obey its parents is coddled as a "self-expressionist." Young people who disregard the requirement of premarital chastity claim to enjoy "the new freedom of our new age."[16]

People try to disguise sin . . . they like to call it a "mistake," an "error in judgment," or some other harmless term. This is just about as true as calling the conflagration which almost destroyed Chicago a "bonfire," the hurricane which leveled Okinawa "a lusty breeze," or the World War "an international unpleasantness."[17]

For Pharisees

You say . . . "My life is an open book." How about the uncut pages and the suppressed chapters that you are really ashamed to have anyone read? To enter the Kingdom, you need much more than that self-satisfied claim so often expressed in your letters to me, "I don't smoke, drink, or play cards."[18]

Progress?

Whatever progress this generation sees is largely scientific or mechanical, not spiritual or moral. We boast of stratospheric flights streaking across the continent in less than twelve hours; but the airplane also helps a criminal commit forgery in Los Angeles before breakfast, bigamy in Chicago before lunch, murder in New York before dinner—all on the same day.[19]

Education Fosters Morality?

A tramp can steal a bag full of wheat from a barn, but a Phi Beta Kappa scholar can corner the wheat market and make the masses suffer.[20]

Salvation Through the One Foretold

One of the most positive and easily understood proofs for the truth that, according to God's plan, Jesus, the Son of God, died for everyone is the astonishing fact that each major part of our Lord's suffering was foreseen and foretold long before it happened.

Think of it, within less than twenty-four hours all these prophecies were fulfilled! First, the Savior was to be betrayed. Second, the traitor was to receive thirty pieces of silver. Third, this money was to be thrown down in the Lord's house. Fourth, it was to be used in purchasing a potter's field. Fifth, Christ was to be forsaken by His disciples. Sixth, He was to be accused by false witnesses. Seventh, He was to be beaten. Eighth, He was to be spat upon. Ninth, He was to keep silent before His oppressors. Tenth, He was to be wounded, bruised, beaten with stripes. Eleventh, He was to have His hands and feet pierced. Twelfth, He, the Son of God, was to be numbered with the transgressors, crucified with thieves. Thirteenth, He was to plead for those who persecuted Him. Fourteenth, the jeering mob would wag their heads. Fifteenth, they would ridicule Him with taunting sarcasm. Sixteenth, they would stand and gaze at Him. Seventeenth, they would divide various articles of His clothing among them. Eighteenth, they would cast lots for one piece of His apparel. Nineteenth, He would be naked on the cross. Twentieth, He would be tortured by thirst. Twenty-first, He would cry, *"My God, My God, why hast Thou forsaken Me?"* Twenty-second, His murderers would give Him gall and vinegar. Twenty-third, the mob would tauntingly ask, *"Let God deliver Him!"* Twenty-fourth, He would cry with a loud voice. Twenty-fifth, He would be pierced, but, twenty-sixth, not one of His bones would be broken. Twenty-seventh, He would be laid, not into a criminal's grave but into the tomb of a rich man.—Now, if these clear, precise prophecies were fulfilled in less than one day and night, how can anyone doubt that the Bible, with the whole record of your salvation, is entirely right, absolutely unbreakable, positively sure?

Now draw this definite, personal conclusion from these twenty-seven prophecies fulfilled in less than twenty-four hours: God never fails. *"Heaven and earth,"* He says, *"shall pass away, but My words shall not pass away."* How different the pledges men make! Goebbels assured the German people that their cities would never be bombed, but many have been wiped out by aerial destruction. Prime Minister Churchill declared that this would not be a peace of vindictive hatred, but he has clearly changed that position. The

Polish people were solemnly guaranteed that their territory would be fully restored; that likewise has been cast away. Happy couples pledge themselves to lifelong loyalty; yet last year more than 300,000 marriages were broken by divorce. I challenge every skeptic, I include especially the loud-mouthed atheists, to prove that even one of Christ's personal prophecies concerning His life, death, and resurrection has not been truly, blessedly fulfilled.[21]

The Easter Victory

The Bible teaches that our risen bodies are to be like the glorified body of our Savior. What comfort to know not merely that our personalities survive death but that our own forms and features will be restored; that although our bodies may be crippled and diseased, they shall be re-created without injury or loss of members!

Do not sneer at this sacred truth by declaring that when a man dies, he is dead forever, or by claiming that no body decayed in the grave, blown into a thousand bits, or decomposed on the ocean floor, can ever be resurrected! Modern unbelief teaches that men can do almost anything, while God, if indeed there is a God, can do little. People applaud the shipbuilder who makes thousands of tons of iron and steel built into a battleship float in the water; but, they say, God's prophet could not make the axhead float in the Jordan. They honor radio engineers who have shown that the air all over the world is filled with many different sounds, which can be heard when selected by a radio receiver; but emphatically they deny that the God who made the air and the sound waves can be everywhere, that the Spirit can work in the hearts of men thousands of miles apart. Much admiration is showered on a St. Louis scientist who has made a human heart beat after the body was dead; but skeptics ridicule the idea that the great God can revive a dead man's spirit. We admire the startling processes of modern industrial chemistry, by which coal tar, distilled and processed, can be changed into attractive crystalline plastics; but why do skeptics refuse to concede that Christ can resurrect our remains and *"change our vile body that it may be fashioned like unto His glorious body"?* Presidential medals are showered on botanists who develop special seeds that, sown into the ground, decay, yet produce the germ from which beautiful, multicolored flowers emerge. But why do haughty men insist that the omnipotent Creator, who first made man from the dust of the ground, cannot remake him in heavenly radiance?

End all doubt on Easter! Throw off all denials before the open grave, and with the mind of Mary Magdalene, who was the first to meet the risen Christ, greet your resurrected Redeemer today with trusting faith! Learn to welcome death and, in the spirit of Christian martyrs who rejoiced that they would soon behold their lord, conquer the fear of *"the last enemy"* through the love of Christ! Don't shriek or scream at a funeral as though there were no hope for those who have the Lord Jesus! Don't clench your fist against the Almighty, as though He were heartless in permitting bereavement to enter your home! Defy Satan, hell, and the grave with this powerful cry of triumph: *"O death, where is thy sting? O grave, where is thy victory? . . . Thanks be to God, which giveth us the victory through our Lord Jesus Christ!"*[22]

Meeting Adversity

As we see the stars only in the darkness, so often the night of adversity must come before we can see clearly the radiance of the Savior's help. There is no rainbow without the rain; and much of the beauty and happiness of our faith is unnoticed until the tempests of life strike us. . . . God sometimes takes our money lest our money take us.[23]

Keeping Faith

Do not rely only on your baptism or your early Christian training at home! If your religion is in the past tense, it can have no present blessing and future promise. You cannot enter heaven by proxy, through the faith of a God-fearing husband, wife, parents, or children.[24]

Modest Petitions

We often timidly ask God for the molehills of grace, and He places us upon the mountains of His munificence.[25]

We too often request a mite, yet our Father enriches us with much. We request the iron and slag of the commonplace; mercifully He grants us the gold and silver of His mercy. We seek temporal blessings, and lo! His love provides eternal benedictions.[26]

Varieties of Prayer

You can pray without Christ or against Christ; but if your petitions are even longer than the Senate filibuster; if you pray louder than the shrieking dervishes in Arabia; if you develop more oratory than Demosthenes or Cicero, your Christless prayers would be answered just as little as the rag prayers that Syrian Moslems tie on trees or the petitions that Tibetan monks multiply on their creaking prayer wheels or that the Zulus chant as they toss another stone on their prayer heap.[27]

It is not the length of a prayer—for Jesus warned against padding our petitions; it is not the place or the time of the prayer—for you may come before God wherever you are and whenever you need His guiding hand; it is not the language and style of prayer—for the lisped trust of children means more in the sight of God than the studied rhetoric of formal but empty prayers; but it is the Christ-centered faith of prayer in Jesus' name, submissive to the will of God, that guarantees the divine response.[28]

Don't Date the Second Coming

The tokens of Christ's return, fulfilled as never before, combine to preach one all-important message: Jesus is coming! According to the clear Scriptures Christ will return, not to build an earthly kingdom of glory (for He Himself emphatically stated, *"My kingdom is not of this world"*), not to rule in a millennial reign over this sin-saturated globe, but to judge the quick and the dead, to pronounce the doom of all unbelieving, unrepentant sinners, to take His trusting followers home to heaven. How much precious time is wasted in pulpit speculations which seek to make Ezekiel's thirty-eighth and thirty-ninth chapters and similar passages predict the outcome of this war and the detailed trend in tomorrow's political events—employing the very passages for which ten years ago men gave an altogether different interpretation and which twenty, thirty, forty years ago, and so on, were given still other explanations! When some of you preachers foretell the world's end on a certain date and that time comes and goes, just as a hundred contradictory dates selected for the final moment of human history have come and gone, can you not see that you are making men and women lose faith in the Bible? You have never saved anyone by insisting, for example, against all evidence, that the Biblical Tubal is the Russian city Tobolsk or that Meshech is Moscow. You will not bring one soul closer to heaven by teaching that Mount Zion in Jerusalem will be made higher than the Himalayas, that the Jews in their entirety will become Christians, and that all nations will stream to Palestine.

Stop this speculation! Preach prophecy and fulfilment as the Scriptures and history clearly portray God's miraculous power to foretell the future! Preach the Law and the Gospel! Preach the atonement and the resurrection! Tell your congregations that Jesus is coming for judgment on unbelief and for the salvation of His believers! Tell them to watch for that coming! [29]

Because of the sermonic format, W.A.M. could vent his strong sense of humor less often over the air than in the *Messenger.* Still, he tried to insert a pleasantry from time to time, which hardly detracted from the serious thrust of his message.

On Missing the Meaning of Christmas

If you would inquire of people who crowd downtown streets in this holiday rush, "Do you know anything about Mary and Joseph?" many of them would counter: "Mary who? Joseph who?" If you would say to our financiers, "Do you know the way of redemption?" many would answer: "What redemption? Redemption of war bonds?" If you would put the question to brokers, "What do you think of Bethlehem?" many would demand: "Bethlehem? Bethlehem Steel?" [30]

Moses and the WFA

When Moses heard the sullen, resentful murmuring of the masses against him, he did not wash his hands of the whole Exodus program for liberating his people and in deep-rooted disgust resign as national leader. Neither did he give a snarling, sarcastic reply of rebuke, nor did he institute a WFA, a Water Finding Authority. He did what every national leader should do in any crises, *"he cried unto the Lord."* [31]

No Mail in Hell

God keep our churches free from the darkness of denial by which the leader of one of the modern creeds declares: "If my future state depends upon putting my whole trust in the death of Jesus Christ on the cross nineteen hundred years ago—well, you can put my future address as: Hell"!—He certainly knows where he's going, but why give out the address? He won't get any mail there. [32]

7
SPEAKER

A Mutual Broadcasting System executive once styled Dr. Maier's sermons as "the soapbox delivery of a Harvard script." Indeed, the speaker devoted much attention to his Harvard script—dictating, rewriting, and polishing it into a broadcast manuscript that was always longer than he could deliver over the air. In the 1930s the sermon scripts grew to 14—15 pages, or about 140 percent of what he could preach in the 19 minutes allotted him on *The Lutheran Hour.* During the 1940s scripts were regularly 22—24 pages long, or nearly twice broadcast length. Since all the material was later published by Concordia in book form, the effort was not wasted.

The problem was that the speaker never ceased being the scholar. "The themes are important," he explained. "I must exhaust my subject." The themes which he selected reflected the seasons of the church year, national moral issues, doctrines of the Christian faith, and particularly the spiritual needs of his listening audience as these surfaced in the mass of response mail.

The next four addresses reflect seasonal themes. Like all subsequent sermons in this anthology, they are edited to

107

approximately the delivery length required by *The Lutheran Hour.*

Advent-Christmas (1936)

Good Tidings of Great Joy

"Behold, I bring you good tidings of great joy, which shall be to all people. For unto you is born this day in the city of David a Savior, which is Christ the Lord."—Luke 2:11

Let me recall the amazing contrasts that we find in Christmas. Do you know, for instance, that in the third gospel's account of the Savior's birth the entire record of this history-molding, world-moving event is told in only 273 words? Yet all the millions of volumes written since men first engraved their history in Mesopotamian clay and painted their achievements on Egyptian temple walls have not even faintly approached the mighty influences exerted by this short, concise account of the first Christmas.

Of these 273 words more than four-fifths are plain, everyday words of one syllable, so simple that your children can understand their promise; yet they conceal a divine mystery and a heavenly miracle so profound and inscrutable that the wisdom of the ages cannot plumb their depths. These unpretentious Christmas lines were penned not by a professional writer but by an eager young man whose lifework seemed to lie in medicine, Luke, *"the beloved physician";* and he received not a penny for his gospel. Yet cold commercialism has capitalized his story, drawing billions of dollars of profit from the event that it commemorates.

A few shepherds were the first to behold the Christ Child; yet priceless canvases immortalize the manger at Bethlehem. Viewed casually, the background of the Savior's birth seemed to hold no hope of promise: a stable; a Galilean man and woman, strangers, eighty miles from home—and there was *"no room . . . in the inn."* Politicians would have been disappointed, patriots disillusioned, publicists embarrassed. Yet that helpless Infant, cradled in a remote caravanserie of far-off Judea, is the universal figure of all history, the most decisive and blessed influence in the lives of hundreds of millions throughout the earth, because He is the Savior of their souls. Recite the morals of Marcus Aurelius to a coolie in China, and he will shake his head in bewilderment; but picture to him the endless mercies of the Christ Child, and he may be ready to offer his life for that Redeemer. Preach the philosophies of Plato to the Bushmen of Australia, and they will turn away unmoved and unaffected; but bring them the message of Christ, and some of them will resolve with eager penitence, *"Let us now go even unto Bethlehem and see this thing which is come to pass, which the Lord hath made known unto us."* Born at the beginning of the first century, Jesus was never more needed than in our twentieth century. Notable figures of the past live on in history, in books, in inscriptions on monuments; but the Christ of Christmas seeks to live in our hearts.

Only by centering our faith and hope on the Christ of the manger can we have this supreme and abiding blessing which makes Jesus our Immanuel, our God-with-us. In Correggio's *Holy Night,* one of the most famous of all Nativity paintings, the artist depicts the newborn Child not only as the center of interest but, for the first time in the history of painting, as the Source of light, which illumines the face of His mother, the shepherds, and even the countenances of the exultant angels above. Only when we behold *"His glory, the glory as of the Only-begotten of the Father,"* and find in Him *"the Light of the world,"* can Christmas truly emerge from carnival and color into its radiant fullness as *"the day which the Lord hath made,"* the festival of soul-rejoicing and tarnish-proof happiness.

Let us then on this Christmas morning turn our hearts and minds to the Christ Child and to these

"Tidings of Great Joy"

which come to us and *"to all people,"* as we hear, believe, and trust the heavenly proclamation, *"Unto you is born this day, in the city of David, a Savior, which is Christ the Lord"* (Luke 2:11).

The Joyous Message of the Christ-Child's Redeeming Grace

These words express the two sacred, eternal, central truths of the Christmas tidings. Because these are life-and-death truths, because your joy and happiness here and hereafter will be made or unmade by your accepting or rejecting these verities, I ask you to behold with me once more the cradled Child of Bethlehem, upon whom the eyes of the entire world, willingly or unwillingly, today focus their attention; for He is, as the angel carols, *"a Savior,"* a Deliverer, a Redeemer.

Some of you will object immediately, "Why do I need a Savior?" You speak in the tone of our times, when men have frantically tried to get rid of that brief black word "sin" by changing its name (in its latest guise it is labeled "social maladjustment"!), by silencing it out of existence, by employing psychological make-up to disguise it. On Christmas Day let us see eye to eye in regard to Heaven's foundation truth, that the Christ Child is our Savior from sin. Of course, if you are the man or woman who has never done, said, or thought anything that distresses your God, injures your fellow-men or yourself; if you are a paragon of perfection—turn off your radio! You do not need my message! You do not need Christmas! You do not want the Christ, who said, *"They that be whole need not a physician"!* But in all my life I have never met a sane, normal man who with all the mask of his own self-righteousness could stand before his God and bring an unblemished life record for divine approval and reward.

You know your own life better than I do. Conscience, the mysterious bar of justice within you that sits in judgment over every thought, word, and deed, has indicted you. I am simply bringing you the plain truth that Christmas asks us not to excuse or disguise our weakness and selfishness, envies and jealousies, untrue words and unkind actions, rebellious denials of God and ungrateful neglect of His mercies but to believe, with all the radiance and rejoicing of this blessed day, that here, *"in the city of David, a Savior"* was born.

That Redeemer our Christmas text calls *"Christ."* Have you ever studied the endless wealth of mercies that lie in this much-used, but much-misunderstood name? *"Christ"* means God's "Anointed," the promised Prophet, Priest, and King, through whose redeeming grace men are to be blessed in life and death. How the whisper of Old Testament prophecy, spoken through mysterious centuries, swells into the chorus of New Testament fulfillment! How the dawnings of hope even at the closed gates of Eden burst into radiant brilliance when the great Anointed, the Messiah, the Christ, was born! But a dark, spectral shadow beclouds the career of this Christ. He was to be rejected as a servant instead of being acclaimed as a king. The price of blood was to rest on His head in place of a crown of glory. The royal city that had stoned the prophets and killed God's messengers was to pay thirty pieces of silver for that Christ, drag Him to a skull-shaped hill, and in the torture of a punishment so brutal that it has not been legally invoked in the last fifteen hundred years, nail Him, its own promised Messiah, to the shame and agony of a cross.

That death blesses us with life, and Christ's resurrection seals for us the everlasting glories of heaven; for the Savior—and we now approach the second of the sublime *"tidings of great joy"*—that Christ, is God incarnate. The Child in the manger (how human reason staggers before this mystery!) is God, the merciful, everlasting, almighty God. As He had to be man to fulfill the Scriptures and suffer and die in our stead, so He had to be God to pay the price demanded for the atonement of all human sin. If you believe that Jesus, who five times calls Himself the Son of God and twenty-seven times calls God His Father, is your Lord; if, as you glance through the Old and New Testaments, you read that in prophecy and in fulfillment He is hailed as divine; that His teachings, His miracles, His power combine to prove that He is "true God, begotten of the Father from eternity, and also true man, born of the Virgin Mary," then you have the pure gold of enduring faith and no tarnished brass of unbelief. With this Christmas gift, the greatest that even God could bestow, you know that through the mercies of Christ the rejected are restored, the alienated reconciled, the unclean purged, the condemned pardoned; you understand that everything you need for body and soul, time and eternity, your faith and life, your hopes and fears, is freely given you.

No wonder men traveled from afar to behold the Christ Child, and today from the ends of the earth great multitudes have come to Christ. No wonder that for thousands of years the pleadings and prayers of men were focused on that first Christmas, that humanity sets its clocks at the cradle, and the world changed its calendar since the Savior's birth. And if by the Spirit's power you give your soul this Christmas present of Christ, a new life, a new age, a rebirth in faith, in joy everlasting, begins for you.

The Joyous Message of the Christ-Child's Universal Grace

We hear the angelic promise that these tidings of great joy are to be *"to ALL people,"* and we are reminded that Christmas is everyone's day. It is the day of the child; for how gloriously has childhood been hallowed by that Babe, the brightness of the Father's glory incarnate as an Infant! I ask you parents, confused by cares and disturbed by your inability to make this Christmas the

111

joyful festival in your home that you desire, not to let these blessed days close without taking your children into your arms and impressing upon them the blessed truth that beyond all the Christmas lights they must find *"the Light of the world";* above starry, glittering decorations they must follow the star that stopped over Bethlehem; beneath all the eager, impatient anticipation of Christmas gifts they must have the one Gift that exceeds all others.

If we build for tomorrow with granite, iron, or steel, no matter how securely we rear the structures, we cannot build with confidence since the tremors of a quaking world and the rust of decay may destroy our choicest architecture. But if we build with God-fearing, obedient children who have faith in Christ, we are building with permanent hope. Fathers and mothers of America, on this day when childhood is raised to its greatest glory by the Christ Child, I ask you to drop everything, no matter how important it may seem to you, that prevents you from bringing your own flesh and blood to the Savior. God pity the parents in whose homes Christmas means nothing more than merriment!

Christmas is the day for mothers. Through nothing else has motherhood been more highly exalted than through the birth of Christ. When *"the Word was made flesh,"* when the Savior was born of the virgin, motherhood was enshrined in the highest glory that we can contemplate. The picture of her who was *"blessed . . . among women"* singing hymns of praise to God during those mysterious but blessed days before the birth of her Son symbolizes the faith that should live in the hearts of wives and mothers of our generation. So let me ask the young women, "Do you have the faith of Mary? Is Christ your Savior, personally and unmistakably? Do you pray to God for strength and divine help in leading a clean, chaste, life? Do you look forward to the time when with a Christian husband you will have your own home and your first baby? If you do not know these joys and this heavenly power for your earthly problems; if you are one of the blase, sophisticated young women who are trying to find happiness without or against God's law, let me, in the name of this Christ of Christmas, speak pleadingly to each one of you and beg you to turn in contrite faith to the mercy of that Christ Child who not only forgives and cancels our sins but through His Word strengthens us for the highest blessings of the truly abundant life! Are you who within the next weeks or months will shelter within your arms a new gift of God, a tiny, precious mite of love, small and

112

weak as the infant Jesus, humming Christmas melodies or singing, as Mary did, *"My soul doth magnify the Lord."*? Or is it true that for years you have not opened your soul, wide and free and happy, to chorus with the herald angels, "Joy to the world, the Lord is come"? If you have been stunting your own soul, may these days sing to you the greatest message that ever came to earth, the Christmas promise of pardon, the Christmas hope of a better, happier, more radiant life.

Christmas is the workingman's day. It is not accidental that the first witnesses of the Savior's birth were men of the laboring class, common shepherd folk from the nearby fields. Yet how often we fail to find the significance of labor bowing before Christ! Many in the great army of America's workingmen and women have been exploited and misled. Others have been disappointed and distracted by the continued reverses of the last years and hardened by the cruelties of our industrial collapse. Still, if every one of the 40,000,000 workers in America could hear the bells of Christmas ring their glad tidings over the cares and worries about employment and come as the shepherds did to the Christ Child, a new sense of blessing would rest on these toilers. Workers of America, never before have as many appeals petitioned your support. You are asked to take up flaming firebrands and, destroying our Government in the fires of Communism, to make the Soviet States of America rise from the ashes. Rival coalitions are bidding for your support. Politicians are bargaining for your votes. But I ask you on Christmas to bring labor to Christ. I ask you, the factory workers, the tradesmen, the miners, the carpenters, the metal workers, and all others engaged in constructive enterprise, to tear out the propaganda of hatred from across the seas that puts the true church of Jesus Christ and the workingman into opposing trenches. He chose twelve workingmen to be His disciples, and today He calls to you who may have opposed Him, who sing the *Internationale* instead of Christmas carols, who crowd labor halls but remain at a contemptuous distance from the Savior, and He asks you to hasten and with the shepherds to find *"the Babe lying in a manger."* Life could never be the same again for these Judean shepherds. With Bethlehem began a new and glorious confidence. And I promise you that with pardon and joyful trust in Christ you will rise to heights of happiness you have never scaled before.

Christmas, as we embrace the entire Nativity cycle, is also the rich man's day. When the Magi brought their treasures to the Christ Child, they represented wealth bowing before the Savior. The Christmas season has an emphatic appeal for the aged too. When Simeon and Anna, advanced in years, welcomed their Redeemer in the temple, you who have traveled far along life's way were given a strong and personal example for your trust in Christ.

Christmas is everyone's day; and though a hundred forces may surround you to contradict this promise, these glad tidings of a Savior are directed *"to ALL people."* Are you poor? Your Savior was born in a stable. Are you neglected? Think of the overcrowded inn. Are you harassed and persecuted by hostile forces within and without your own life? Listen to the voice of lamentation in Rama when bloody Herod massacred the children in Bethlehem and the Holy Family fled to safety in Egypt. Does it seem as though your Christmas must be tear-filled and sorrow-laden because of sickness, family trouble, or the pain of death? Remember that He who came into the flesh was *"touched with the feeling of our infirmities"* and that every sorrow, no matter how deep-rooted it may be, can vanish before the joy-filled message of Christmas salvation.

Almost six hundred years ago the plague of the Black Death, one of the greatest pestilences of all history, swept over Europe, leaving piled corpses in its terrifying swath. "Men," we are told, "fled in terror of their fellow-men in awful fear of their breath or touch and for weeks sustained a strange, weird siege of solitude." This dread fear of contamination continued until Christmas Eve, 1353, when in the city of Goldberg, Silesia, a man who thought he was the only survivor of the entire city went forth at the dead of night. He knew it was Christmas, and he raised his voice to sing:

> To us this day is born a Child,
> God with us!
> His mother is a Virgin mild,
> God with us!
> God with us!
> God with us—against us who dare be!

As his voice rang into the stillness of the night, another voice came through a barred door in response to his own, and then a man joined him in the street. Together they sang into the quiet of the midnight hour, the first songs that had been heard in the city since the pestilence had entered the gates. Their songs brought strange echoes, and from living tombs survivors to the number of twenty-five—all that were left in the town—came forth and with new courage marched through death-stricken streets, singing:

God with us—against us who dare be!

If you and I, kneeling at the cradle, will raise eyes of faith to the Christ Child and exult: "God *is* for us because this Child that is born to us, this Son that is given to us, this 'Immanuel' is *'Wonderful, Counselor, the Mighty God, the Everlasting Father, the Prince of Peace,'"* then the Savior's joy will be fulfilled in us, and we shall know life at its highest and best. To this faith and to this newborn Savior I commend you. God bless you on this Christmas through the Christ Child. Amen.[33]

Lent (1947)

Follow Christ on the Calvary Road!

"As they led Him [Jesus] away, they laid hold upon one Simon, a Cyrenian, coming out of the country, and on him they laid the cross that he might bear it after Jesus. And there followed Him a great company of people and of women, which also bewailed and lamented Him. But Jesus, turning unto them, said: Daughters of Jerusalem, weep not for Me, but weep for yourselves and for your children."—Luke 23:26-28

When President Truman recently visited our good neighbors across the Rio Grande, the Mexican government and its people gave him the warmest welcome any foreign guest has ever received in that country. Schools were closed for the day to let the children greet our President. Mexico City was beflagged as never before; and—this is unusual—the houses on the streets along the presidential party's route were all freshly painted, the babies carefully washed and clothed in their finest. President Truman was to behold Mexico at its best.

It has long been the policy among nations to make rulers of other realms see only beauty. When Marie Antoinette traveled through France, weeks ahead the beggars and the cripples, the poor and the disfigured, were removed from the path of her procession. When Ibrahim Pasha entered Palestine, large squads of laborers had gone before him, widening the road, smoothing its surface, filling its deep declines. Indeed, years ago, when a Russian czar wanted to impress a visiting ruler, he had entire make-believe cities and villages erected along the banks of the Vistula, with many thousands of house fronts, make-believe stores, shells of public buildings and churches. As the royal guest floated down the river in the czar's barge, he was to be impressed by the camouflage of a flourishing, fertile countryside. Royalty on parade must be routed along the most pleasing boulevards and behold only the best.

How different the procession in which Jesus Christ, the King of kings, goes from Jerusalem to His death cross at Calvary! Here marches the Son of God and the Savior of the world, not on any diplomatic errand of promoting goodwill between neighboring nations but on the holiest mission this earth can ever know, the reconciling of mankind with the Almighty. Yet despite this mercy He is made to suffer crushing sorrows. Agony, not applause, burning grief instead of warm welcome, cries of hatred instead of homage meet Him as men blasphemously show Jesus their worst rather than their best.

We do not begin to treat our worst criminals on their last journey to the gallows with the viciousness heaped on our Lord. A few days ago in Seattle the sheriff took Garland Wilson, a condemned murderer, to the death house in a distant penitentiary. He rode to the death house in a large limousine, stretching lazily as he remarked how good it was to get out of jail for a while. The only inconvenience he suffered was that, handcuffed, he found some difficulty in lighting his cigarette. Otherwise, from time to time, he whistled softly and expressed the hope that his lawyer and his chaplain would appeal to the governor and save him from the gallows. But Jesus did not ride to Calvary; He had to drag Himself to gory Golgotha along a *via dolorosa,* a way of sorrows, every inch of which was marked both with excruciating pain for Him and with powerful lessons for us. To learn these, I plead with you:

Follow Christ on the Calvary Road!

Witness His deep devotion to your souls on that death march! Study His words of warning love as you hear our text (Saint Luke twenty-three, verses twenty-six to twenty-eight): *"As they led Him* [Jesus] *away, they laid hold upon one Simon, a Cyrenian, coming out of the country, and on him they laid the cross that he might bear it after Jesus. And there followed Him a great company of people and of women, which also bewailed and lamented Him. But Jesus, turning unto them, said: Daughters of Jerusalem, weep not for Me, but weep for yourselves and for your children."*

See Him Suffering for You!

According to custom the Romans should have required that two days intervene between the verdict of guilty and the execution of the death sentence; yet here again, as in every aspect of our Savior's suffering, right was swept aside by the hatred and haste which marked the blood lust of our Lord's enemies. The law granted Him two days but His enemies less than two hours.

When the preparation for the cruel cavalcade to the cross began, Pilate's soldiers tore the purple robe of mock royalty from Christ. That garment, their greed and unbelief concluded, was too valuable to waste on Him. Usually a centurion, in command of a hundred troops, was in charge at public executions. We know that an officer of this rank supervised the Savior's crucifixion. Tradition calls him Longinus, but his real name, like that of many heroes of the faith, is unknown. We are sure, however, that he should be the model for every soldier, officer, or enlisted man today. He took reverent time to behold Jesus. While others scoffed and ridiculed, he kept on regarding the Crucified without their hatred and prejudice. It took courage for him, when the skies darkened over Golgotha and the earth shook beneath it, to cry out: *"Certainly this was a righteous Man!"* and: *"Truly this was the Son of God!"* The first convert at Calvary a military officer!

It was customary also at many executions that a herald went ahead of the death procession, declaring, either with repeated announcements or with a printed sign, the crime for which the prisoner was to be executed. The purpose behind this was to give anyone who could speak a plea or bring new evidence in behalf of the condemned man a final opportunity to raise his voice. We do not know whether a herald thus preceded Pilate's soldiers, although legend has it, in the Talmud, that for forty days before the crucifixion, a messenger went about declaring: "Jesus of Nazareth goeth forth to be executed. If anyone can say a word of defense for Him, let him speak!" Yet we read, "No defense was found for Him." The Bible supports this tragic silence. Not a single person throughout the length and breadth of Judea, Samaria, or Galilee, among the tens of thousands who had been benefited and blessed by God's

Son, stood up publicly to intercede for Him. Was there ever such utter ingratitude?

Often the death parade chose the longest possible route to the place of execution since the condemned prisoner was to be made a public spectacle, a warning to the curious masses. Perhaps our Savior was spared this added humiliation. We do know, however, that He could not escape one of the heaviest of all burdens: He had to carry His own cross. Again we are not sure exactly what shape that ghastly instrument of torture took, although we are certain that Christ's countrymen shrank back from touching it. That, they declared, would have made them unclean. To the Romans, likewise, the cross was an emblem of the deepest disgrace. No soldier would lower himself by bearing this bloody burden; so the Roman legionaries pressed its heavy timbers on Jesus' bleeding back and pushed Him forward on His pathway of pain.

Stop, repentantly, to behold Jesus as He starts carrying His cross to Calvary! Concentrate your thoughts on the Son of God bowed beneath those accursed timbers! If you have never realized this before, do you now, personally and penitently, understand that this Christ, going to Golgotha, is innocent, absolutely unstained by any suggestion of sin? Do you really know that He is the victim of the worst injustice, the most criminal falsehood men have ever seen? Even more: As you behold the Man of Sorrows dragging His broken body beneath the weight of that cross without once accusing His cruel foes or screaming under the agony wounding His spirit, do you understand that the stainless Savior, *"brought as a lamb to the slaughter,"* here lifts the load which should have been placed on your shoulders, here, on the highway to His dismal death, suffers in your stead? For almost fourteen years in this mission of the air, we have reemphasized in hundreds of different ways the one supremely sacred truth that *"He was wounded for our transgressions, He was bruised for our iniquities."* If we could broadcast for fourteen centuries, this would not be long enough to exhaust the love of the cross-carrying Christ and to tell you that He goes the grim road to Golgotha not, as the two thieves and murderers who went with Him, for His own sins. Son of God that He is, He had no transgressions of His own. He took your iniquities upon Himself. What matchless mercy! Each inch of that heartbreaking way to Calvary was marked by gripping grief of soul as the wrath of the Father singled out His own Son to assume the sentence of your sin.

Legend has it that when our Lord was passing through a busy section of Jerusalem, lurching under the heavy beams of His cross, a fellow countryman, Ahasuerus, spied the death march, ran out of his house, and with devilish delight kicked the Cross-Bearer so that He began to stagger beneath His load. Then, the story concludes, Christ cursed him to wander restlessly all over the face of the earth until the end of time. This is mere fiction, and it goes too far. On the Calvary road the Redeemer of the race cursed no one. Even then He was praying for His persecutors, as He did on the cross.

Look once more at the cross-bearing Son of God and realize what He has done for you! His was the bitterness of death but yours the sweetness of salvation. The suffering was His but the healing yours; He endured rejection, but you gained redemption; He shed His blood, but your soul was cleansed; He won the crown of thorns, but the crown of life is for you. The torments of hell were for Him but the hallowed joys of His Father's house for you. Don't let this Sunday pass as you have many others in which you came close to your salvation but not close enough to call the Crucified "My Lord." Those who continually refuse to accept Jesus may find that divine patience runs out. Today, right in your own room, in your family circle, in automobiles or speeding trains, in hospitals or old folks' homes, in penitentiaries, or any place where this broadcast is heard, follow Christ on Calvary's road, receive Him as your Redeemer and Ruler, your Savior and Substitute, your good and gracious God! You need only believe, only give Him your contrite heart; then He will give Himself to you.

You can learn another blessed lesson on the Calvary road. When you are called to bear a cross of affliction, you will know that Christ has carried an unspeakably heavier load than whatever may burden you. He, the Son of God, endured every grief which will ever grip you; only He suffered immeasurably worse sorrows. We have a Savior who was *"touched with the feeling of our infirmities."* He knows our pains and problems because He felt them all in a degree far too great for the human mind to fathom. During the Civil War, "Stonewall" Jackson's men were once overtaken by a severe snowstorm. In the morning when, half frozen, they crawled from beneath their snow-covered blankets, some began to curse him for their plight until they learned that Jackson himself had slept with them in the snow. He suffered what his soldiers suffered. In a much higher manner "Jesus knows our every weakness." Are you poor?

He was so destitute that His only possessions were bloodstained garments with which He was clothed—and even these were soon to be taken from Him. He staggered under the same miseries, although vastly multiplied, which make you groan. Take every fevered anxiety to Him, *"casting all your care upon Him; for He careth for you."*

Are you lonely? Think of Him dragging His cross alone through the crowded streets with no one to wipe the blood and the sweat and the tears from His face! Hear Him as in earth's deepest loneliness He screams: *"My God, My God! Why hast Thou forsaken Me?"* He knows the turmoil of your soul, and though He was forsaken, even by His disciples, He promises you, through faith: *"I will never leave thee nor forsake thee."*

Are you beset by enemies? See how Jesus was surrounded by coarse, cruel soldiers on the Calvary highway, how He was mocked on the cross by brutal men, and then find comfort in the guarantee of His grace: *"If God be for us, who can be against us?"*

In all this I have been trying to tell you Jesus was *"tempted like we are, yet without sin."* No burden you carry is unknown to Him; and because He is your almighty Lord, He not only understands your misery, but He also assures you, *"Your sorrows shall be turned into joy."* Your adversities will become your advantages, your tears your triumphs through Christ, whose errorless Word promises: *"All things work together for good to them that love God."* As the greatest suffering ever witnessed—the crucifixion—was followed by the greatest miracle—the resurrection—so, in our incomparably smaller afflictions, as believers, the crown always follows the cross.

The pain and disgrace of bearing the cross suddenly ended for the Savior. Our Lord had not slept a moment during the last twenty-four hours; instead He was tortured, tormented, scourged, slashed, mocked, and marred. Neither food nor drink had crossed His lips; and far worse than this physical pain was the agony of His soul as He paid the appalling price for your redemption. No wonder, then, that Christ collapsed under the pressure of the cross and that the soldiers, eager to be through with the ghastly business of killing, *"laid hold upon one Simon, a Cyrenian, coming out of the country, and on him they laid the cross that he might bear it after Jesus."*

Some say that Simon was a black. We know that he did come from sunbaked Cyrenian Africa. I wish that we could prove that this cross-bearer was a member of the race long burdened by the cruelties which the white people have laid upon their backs. Did you read the newspaper story of a frail black woman who for the last thirty years worked in unpaid drudgery for seventeen hours each day as a veritable slave to a socialite Boston couple? She was not permitted to see relatives or friends; her food was the leftovers; her clothes the castoffs. She slept in a cellar cubbyhole large enough only for a cot. She was not allowed to attend church nor to read Scripture. But she recalled: "I had learned some Bible passages in school, and I still remember them. They were a comfort to me during all those years." "Could anything be more cruel?" you ask. "Yes," we answer, "the persistent policy of some white churches to bar the black from the privilege of joint worship!" The Holy Spirit help us recognize clearly that *"God is no respecter of persons,"* that He loves the souls of all men, whatever the color of their skin may be.

To Simon this cross-bearing was anything but a privilege and an honor. He probably regarded it as a curse; but we have reason to believe that by lifting Christ's load he was brought close to the Savior, just as the hardships some of you were called upon to endure for Jesus have led you close to your Lord. Are you willing to do what Simon was forced to do: face scorn and ridicule for the Redeemer's sake? Are you ready to stand up for Jesus though the masses may point the finger of scorn at you? The world today needs brave people who valiantly testify to Christ, and if need be, suffer with Him. Courageous cross-bearers have this promise: *"If we suffer, we shall also reign with Him."*

Hear Him Speak Warning to You!

It was probably just outside the city wall that our Lord collapsed, and by this time, as our text records, *"there followed Him a great company of people."* It was a holiday in Jerusalem, the day before the Passover festival, and visitors had hastened to the holy city even from distant nations. When they heard that Jesus was to be crucified, the same morbid curiosity which led the women of Paris to sit and knit by the side of the dripping guillotine made many eager to catch a glimpse of the widely discussed Preacher from Galilee. Large numbers marched out to Calvary to sneer at the dying Savior, some perhaps who only five short days before had greeted Him with the hosannas of welcome when He held His humble but triumphant entry into Jerusalem.

Some followed Christ with no curiosity or hatred in their hearts. These, according to our text, were *"women which also bewailed and lamented Him,"* the mothers, wives, and daughters of Jerusalem's citizens, high and low. The Almighty has blessed womanhood with a feeling of sympathy for the suffering, and when the *"daughters of Jerusalem"* beheld Him, they saw the deep gashes left by the thorny crown, the imprint of brutal blows on His countenance, and they screamed in piercing lament.

We might think that Christ was too completely gripped by His own grief to have a thought or word for these wailing women. But on the Calvary road He was never too self-engrossed to speak to others of their salvation or warn them of the dangers surrounding them. Hear him tell the women on that day of woe: *"Daughters of Jerusalem, weep not for Me, but weep for yourselves and for your children."* Our suffering Savior was touched by their sorrowing compassion. Our Lord was too human to be ungrateful for their sympathy, but He was too divine to be unmindful of their peril. His all-knowing eye penetrates the fearful future ahead for the sons and daughters of those lamenting women. These children, reared in the rejection of their Redeemer, would pay an appalling penalty for their unbelief. The city that had stoned the prophets and now, in the climax of its crime, was to crucify the Son of God would be leveled to the ground by Roman conquerors in a massacre and murder such as men have seldom seen. The children now playing in the Jerusalem streets would be captured, tortured, sold into slavery, killed by the thousands.

Today the Savior has the same word of warning for many American parents: *"Weep . . . for your children!"* *"Weep,"* He cries out, "for your sons and daughters who have been brought up without Baptism, without Sunday school, without church membership, without family devotions, without the example of our Lord's power in their parents' lives!" Agonies far worse than those which marked the devastation of Jerusalem await them in an endless hereafter unless they come penitently to Him who alone is *"the Way, the Truth, and the Life."* *"Weep . . . for your children,"* parents throughout the land, if you have neglected them, failed to guide their souls to Jesus, permitted them to spend their leisure hours with unbelievers, reading suggestive books and taking part in sensual amusements.

"Weep . . . for your children!" Christ repeats to our entire country if, despite the unparalleled blessings with which the Almighty has endowed us, we spurn His mercies, and His outraged justice permits the fearful forecasts of a Third World War, with its superatomic destruction, to overtake us. The bombs that fell on Japan helped create five new and deadly poisons, with which the children of Hiroshima and Nagasaki must now contend; but what will be the horror awaiting our youth in the new atomic warfare ahead, the secrets of which, we are now solemnly assured, several other nations share?

To prevent this, to give America the defense of that righteousness which *"exalteth a nation"*; to assure for our children the hope and happiness Heaven wants them to have; to keep the Savior with our country, our churches, our homes, especially with our souls, let every one of us in this mission of the air follow Christ on the Calvary road and find in Him our God, going to Golgotha to be crucified for our sins! Take one last glance at the cross before the Redeemer of mankind is affixed to the beams and it is raised to tower over the whole gruesome scene! A Roman soldier is hammering Pilate's superscription to the top of the cross. You know what he penned in the sarcasm of his unbelief—a title proclaiming Christ the King of His people. Today I ask you, with the Spirit's help, to write your own superscription to the cross. What shall it be?—In a cemetery at Stroudsburg, Pennsylvania, you will find this inscription on a tombstone over the grave of a Civil War veteran: "Abraham Lincoln's Substitute." There lies the man whom President Lincoln chose to take his place in battle, according to the customs and provisions of the draft laws at that time. Believing that Jesus Christ, the Son of God, was nailed to the cross to take your place in fulfilling Heaven's holy law and in paying the fearful price required to remove your sins, will you not write this title of triumph and faith, ever to remain atop that gory timber, "My Substitute"? God grant you will! Amen![34]

Easter (1937)

The Resurrection Reality

"God hath both raised up the Lord and will also raise up us by His own power."—1 Cor. 6:14

On this glorious Easter Day, as we stand in spirit before the

123

Savior's open grave, let us ask ourselves frankly, What is it that magnetizes the faith of Christian hearts all over the world and draws them to this broken sepulcher? History knows far more pretentious burial places than Joseph's grave, where the lifeless body of the Savior was laid to its repose. Recent excavations have uncovered the extended tombs of the kings in Ur of the Chaldees and shown us that at the death of the ruler his entire court was buried alive. In Egypt the tomb of Tutankhamen, with its lavish wealth and its artistic adornment, has impressed even our age. In the Red Square at Moscow the remains of the Red Dictator Lenin, preserved by a mysterious process, are regarded with an admiration that approaches worship. But even the site of our Savior's grave is not definitely known. Mohammedans heckle Christian missionaries with the challenge: "We have the tomb of our great prophet Mohammed here in Medina, while you Christians have nothing."

Yet at Easter we have everything! While all other tombs are evidences of death and decay, Christ's tomb alone is the evidence of life. We hear the angel challenge, *"Why seek ye the Living among the dead?"* and we recall the burial place enshrined in the grateful memory of our nation, Flanders' fields, where

> . . . poppies grow
> Between the crosses, row on row;

the burial vault of George Washington at Mount Vernon, the sepulchers of other distinguished leaders and statesmen, all of which commemorate brilliant or generous lives that ran their course only to end in inevitable death. But our Savior's grave offers life, hope, and blessing! Even though we may never be able to mark the garden grave of our Lord, the reality of His resurrection must be a strong and vital power in our faith and lives. Even though the ranks of twentieth-century scoffers are daily swollen by those who demand, "Where is the proof of the next life, the evidence of the resurrection?" we must cling to the Easter pledge of Heaven.

To strengthen our faith and remove all distrust of the Easter message, let us consecrate our thoughts in this festival broadcast to

The Resurrection Reality

and, taking the words of St. Paul, 1 Corinthians, chapter 6, verse fourteen, *"God hath both raised up the Lord and will also raise up us by His own power,"* find faith and hope in the Savior's resurrection and in our eternal Easter with Him.

Walter A. Maier

These photos were graciously provided by the Concordia Historical Institute, from their Walter A. Maier collection.

Dr. Maier in his study at his St. Louis home. An accomplished Semitic scholar and a Harvard Ph.D., Maier taught Old Testament exegesis at Concordia Seminary for many years.

Walter A. Maier as a student.

Walter A. Maier as seen in 1944.

Dr. Maier is greeted by Indiana Governor Henry Schricker at an Indianapolis railroad station prior to a speaking engagement in that city.

(A George Nelidoff Photo)

Walter Maier striking a familiar pose at a microphone. He began broadcasting in 1930, and his Lutheran Hour messages continued until his untimely death in 1950.

Dr. Maier with Dr. Eugene Bertermann on his last Rally Day, in December 1949.

Maier speaking to a capacity crowd of 25,000 at the 1949 Lutheran Hour Rally at the Chicago Stadium.

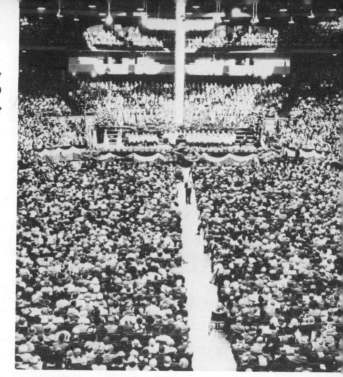

Dr. Walter Maier in a familiar setting, this time addressing an All-Lutheran Rally in Ocean Grove, New Jersey, on July 16, 1949.

*The Lutheran
Hour floral
arrangement
at Dr. Maier's
funeral.*

*Dr. Maier's funeral, Saturday,
January 14, 1950, in the
Concordia Seminary chapel.
Dr. Maier's pastor, the Rev.
Herman A. Etzold, was the
preacher.*

*The Walter A. Maier
Memorial, dedicated
October 7, 1951.*

"God Hath Raised Up the Lord"

First of all, let us impress this conviction deeply in our minds: The resurrection of Jesus Christ rests on fact as well as faith. Repeatedly do Old Testament passages foretell His resurrection. Emphatically did Jesus Himself, before He went the way of the cross, tell His friends and His enemies that on the third day after His crucifixion He would rise from the dead. Six different and independent accounts, one in each of the four gospels, one in the Book of Acts, and one from the pen of St. Paul, recount His triumph over death. Scores of passages in the remainder of the New Testament speak of the Savior's resurrection with a clarity that tolerates no uncertainty. Do you know any other fact in the history of the first century that has as much support as the resurrection? Historians today accept thousands of facts for which they can produce only shreds of evidence; yet there are some who refuse to believe this epochal event and the hundreds of New Testament witnesses who talked with the risen Christ, walked with Him, ate with Him, knelt before Him, and acclaimed Him their Lord and Savior. Today we send a man to death in the electric chair on circumstantial evidence; but the enemies of Christ are not ready to let Jesus live, even though overwhelming testimony proves His resurrection. If the Easter record is not in every claim the account of history, if the statements of those who testified to the Easter truth are not accepted as conclusive evidence, then no testimony and evidence whatever can establish any truth in any age of history.

The proof that *"God hath raised up the Lord"* comes to us from other convincing sources. What was it that took the first company of the disciples, cowering as they did behind locked doors, and transformed them into a band of confident champions of their crucified Lord? Not a dead Savior but a living, conquering Christ! What power and influence changed the cross from an instrument of bloody torture to the most beloved of all symbols? Uncounted thousands had been crucified before the day of our blessed Savior; and you know that, if He had not risen from the dead, no right-minded person would have glorified anything as hideous and repulsive as that timber and crossbeam stained with the Savior's blood. What gave the great army of Christian martyrs and missionaries the love and the power to face death, to penetrate poisonous jungles, to cross barren deserts, to hasten to the ends of the earth in their zeal for winning disciples for the Savior? Only blind fanaticism could lead them to serve a dead Lord, whose resurrection promises had failed and whose body had moldered in the grave. There is no fanaticism in our faith. We have the eternal facts, the everlasting truth of the Savior's conquest of death.

Jesus had to rise again and by this miracle of all miracles place the seal of assurance on the forgiveness of our sins; for a dead Christ could be no Savior. An unopened grave would mean an unopened heaven. By bursting the bonds of the grave, Jesus proved Himself the Conqueror of sin and showed the everlasting validity of His atonement. The sacrifice on Calvary had fulfilled its purpose, the ransom price paid for your sins and mine had been accepted.

No wonder that great men of God have found their highest comfort in this resurrection reality: *"God hath raised up the Lord."* Luther would dispel all despondency with the one word *vivit,* the Latin for "He lives." Many times he seized a piece of chalk and wrote this *vivit* on his study table or voiced it in triumph. When asked for an explanation, he answered: "Jesus lives, and if He were not among the living, I would not wish to live even an hour." Let us all try with the Spirit's help to engrave this Easter truth "He lives" in our hearts.

"God . . . Will Also Raise Up Us by His Own Power"

With faith in Christ's resurrection our text offers this pledge: *"God . . . will also raise up us by His own power."* The open grave becomes the pledge of our immortality; the Savior's resurrected body, the promise of our glorified bodies; the Easter cry, *"O death, where is thy sting?"* the echo of our own triumph, *"O grave, where is thy victory?"* With faith in the Easter morning greeting *"He is not here, He is risen"* the great problem of the human soul and its destiny, that ageless perplexity which has baffled the choicest minds, brings a blessed and personal solution for every one of us. At the empty tomb we learn that the one short, perplexing life which is ours does not complete our destiny; that the grave is not the last, futile chapter in our life's story. With the great stone rolled from the entrance of the Savior's rock-hewn grave, we must catch a foregleam of a new and blessed existence that starts when this life stops.

Only in the power of Christ's resurrection can we gain strength and assurance for our own eternal Easter. Men may dream dreams of a hereafter and draw pretty pictures of the life to come; but our resurrection reality must be woven of firmer texture. Ask the botanist, and he will point you to the lily, which in its white beauty has become the flower of the Easter Festival. Its bulb lies buried and unseen in the black ground until, by the mysterious force of life, a shaft of green breaks through the earth, and as the sun smiles with its sustaining warmth, the tender stalk grows in height and strength, a cluster of buds appears, and then a lily in all its fairness and fragrance. So, we are told, the grave becomes the garden of God's new creation. The lifeless body reposes in its dark embrace; it decays; yet by the power of God a new body, pure and sinless, arises. Ask the naturalist, and he will offer a picture of the resurrection in the spring and autumnal migration of the birds. He will show you winged creatures that fly 7,000 miles, from the Yukon Valley to southern Argentina, guided by their instinct; and he will conclude that an inborn sense of immortality will irresistibly summon man to seek and find his everlasting home in a better and happier land. He will tell you that we are all like the homing pigeon and that, when we are released, we shall fly back to God, whose love created us. The philosopher has a dozen arguments for life after death. He believes that death cannot end all, because our lives are so incomplete and unfinished, that there must be a continuation, just as he insists, there must be a reward or retribution in the next world, by which all the injustice and unfairness of life can be adjusted, its wrongs righted, its losses compensated.

We need not argue the reality of our resurrection on these grounds nor rest our hope for a reunion with those who have gone before us on the reawakening of nature or on the claims that the higher forces which created man could not brutally destroy him forever. In the word of Jesus we have surety, conviction, truth. When our Lord promises, *"He that believeth in Me, though he were dead, yet shall he live";* when He adds certainty to certainty by repeating, *"Because I live, ye shall live also"; "Where I am, there shall also My servant be"; "If a man keep My saying, he shall never see death,"* the issue is closed. The resurrection is not a matter of speculation and guess and conjecture. It is the unchangeable truth of God Himself, bestowed through the only sure antidote to death, the blood of Jesus Christ, which forever removes the cause of death, the sin that would separate us from God.

We know, of course, that there have always been Sadducees

who deny the resurrection. One of the very first records of Christianity outside the New Testament is a letter dated in A.D. 112 sent by Pliny the Younger, the acting Roman governor of the province of Asia, to Trajan, emperor of Rome. The governor reports that in Syria a sect has arisen called the Christians, and "these foolish people," the governor writes, "think they are immortal; they go to their death as to a triumph, and no threat of punishment has any effect on them."

This verdict of "foolishness" is repeated today. The many contradictions raised in the name of science to which skeptical minds refer in their attack on the resurrection need not disturb us, for they are simply the continuation of scientific errors of the past. For instance, Lavoisier, one of the greatest figures in the history of chemistry, stubbornly taught that heat was a substance. Plato believed that the stomach shared mental activity with the brain. Nineteenth-century scientists claimed that tooth decay came from worms. For a long time psychiatrists declared that "most criminals were feeble-minded"; ancient phrenologists taught that insanity was produced by too much heat or cold in the brain, and their more modern associates held that each cranial bump indicated a particular characteristic. These falsities, as hundreds of other scientific theories, have been disproved; yet each mistake of the past entitles us to ask, If the scientific world cannot solve questions pertaining to the teeth, the stomach, the brain, the skull, and the forces of nature that surround us, why should atheistic and infidel scientists dare to deny the resurrection of the body?

We must cling to this doctrine of our resurrection even though its promises seem far too merciful and abundant for our sin-bound lives. When Dr. Morrison was translating the Bible into Chinese and came upon the passage *"We shall be like Him; for we shall see Him as He is"* (1 John 3:2), one of his assistants, a native scholar, exclaimed, "My people can never believe that they shall see their Savior and their God face to face. Let me rather translate, 'For we may hope to kiss His feet.'" But Dr. Morrison replied: "Give the Word of God as it is." And when we take God at His promises and penitently trust in the love of our Savior, all sin and selfishness that would tear us away from God vanishes, and unworthy, unholy, unhappy as we may be, we are blessed by the promise that *"we shall see Him as He is."*

Many of you sang this morning in one of the last stanzas of the hymn, "I Know that My Redeemer Lives," these reassuring words:

> He lives and grants me daily breath;
> He lives, and I shall conquer death;
> He lives my mansion to prepare;
> He lives to bring me safely there.

Samuel Medley, who wrote these lines, was converted to the faith from a wild and dissolute life, and overcoming sin, he could die in the hope of his Easter hymn and on his deathbed declare, "I am a poor, shattered bark, just about to gain the blissful harbor, and oh, how sweet will be the port after the storm! Dying is sweet, sweet work! I am looking to my dear Jesus, my God, my Portion, my All in all." So, in the radiance of the Easter mercy and in the power of the resurrection glory, may the Spirit of God bring into your penitent, believing hearts the assurance that, since Christ *"was delivered for our offenses and was raised again for our justification," "the gift of God is eternal life."*

We must build our hopes on the reality of the resurrection, even though the human mind staggers when it is asked to believe that the body, returned to the dust whence it sprang, can be revived and rebuilt, that our human frame, with all its blemishes and imperfections, can be molded in a new and perfect form. One day in the laboratory of Michael Faraday, the great chemist, a workman accidentally knocked a silver cup into a jar of acid. The cup was consumed by the powerful solution. When Faraday, that stalwart confessor of Christ, heard of the disappearance of the cup, he threw some chemicals into the acid, and soon the dissolved particles of silver were precipitated. The metal was reclaimed, sent to a silversmith, and recast into a graceful cup. Does not the inference suggest itself that, if a chemist can perform this reconstruction, surely the almighty God can gather the particles of our body, though they be scattered to the four winds, and change that which is sown *"a natural body"* into *"a spiritual body"?* And if you tell me that this is only an analogy, then I point you to those resurrection miracles which prove the power of God—not only the reawakening of Jairus' daughter, not only the restored life of the widow's son at Nain, not only the resurrection of Lazarus after decomposition had started, but on Easter particularly to the triumph of our Savior over the grave and His victorious promise, *"Because I live, ye shall live also."*

Unless we believe that through the Savior's resurrection, life and eternity are ours, we have no guideposts to lead us through the maze of life. In the catacombs at Rome the burial places of the pagan dead and of the early Christians are marked by a notable contrast. The heathen graves are inscribed with dedications to the gods of the lower world, and sometimes they abound in sarcasm and resentment. Death is often pictured as an eternal sleep or an unhappy existence of gloom and hopelessness. But the favorite expressions on the Christian graves are: "He rests in peace," or, "He lives forever," or, "Weep not, my child; death is not eternal."

Easter is the day of comfort particularly for those whose hearts ache under recent bereavement. Self-confident men and women who can speak boldly on the topics of the day are often strangely muted when they are confronted by the enigma of death. Even Christians who in theory accept the doctrine of the resurrection sometimes question it when death touches their home. I read somewhere of a teacher at a theological seminary who spoke with calm assurance when his lectures on the New Testament brought him to the resurrection of the body. It was easy for him, with his young wife in a home that had not been tried and tested by the most serious of all emergencies, to speak with reechoing confidence. But when death took his five-year-old son, that father ran distractedly from one of his friends to the other, asking if they really believed that his child was now in heaven.

May God give you all, through the risen Christ, the faith that is fitted for these crucial tests! May He lead every one of you, and especially those who are too ready to charge God with heartlessness and cruelty, on this day to stand at the open grave and to hear the promise: *"God . . . will also raise up us by His power."* When the armies of Napoleon swept over Europe, one of his generals made a surprise attack on the little town of Feldkirch on the Austrian border. It was Easter, and as the formidable French army maneuvered on the heights above Feldkirch, the council of its citizens was hastily summoned to deliberate on the alternative of surrender or defense. It was in this assembly that the venerable dean of the church arose to declare: "This is Easter Day. We have been counting on our own strength, and that will fail. This is the day of our Lord's resurrection. Let us ring the bells and have services as usual and leave the matter in God's hands." His counsel was accepted, and in a moment or two the church belfry chimed the joyous bells announcing the Savior's resurrection. The enemy, hearing the sudden peal, concluding that the Austrian army had arrived during the night, broke up camp, and before the Easter bells had ceased, the danger had been lifted.

Let the joy of Easter ring in your heart, and all the doubt and sorrow and gloom and despondency that surround you will similarly vanish. God grant every one of us in this wide Easter congregation of the air the faith and the victory that will unite us through the blessings of these resurrection realities in the eternal mansions prepared by Him who lived for us, who died for us, but on that first Easter Day rose again for us! Amen.[35]

Pentecost (1945)

Come, Holy Spirit!

"When the day of Pentecost was fully come . . . they were all filled with the Holy Ghost. . . . And the same day there were added unto them about three thousand souls."—Acts 2:1, 4, 41

A few years ago on the night before Easter, so it is reported, a new play opened in one of Moscow's leading theaters, a blasphemous comedy entitled "Christ in Tuxedo." A packed house saw the first act, with a scene featuring a church altar arrayed like a saloon bar, with bottles of beer, wine, and vodka. Fat priests sat around the altar raising their arms in drunken toasts. Nuns squatted on the sanctuary floor playing cards. It was just another of those degrading, damnable exhibitions of atheism which repeatedly marked the Red rebellion against the Savior. The second act featured Comrade Alexander Rostovzev, a Moscow matinee idol, a dyed-in-the-wool disciple of Marx and a sneering enemy of Jesus. You can imagine, then, how the audience roared when Rostovzev walked out on the stage impersonating Christ, dressed in a flowing oriental robe and carrying a large New Testament. Soon after his entrance he was to read two verses from the Sermon on the Mount, remove his Palestine gown, and cry out, "Give me my tuxedo and top hat!" Rostovzev, as directed by the script, began to intone slowly: *"Blessed are the poor in spirit, for theirs is the kingdom of God. Blessed are they that mourn, for they shall be comforted."* Then, instead of following his cues and putting on the tuxedo, he stopped as though paralyzed. An uneasy silence gripped the spectators when the smooth, suave actor, his whole body shaking, started to read again: *"Blessed are the meek, for they shall inherit the earth. Blessed are they who hunger and thirst after righteousness, for they shall be filled. Blessed are the merciful, for they shall obtain mercy."* He finished the forty-one remaining verses of Matthew's fifth chapter before a stunned audience. Backstage other actors in the cast, perhaps thinking that he was drunk, coughed, called, and stamped to urge the star of Moscow's stage on with his forgotten blasphemies. But Rostovzev was no longer a blasphemer. Christ's Word had conquered and converted him; for there, before the footlights, he who had reviled the Crucified now made the sign of the cross in the Russian Orthodox tradition and cried out in the prayer of the penitent thief: *"Lord, remember me when Thou comest into Thy kingdom!"* That was too much for the management. The curtain was lowered, someone announced that Comrade Rostovzev had taken ill suddenly; the performance was canceled.

That startling change from blasphemer to believer was the work of the Holy Spirit, the same enlightening God who took St. Paul, bent on destroying the early disciples, and made him the mightiest apostle of all; the same gracious God who now appeals to you, the unsaved, on the way to hell without Jesus, and would put you on the sure road to heaven with the Savior.

That Holy Spirit believers throughout the world honor today, on Pentecost, the birthday of the Christian church. Because every one of us should personally have the same Spirit who this day descended on the disciples, join me across America today in this Pentecost prayer:

Come, Holy Spirit!

Learn the divine blessings He can give you from our text (the Book of Acts, chapter two, verses one, four, and forty-one): *"When the day of Pentecost was fully come . . . they were all filled with the Holy Ghost. . . . And the same day there were added unto them about three thousand souls."*

Come with Thy Blessings for Our Faith!

Pentecost, as its name indicates, fifty days after Easter, was a holiday in Jerusalem, a sort of Thanksgiving Festival on which the earliest wheat harvest was presented to the Lord. What a happy day for giving the Father the firstfruits in the harvest of human souls won for Christ and His church! The disciples, obeying their risen

Lord's command, had stayed in Jerusalem since the ascended Savior left them ten days before. How much they would have missed if, driven by a desire to make money, they had gone back to their fishing boats in Galilee!

Nobody knows the place where the disciples assembled; perhaps it was that unmarked upper chamber in which Jesus Himself had instituted the Lord's Supper. While that hunted band of believers prayed and worshiped together, it happened. Christ kept His word to them. He had pledged His followers: *"Ye shall receive power, after that the Holy Ghost has come upon you,"* and now, in fulfillment, the Holy Ghost came. At first nothing unusual was to be seen, but a strange noise, *"as of a rushing mighty wind . . . filled all the house where they were sitting."* No twenty-one-gun naval salute has ever had the force of that reverberating, galelike, rushing sound from heaven; for it was the Comforter, the Sanctifier, coming into the souls of His servants. A few moments later little fiery flames appeared and descended on each of the disciples. They were men of different stations and positions in life, but each of them needed the Holy Spirit fully to believe, worthily to accept Christ as his Savior; and here, descending gently on each one as a blaze of purifying fire, came that enlightening, sustaining Spirit, whom we worship as our God.

I make neither apology nor defense when I declare that the Holy Spirit, in the fullest sense of this exalted term, is our God. The Bible, which calls the Holy Spirit God, gives Him divine honor, ascribes divinely blessed work to Him, and makes Him, together with the Father and the Son, our true and triune God. The Father created our earthly life, but the Spirit creates us anew in the heavenly life. The Son died for our redemption, but the Spirit brings the message of His mercy into our hearts. You may not hear much of the Spirit in many modern churches, but this omission helps account for the fact that, while with His help Peter, a Galilean fisherman, could preach a heart-searching sermon, which won thousands of converts for Christ, many a highly paid D.D., Th.D., S.T.D., without the Spirit has never been able to bring a single soul to the Lord Jesus.

Only God could show the mighty Pentecost power which the Spirit exercised on the first disciples. Think of it! A short week and a half before, these men were so saturated with ambition for earthly power that they asked Christ immediately before His ascent the political question when He would make Israel a world power again—strangely enough the very issue which modern but misguided pulpits often discuss, rather than the answer to the personal and pointed question, *"What must I do to be saved?"* Now, when the Holy Spirit filled their lives, He purified them and, as Jesus had promised, guided them into all truth. Read Peter's address on Pentecost, his first recorded sermon, and you will notice that he does not spend his time discussing various theories of the millenium nor advancing his own opinion on the political future of his countrymen nor speculating on vague issues of prophecy nor featuring a dozen different moral side issues, which so crowd and clutter many sermons today that no room remains for the one imperative issue, the salvation of souls. Illumined by the Spirit, Peter, who before had manifested ignorance, weakness, and often only a hazy understanding of our Lord's self-sacrifice for the atonement of the world, finds his faith purified. The blinders drop from his eyes; the mist of error vanishes; he sees Jesus and His saving Word with a clearer understanding that he ever had before. The New Testament gives us only twenty-three verses of his sermon, but fifteen of these are direct quotations from the Old Testament and Peter's own explanation of them.

This, then, is the first Pentecost blessing in the faith of believers: the Holy Spirit leads them, not to tradition, not to human keys to the Bible, not to church council decrees, not to their emotions but back directly to the source of all truth, Sacred Scripture. May you who love the Lord Jesus find a powerful lesson here! If you are dissatisfied with your spiritual life; if the joy and fervor of your faith are disappearing; if your heart is riveting its desires on earthly schemes; if you doubt your Savior's grace, with deep sincerity pray today and every day: "Come, Holy Spirit, come to cleanse, refine, purify, guide, teach my heart as Thou didst the disciples'! Bring me back all the way to the Bible with its bountiful promise of my redemption!"

Even more startling is the faith-bestowing power with which the Spirit leads unbelievers to Jesus. In the crowd of thousands soon gathered before the disciples were many scoffers and sworn enemies of our Lord, some probably who were directly involved in His crucifixion. Peter did not spare their feelings, just as no real Christian pulpit today will gloss over popular sins to make people feel good. Instead Peter told that hostile mass directly and unhesitatingly, *"Ye have taken and by wicked hands have crucified and slain"* Jesus of Nazareth. Publicly he accused them of their savage sin of murdering Christ, and then the Holy Spirit began His blessed work in their hearts. He convicted them of their terrifying transgressions, and three thousand of them cried: *"What shall we do?"*

More than ever before we must pray: "Come, Holy Spirit, to prick the hearts of the self-righteous and self-satisfied who smile at evil, shake hands with hellish forces, acclaim atheism, and stubbornly seek to defend evil!" Great numbers within our borders are losing their sense of sin, its hideousness, its soul-destroying, damning guilt.

Therefore we pray for you who are still far from Christ, who with your private, personal, concealed transgressions long for a peace which your position, your money, your influence, your friends, your college degrees, your self-confidence can never give, "Come, Holy Spirit." I tell you who want pardon for your sins and peace for your souls: Fall on your knees and plead: "Come, Holy Spirit! Lead me to the Lord Jesus! Show me beyond question, as Thou didst show those three thousand, that He, my God, is also my Savior; that with a love surpassing my poor powers of understanding He transferred my transgressions, their guilt and punishment, to Himself, freed me forever from their curse, saved me from eternal damnation, restored me to the Father!"

God grant that this will be a real Pentecost for you as the power of the Spirit descends on your lives! Don't make the mistake of which Aaron Burr, later Vice-President of the United States, was guilty. Despite the appeal of his grandfather, Jonathan Edwards, Burr left Princeton University an unbeliever. Once, when he was ready to accept Christ, the president of Princeton told him to think the matter over carefully so that his judgment would not be too hasty. That was bad advice; and Burr, a brilliant student, left college, telling God, as he later explained to his friends, "that if He would let me alone, I would let Him alone, and that settled it." But later in life, after receiving high honors, he was charged with murder, betrayal, and fraud. He left this country, and when he returned, an old, broken, friendless man, he admitted, "Sixty years ago I told God that if He would let me alone, I would let Him alone, and God has not bothered about me since." May the Holy Spirit refuse to let you alone but instead prod your conscience, call you to the comfort in Jesus, and guide you to your sure salvation!

The power of Pentecost is not past. The Spirit, our almighty God, can still perform wonders. The amazing blessings with which He has remembered this radio mission are in some ways even more startling than those first conversions. There in Jerusalem the crowd could see the disciples; but what shall we say when—all praise and honor to the Lord—we broadcast the message of repentance and return to God in His Son here in St. Louis and a hundred, a thousand, five thousand miles away truth-seeking souls actually turn to their Savior without ever having seen the speaker? An image maker in Costa Rica heard the broadcast and came to Jesus; a listener in Argentina who never before knew the Gospel until our broadcast brought it to him gave his life to the Lord. A cabaret singer in Ecuador, living in sin and unbelief, listened to our message of the Redeemer's love, fell on his knees in repentance and faith, and dedicated his voice to sing hymns of praise to God. A Chinese young man in the Dominican Republic, a Cuban student in the West Indies, a sailor in the South Pacific learn the Gospel of grace and plan to give themselves to Him in the ministry. In our own country a soldier saved from suicide for Christ; a profane bartender, repentant and reborn into a new and radiant life; a New York atheist converted; a scoffing Texas woman made a humble worshiper; a murderer in a Minnesota penitentiary baptized; a convict in a Michigan prison led to his Savior; an Indian spiritist medium recalled to her Redeemer—these are only a few of the startling miracles the Almighty has permitted us to see in our mission of the air.

Come with Thy Blessings in Our Life!

When the Holy Spirit thus enriches you with faith, He will bless you with new life. You will be reborn a new creature in Christ. See how completely Pentecost changed those first disciples! Peter and the others had been cowards, shamelessly deserting Christ and full of fear hiding themselves behind locked doors; yet when the Holy Spirit descended upon them, all fright disappeared. You too may be afraid to stand up for your Lord; you may keep your lips sealed when your mouth should be open, testifying that *"Jesus Christ . . . is our Hope";* but when the Spirit takes mastery over your life, this terror will vanish as the fog before the sun. That is why sixteen-year-old girls in Rome's blood-stained arenas, faced with the horror of

142

being torn to pieces by panthers, tigers, lions, could bravely sing their hymns of praise to the Savior. Pray, "Come, Holy Spirit!" and as in answer He enters your heart, He will strengthen you with the courage in Christ to face the worst that life or death itself may bring.

Pentecost gave those unlearned disciples the wisdom required to preach the Gospel; it enriched them even with instantaneous knowledge of many hard, foreign languages. The Holy Spirit can grant the same enlightenment today, although this need is not nearly so great now since the Bible has been translated into more than a thousand different languages. If you hesitate to speak out for Christ because you have never attended a theological seminary and it is not easy for you to talk publicly, then pray, "Come, Holy Spirit!" As we are told of the apostles, *The Spirit gave them utterance,* so fitting thoughts and expressions shall be given you. The very words you need will be placed in your mind and on your lips.

See what the gift of the Holy Comforter did for the church! On Pentecost morning one hundred and twenty believers, on Pentecost evening three thousand one hundred and twenty! And that was only the beginning! Preaching Christ Crucified, the church moved as a mighty army, and wherever the Gospel was proclaimed, the fortresses of paganism, idolatry, and superstition collapsed. Tertullian, leader of the second-century north African believers, could tell the heathen world: "We [the Christians] are a people but of yesterday; yet we have filled every place belonging to you—cities, islands, castles, towns, assemblies, your very camps, your tribes, companies, palaces, forums. We leave you your temples only." Soon after, in the third century, Emperor Maximianus could write officially that almost all his empire "had abandoned the worship of their ancestors for the new sect," the Christian faith. The historian Gibbon, an enemy of Christianity, admits that the onward rush of the Gospel "finally erected the triumphant banner of the cross on the ruins of the Capitol" in Rome. That forward march was led by the Spirit and was marked by the shedding of much martyr blood. When you read today that some of our large denominations show an annual decrease in membership or some a gain of only 4 or 5 percent over a ten-year period; when the International Sunday School Council in America estimates a loss of four million in Sunday schools during a recent ten-year period; when many of you know better than I can tell you that you belong to dwindling, decreasing churches which do not have the pure, powerful Gospel and therefore not the Holy Spirit, you can understand first why it is necessary to plead as never before in our generation, "Come, Holy Spirit, reform, restore, rededicate apostate churches to Christ!"

See what the Holy Spirit did for the world at large when the apostles, led by Him, spread the message of the crucified Savior! In the words of their own enemies, they *"turned the world upside down."* Today you have the choice either of remaining silent while this generation goes farther from Christ or of praying, "Come, Holy Spirit, help me turn this world of hatred, violence, crime, greed, destruction, upside down through Jesus!"

Because He is our only and last Hope; because the world today needs, more than a hundred international conferences, the spreading of His saving Gospel and the presence of His regenerating Comforter, stand by us with your prayers as we consider plans to proclaim this rebuilding message of redemption throughout the war-torn world! Join us now from coast to coast in pleading: Oh, come, Holy Spirit, to give us the faith, the courage, the comfort, the wisdom, the power, the blessing by which we, as Thine apostles on the first Pentecost did, use all the major languages of our day in bringing sinners to their Savior! Come richly, come continually, come quickly! Come, O Holy Spirit, for Jesus' sake! Amen.[36]

8

ILLUSTRATOR

Aside from delivery, which can hardly be reproduced on the printed page, probably the most characteristic hallmark of Maier preaching was its rich use of illustration. This technique, of course, goes back to Jesus Himself. How frequently Christ began one of His discourses with the words, "The kingdom of heaven is like—" and a parable followed. In fact, Matthew summarizes: "All this Jesus said to the crowds in parables; indeed he said nothing to them without a parable" (13:34).

Today sermon illustrations are near equivalents of such parables. Dr. Maier sedulously collected and cultivated them by means of a vast topical reference system that filled several dozen filing cabinets at his seminary offices. Occasionally he borrowed some of the best illustrations of others—with due credit. More often he developed them himself, mining his nuggets from church or secular history, the physical world, the arts, sciences, literature, newspaper and magazine reports, and most importantly, the experiences of everyday life.

The following examples of his illustrations are roughly arranged in a vector from sin to salvation.

On Indifference

We stand aghast at the unconcern of human leaders in the pivotal moments of history. When Rome was besieged by Alaric and his Goths, Emperor Honorius was more concerned about the safety of his prize poultry than the destiny of the imperial city. After a panting messenger brought the news "Rome is lost," he sighed in relief when he learned that it was not his favorite pullet, named "Rome," but the capital that had been destroyed! There have always been those who have toyed and dallied when they should have led the forces of righteousness and truth.[37]

Consequences of Godlessness

No country which builds its foundation on anti-Christian principles can truly prosper; often not even an isolated community, established in defiance of God and in ridicule of our Lord's redemption, can maintain itself. We have a glaring example of that in the town of Liberal, Missouri, south of Kansas City, founded by freethinkers and infidels. This community was so liberal that no churches were permitted within its bounds. Its printed literature boasted that it was the only town of its size in the United States "without a priest, preacher, a church . . . God, Jesus, hell, or devil." Yet a St. Louis newspaper reporter who visited Liberal during its boom said that the whole place was "nothing else *but* hell and the devil." His account was so horrifying that the reporter was arrested and his newspaper, the St. Louis *Post-Dispatch,* sued for $25,000 damage. The court investigated the facts, found the reporter right, acquitted him, dismissed the damage suit, and made the officials of the freethinking town pay the charges. Today, Liberal, Missouri, is a changed community. Why? It has three Christian churches. As one of the founders of Liberal admitted, "It will never do to establish a society with infidelity as its basis."[38]

Only God Transforms

Modern science and industry can produce amazing transformation. Visit a paper factory and you will see how dirty rags, thrown into a large hopper, cut into pieces, treated with acids, finally emerge as white, spotless sheets. But no industrial process can take human beings despite claims of many righteousnesses—the Bible calls these *"filthy rags"*—and make them clean, stainless. By the marvels of modern chemistry coal tar, black, sticky, smelly, altogether unpromising, can be converted into a rainbow of wonderful colors, an array of perfumes, a number of useful plastics, an assortment of explosives, and many other materials. But the soul will not yield to such treatment, and neither education, medical care, social improvement can transform black, sordid, corrupt characters and endow them with beauty, strength, and power. At best, evil may be concealed or disguised; but as little as you can restore a rotting, worm-eaten apple by polishing its skin, purify water by painting the pump, bring life into a corpse by putting rouge on its cheeks, so and even more impossible is it to change the soul by culture, medical or social science. You need God for that! [39]

Fear as Prod Toward God

Not long ago I had to fly from New York to Pittsburgh. On the seat beside me was a successful young scientist, who in the course of our conversation admitted that he had never found much reason to attend church. His closest approach to religion was the rather vague intention to send his little daughter to Sunday school. After our short conversation he moved to the single seat across the aisle, perhaps to read privately a certain salaciously illustrated magazine that unfortunately claims many readers among the so-called upper classes. Suddenly we were asked to adjust the safety belts, for we were running into an electrical storm. Soon the furious wind shook the plane as though the huge transport were but a plaything for the elements while lightning lit up the heavens and thunder reechoed across the whole firmament. That self-confident young man who had just admitted scant interest in spiritual things now turned white, dropped his magazine, came over to sit beside me, and asked distractedly: "Do you think the lightning will strike us? You were right; we can be nearer to God than we believe." Every one of you can be nearer to God than he imagines in this day's quick change and sudden sorrow. [40]

Work-Righteousness

In Los Angeles a stunt performer, a so-called "human fly," started to climb up the face of a large department-store building. Many thousands on the street below watched him as he went up slowly and carefully, by cornice stones, window sills, crevices, and protruding bricks, raising himself from story to story, until he had

147

almost reached the top. There he paused for a moment, searching for something which would help him over the top. Finally he selected what looked like a gray, discolored brick jutting from the wall. He stretched out his arm for it, but it was just beyond his reach; so he leaped up to clutch the support. Then horrified spectators saw him crash to his death on the ground. In his hand they found a spider's web, evidently mistaken for a solid stone. Everyone who tries to climb to heaven by his own efforts is doomed to similar disaster. Especially in the hour of danger, those who substitute for our Lord's completed redemption their own faulty righteousness will find that they have grasped for cobwebs instead of clinging to Christ, the solid Rock.[41]

The Nativity

Sir Harry Lauder, whose son died in World War I, tells us of a child who, walking hand in hand with its father, noted many buildings marked with service flags. When their purpose was explained, the boy clapped his hands every time they passed a dwelling so adorned and exclaimed: "Oh, look, Daddy, there is another house that has sent a son into the war! And there's another! There's one with two stars!" As they walked on, night began to fall, and high in the heavens the evening star began to shine in its solitary beauty. Beholding it, the little boy stopped, caught his breath, and cried, "Oh, look, Daddy, God must have sent *His* Son, because He has a star in His window!"[42]

The Symbols of Christmas

Let every gift that you give and receive strengthen within you the deep gratitude for the *"unspeakable Gift"* of Christ the Savior. Let every light that burns within your home testify to your faith in Jesus, the *"Light of the world."* Let the golden gleam of ornaments remind you of the treasures of faith, the hope, and the love that you, with the mind of the Magi, must lay at the feet of the Christ Child. Let the pungent pine direct you to the sweet-smelling sacrifice of Christ Himself in that everlasting love wherewith He *"loved us unto the end."* Let your Christmas cards contain a joyful acknowledgment of your faith in Christ—just as the shepherds *"made known abroad the saying which was told them concerning this Child."* Let the music and song that ring throughout your home be the joyful reechoing of the first angelic chorus over the fields of

Bethlehem: *"Glory to God in the highest, and on earth peace, goodwill toward men."* If you have Christ in Christmas, this festival is not just another holiday but a holy day.[43]

The Resurrection

I call your attention to two recent experiments. One was conducted by England's Ministry of Foods, which examined barley seeds from a jar that had stood in the British Museum for twenty-two years and previous to that in Tutankhamen's Egyptian tomb for 3,300 years. Careful investigation revealed that these thirty-three-century-old seeds still retained their vital properties. Indeed, London experts were able to make some of the grains sprout. Even more astonishing was the second experiment at the Army Air Forces Tactical Air Center, Orlando, Florida, where seeds grown from three small withered peas, likewise taken from the thirty-three-hundred-year-old tomb of King Tutankhamen, not only sprouted but produced pest-proof peas, far better in this respect than the present-day Florida crop. Now, if man can sow seeds in the ground after they have long reposed in darkened tombs and produce notable harvests from them, cannot the Almighty, who made both seeds and men, resurrect our bodies committed to the earth and make them live again in glory?[44]

The German Bible critic De Wette, a radical among radical enemies of the inspiration, declared on his deathbed, "The fact of the resurrection can be doubted just as little as the assassination of Julius Caesar." Even that is an understatement. Do we have the testimony of any eyewitnesses who saw the assassination of Caesar or attended his funeral? Not one! But we do possess the statements of Matthew, John, Peter, Paul, truthful witnesses who actually saw the risen Christ and heard Him speak. Patriarchs foreknew it; psalmists foretold it; prophets foresaw it; evangelists recorded it; witnesses reassured it; apostles reaffirmed it; the empty tomb proclaimed it; our Lord's repeated post-Easter appearances proved it.[45]

Power of the Holy Spirit

A resident of Champaign, Illinois, planted asparagus in his yard three years ago, but it did not grow. Then he built a driveway over the barren patch, using four inches of gravel and two inches of solid asphalt. Now the asparagus is beginning to sprout and split the driveway. The Holy Spirit is far stronger than such forces of nature. If you will not continually resist Him, He can break through the hardest of your sorrows and your multiplied miseries. Through His divine indwelling you can be born again; and if you want to *"see the kingdom of God,"* remember that Jesus Himself has said, "You *'must be born again!'* "[46]

On Repentance

Repentance means more than simply admitting your guilt. The French skeptic Rousseau wrote a book called *Confessions,* in which he describes, often with much detail, his bad habits and vices; but sometimes he gloats over his crimes. Repentance does not mean stopping your sins because you cannot continue them. Recently Great Britain's oldest burglar retired from his evil profession at ninety years, almost half of which were spent in prison. He stopped stealing not because he regarded it as wrong but because, as he stated: "I can't run as I used to. And besides, I'm getting clumsy; I knock things over on the job." Again, repentance is not mere sorrow over your wrongdoing. Judas was seized by remorse for betraying Jesus; but he did not repent. Almost every girl who gets into trouble regrets her downfall, but not all, by far, repent.[47]

Failure to Witness

What a crime for those who know that Jesus died for their sins to keep this assurance of deliverance from their fellow men! When the decisive battle at Waterloo was fought, Nathan Rothschild, a founder of the international banking house, kept close to the front, in the safety of a shot-proof hiding place. As soon as he saw the beginning of Wellington's victory and Napoleon's defeat, he mounted a swift horse and rode furiously to Brussels, where he hired the fastest carriage he could secure and drove at top speed to the Belgian coast. A wild storm raged over the English Channel, and Rothschild had to pay an adventurous fisherman $500 for ferrying him across. Reaching the British shore, he galloped on horseback to the London Stock Exchange. Here he found the bankers dejected, expecting the news of their country's defeat. Without breathing a hint of what he knew, Rothschild and his agents bought up at low prices all the government securities they could. The panic lasted for two days, until the news of Wellington's victory reached London, and the stock immediately rose to fabulous figures. Then in two hours Nathan Rothschild made a profit of $10,000,000 by selling at high quotations the securities he had bought at bottom prices. "What treachery," you declare "to withhold the message of victory!" Yet what greater treachery for some of you to know that Jesus has conquered sin, death, hell, and still to keep the Gospel of His grace from your fellow-men! The first-century church grew, under the Holy Spirit, because those who accepted Christ were constant witnesses to Him. The twentieth-century church will expereince new and necessary blessings if present-day disciples of the Lord declare, *"We cannot but speak the things which we have seen and heard."*[48]

Trials That Temper

The love of God is often most clearly shown in the trials that purify and temper our lives and help us draw others to the love of Christ. Think of the iron ore that is mined in the depths of the earth. Under terrific heat it is smelted and separated from the dross. Again and again the purified metal is refined by fire till its strength is fully developed. Carbon is added, and the iron becomes steel. An electric current passes through the steel, and it becomes a magnet that attracts and holds iron. In a much higher way the love of Christ takes us with all our imperfections and impurities, refines us by the successive trials of life, and charges us with a *"new and right spirit"*; and not only do we emerge from the chastenings of His love truer and purer and stronger, as the tempered steel, but drawn to the cross by the lodestone of His love, our lives may become magnets that can draw our fellow-men, as does the crude iron, to the Christ that lives in our souls.[49]

Advantages in Affliction

Think of the refining, strengthening power of affliction. God employs the sudden reverses of life not only to keep us from pride and self-reliance but to build up our faith. Have you ever walked through a greenhouse to watch florists clip off all buds but one, so that the whole strength of the stock may be concentrated into the full bloom of a large chrysanthemum? Have you ever stopped in a machine shop to hear the emery wheel and the buffer polish the surface of a dull metal to mirrorlike brightness? Have you ever peered into the roar of a smelter and seen the white heat fuse pieces of iron into the strength of refined metal? May we not regard this as a crude symbol of the miraculous process by which God often

151

removes the side issues of life, so that our strength and interest are directed toward spiritual growth? The frictions of destiny add luster to our faith, and the fires of affliction strengthen our courage. The funnel of a tornado cuts its swath of destruction through a city; but the ruins are rebuilt into more modern homes and more attractive buildings. A fire destroys vast areas; but when the ashes have cooled, men build better and more wisely than before. An airplane crashes; but scientists examine the wreckage to find a clue for safer aircraft construction. Many of our material calamities involve a hidden benefit; and in a much higher degree, once you are Christ's, everything that crowds into your life is designed to deepen your conviction, to steel your resistance to destructive impulses of life, and to warm your heart to the need and suffering of others.

In short, view the life that you live in Christ from whatever angle you may, and you will exult, *"All things work together for good!"* As the artist employs dark, somber hues to emphasize the light, so the shadows sharpen the sunshine of the Christian's life. As the great Flemish tapestries were often woven from the back and seemed to present a muddled confusion of loose ends and knots until completed and viewed from the right side, so when we see the face of the finished and holy design created by Christ, the Master Weaver of our destiny, all doubt as to the wisdom and the love of God will vanish. As under the baton of a great musician the minor chords may blend with the symphonic theme, so, because *"all things work together for good,"* there is above all distress a harmony and symphony of Christian life. That symphony always closes with a grand finale, the coda of sustained triumph.[50]

Patience

In fulfilling our promises God often lets us wait. When we become impatient and doubtful, let us not struggle in unbelief but exult in the faith of the prophet: *"Though it tarry, wait for it, because it will surely come."* God's time is always the right time.

You know that a mushroom grows overnight, while it takes years to produce a sturdy oak that can weather hurricanes. The firmer trust in God does not usually come from a passing emotion or a pious feeling at a revival but from long acquaintance with God and His protecting, ennobling, and strengthening of our hearts. Lenses for eyeglasses are made in a quick process; but do you recall that it took the great lens of the Pacific Coast telescope two years to cool?

And if we would look deep into our lives and high into God's mercies, this clarifying of our vision often requires years. You can draw hasty, sketchy lines in a moment; but Ghiberti worked more than forty years on two medallioned baptistry doors at Florence, doors that Michelangelo pronounced beautiful enough to be the gates of Paradise; and if God would make masterpieces of our lives, why should we seek to ruin His artistry by demanding haste? No modern violin can produce the rich tones of the Stradivarius, made of aged, seasoned wood and completed by painstaking craftsmanship. The heart that best sings the new song of faith bears the stamp that this Savior's love has repeatedly placed upon him in long years of blessed faith. No synthetic pearl made in the speedy processes of artificial culture has the luster of the natural gem that has been years in the making; and when you experience a postponement of the answer to your prayers, remember Abraham, who during a delay of twenty-five years *"staggered not at the promise of God,"* and, casting your eyes upon the same Christ whom He worshiped, resolve, *"I wait for the Lord, my soul doth wait, and in His Word do I hope."* [51]

Judgment Day

Have you ever stopped to realize how directly our globe is prepared for destruction—particularly by fire? Examine the surface of the earth, and you will find more than half of it oxygen, potassium, sodium, magnesium—all highly flammable materials! Descend beneath this crust, and you will discover unmistakable evidence of tremendous heat there. In the copper mines of Michigan the temperature rises one degree for each 100 feet you descend beneath the 5,000 foot level. As you see molten rocks flow from the craters of fiery volcanoes, remember that temperatures at the earth's core could wipe out the elements even more completely than you can burn a pile of dead autumn leaves. Peter tells God's truth when he declares, *"The elements shall melt with fervent heat, the earth also and the works that are therein shall be burned up"* (2 Peter 3:10-11).[52]

If mere mortals can set off an atomic explosion which generates a heat of 70,000,000 degrees centigrade, a flash seventy times hotter and brighter than the sun; if the first atomic bombs puny men designed could blast large parts of cities off the map, killing one tenth of a million Japanese civilians and soldiers, cannot the

Almighty, who formed the atom, use it to annihilate His own creation? He who called the world into existence can surely call it out of existence.[53]

Eternal Life

We look for the resurrection of the body not because men have always and instinctively believed in a future life. We need more for the assurance of life to come than the message of reviving spring, the beauty of flowers blossoming after an icebound winter, the symbolism of the butterfly emerging from its cocoon. When life hangs by a slender, unraveling thread, we can find small comfort in the fact that even the Zulus in Africa believe in another world; that the Greeks placed a coin into the mouth of every corpse to pay the fare across the river into eternity; that the Hindus taught the transmigration of the soul; that the Indians buried their dead with arrowheads and earthen vessels for the happy hunting ground. When that thread of life snaps, we must have a faith founded on bedrock, a conviction surer than life itself, a truth that can never waver. This rock-grounded conviction is granted by God's Son, the risen Christ. *"Thanks be to God, which giveth us the victory through our Lord Jesus Christ."*[54]

Why should it be altogether unreasonable that the Lord of life should resurrect our crumbling remains? Part of your present body comes from the earth, even from various remote areas. The cereal you ate this morning, and which builds your physical energy, may have been grown in the soil of Minnesota, Kansas, Georgia, or many other places. The sugar you used may have been the product of a Cuban or Puerto Rican plantation. The coffee you drank came from Central America or Brazil, the tea from India or Ceylon. The vegetables and the fruit for your dinner may have ripened in California, Texas, or Florida. Now, if the Almighty has gathered from the soil of a hundred different locations the material with which your body is built and strengthened, why limit His omnipotence and say that He cannot gather from the good earth of our cemeteries the seed from which our spiritual bodies are to spring?[55]

9
MINISTER

Except at mass meetings, Walter A. Maier could never see his listeners, nor they him. It might be assumed, accordingly, that an inevitable barrier intruded that prevented any pastoral relationships between unseen voice and unseen audience. This is mistaken. After the sermon on each *Lutheran Hour* broadcast the announcer issued this invitation: "If you have no church affiliation and are troubled by a spiritual problem, Dr. Maier will be glad to advise you. Write to *The Lutheran Hour*. . . ."

The mail cascaded in. Along with nonproblem correspondence, the tally eventually swelled up to nearly 500,000 letters a year. A pastoral staff was necessarily involved in replying to this mass response, but major problem mail was still funneled onto the speaker's desk. And he got involved with it, developing a strong sensitivity to the needs, pains, and joys of his invisible congregation, which he reflected in the themes he chose for many of his sermons. His later addresses on *The Lutheran Hour* have a warmer, more personal approach to his listeners than earlier ones, with at least one paragraph spoken on a heart-to-heart basis.

In effect, then, Dr. Maier became a minister to millions despite that statistic, and the following 1936 sermon on the problem of pain is typical of one or two preached on this theme each broadcast season.

Through Trial to Triumph

"God knoweth the way that I take. When He hath tried me, I shall come forth as gold."—Job 23:10

"Why must *I* suffer?" "Why do miseries crowd in on *my* life?" "Why are *my* ambitions always crushed into dust?" These bitter, resentful questions that men have asked since the cradle days of humanity have never been repeated in more piteous protest than in the baffling discouragement of these tragic [depression] years. The sick and the maimed, who face dismal prospects of long and unrelieved suffering, exclaim with impatient bitterness: "If there is any justice in earth or in heaven, why are we the victims of these endless miseries?" The frugal, God-fearing folk who have worked and saved, hoped and prayed, only to have their plans shattered, demand: "Why does the scourge of God beat us while money and pleasure overflow for the open enemies of God?" A bereft mother crushes the lifeless form of her only child in a last embrace and screams: "If there is a God in heaven, why did He rob me of my baby when millions of wives refuse to become mothers or neglect their unwanted children?"

There is one and only one true answer to this everlasting "why" of humanity's sorrow: the solution found in God's never-failing Word. The light for the darkness of our pain and affliction comes to us with practical, everyday force from the Book of Job. Here was a man of affairs, a patriarch of renown and riches, in his day, as the Bible assures us, *"the greatest of all the men in the East."* He numbered his sheep and cattle and camels by the thousands as they roamed over his far-flung pasture lands. He was blessed with seven sons and three daughters. Prosperity had indeed smiled upon Job, the upright and God-fearing. But suddenly disaster swooped down upon his house and his lands. His flocks, his herded cattle, his drove of three thousand camels were taken from him on a single day. And before that sunset a breathless messenger of doom brought the terrifying announcement that his children had been killed. Men have lost their reason and taken their lives for tragedies far less grievous than the ruin that came to Job between dawn and dusk.

156

But he had not yet drained the cup of his suffering to the bitterest dregs. Pain and torture gripped him. He was afflicted, we read, *"with sore boils from the sole of his foot to his crown,"* with an agonizing form of leprosy; so hideous and repulsive was this skin cancer over his entire body that the ancients hesitated to speak the name of this incurable curse. As he sits in his agony, isolated in some remote ash-strewn corner, feverishly scratching the fiery ache of his ulcered body, the taunting sneer of his wife demands: *"Dost thou still retain thine integrity,"* thy faith in God? *"Curse God and die!"*

But Job did not die. And although assailed by fierce despair, he turned to God and found the solution to the problem of his suffering. Let me, under the guidance of God, offer the same help to every distressed soul that may question the "why" of human sufferings. Let me bring you

Through Trial to Triumph

with the immortal words of Job's ageless, deathless faith (chapter 23, verse 10): *"God knoweth the way that I take. When He hath tried me, I shall come forth as gold."*

In Trials We Triumph: "God Knows the Way!"

In Job's own reason and strength there was no gleam of hope for his ulcerated body and his plundered possessions. Even his friends sat before him with closed lips, stunned into speechlessness for seven days. But when God was invoked, the courage of the sufferer showed the strength of iron; as the roots of Job's faith struck deeply into the fullness of divine promises, he rose up to cry in triumph: *"God knoweth the way that I take."*

Today a blinded world, staggering under the impact of one savage onslaught after the other, adds to its miseries by pushing God aside. Let there be no misunderstanding on this one basic fact: If we are to contradict the Bible and to believe that there is no sovereign God in the heavens above; if we are to contradict Christ and to hold that this world is only the haphazard result of an ancient accident in the solar system; if we are to contradict the First Article of the Apostles' Creed and admit that you and I have come up from the amoeba and the ape, all by chance, then there is no key to the mystery of sorrow and suffering; then you and I are but the pitiful playthings of cruel fate; then, though we scream piercing prayers into the black night of despair, the empty echo of our failure reminds us that we are only hopeless atoms of humanity, caught in the riptides and the whirlpools of life's crosscurrents. Destroy faith in God, and life becomes a roulette wheel with mankind inevitably the loser. Wipe out Christian hope, and logically you arrive at the despair leading to suicide.

But if with Job we look beyond the turmoil of earth's agonies to our ever-living, ever-compassionate Redeemer, we too shall find in His cross God's own answer to the perplexities of human pain. If God loved us, weak and sinful as we all are, with the everlasting mercy of the sacrifice that nailed His Son, our Savior, to the cross, how can we doubt that His love will direct the lives of those who penitently accept the mercies of Christ? *"If,"* as the apostle puts it, *"God spared not His own Son but delivered Him up for us all, how shall He not with Him also freely give us all things,"* including His guidance for every turn of human affairs?

In the radiance of the cross and in the light of its love we too can raise our trusting eyes to God above and exult: *"He knoweth the way that I take."* God, whose hand moves the spheres of the universe and directs the course of all history, whose eyes sweep the world and see the path of life before life begins—our God knows the way that you and I take. Once we are Christ's, once our penitent, pleading faith says:

> Take my life and let it be
> Consecrated, Lord, to Thee,

God takes our hand and guides us along the paths of His righteousness. Not a day passes that His watchful love does not guard and bless our progress toward heaven; not a night draws its cover of darkness over land and sea but the vigilance of Him who neither slumbers nor sleeps pierces the darkness to keep watch over us; not a moment of sorrow, not a single temptation breaks over us in which He, the constant Companion of our lives, does not speak to our souls and say: *"Fear thou not, for I am with thee; be not dismayed, for I am thy God. I will strengthen thee; yea, I will help thee; yea, I will uphold thee with the right hand of My righteousness."*

God knows the way that we take, though we ourselves cannot know it. Has He not told us in plain and unmistakable words: *"My thoughts are not your thoughts, neither are your ways My ways"?* Sometimes when God leads us through a barren wilderness, we may dispute His leadership and question His wisdom. Sometimes His guidance seems cruel, and in our short-sighted human vision we may be ready to rise up and accuse God. Yet His paths, far above our poor powers of comprehension, are always the right paths.

Many years ago in western Montana a stagecoach was caught in the grip of freezing cold. A mother and her infant child were the only passengers. When in spite of extra wraps and coverings the fatal drowsiness that precedes death by freezing began to steal over the mother, the driver took away the baby, dragged the mother out on the frozen ground, shook her violently until she was awakened, and then, springing to his seat, drove off, leaving the distressed mother alone in the middle of the road. But when the woman saw the coach speeding away with her child, the horror of losing her baby banished her drowsiness, and she started in mad pursuit. Her blood began to circulate, and when the danger of her freezing to death had passed, the driver slacked his speed, took her back into the coach to her unharmed child, and later reached warmth and refuge. Without that apparently cruel and inhuman extreme the mother would have died.

In much the same way, when the drowsiness of sin overtakes us and deadens our spiritual senses, when our love of God and our faith in Christ are in danger of being chilled to death, God may adopt a sudden terror as a means of sure and quick rescue. Sometimes it takes a shock, a misfortune, a deep-grooved sorrow, to shake us out of our soul's lethargy and arouse us from our sleep. Though we may not understand it, God's mercy saves us from ourselves.

Again, we are prone to blame God as we impatiently mark time and wait for the removal of obstacles and misfortunes; but God knows our way better than we, and His time for help is always the right time. Even if we cannot penetrate God's hidden purposes here, where we see *"through a glass, darkly,"* we shall see *"face to face,"* and we too shall know, because the Savior Himself promised: *"What I do thou knowest not now, but thou shalt know hereafter."* Then we shall discover the answer to the perplexing *why* that we have asked when our wishes were denied, our plans overturned, our happiness interrupted. In that full vision many will be able to see that God permitted their money to be taken away that their souls might be wrenched from avarice and greed and the love of money not become the root of multiplied evils in their lives. We shall be able to understand how the sudden death of a promising young man became the means of bringing his father to repentance and to salvation; how long and weary years of sickness and deformity provided opportunity for prayer and spiritual growth; how family trouble and the breaking of homes may save a believing husband or wife from unbelief.

After Trials We Triumph: "I Have Come Forth as Gold!"

Job knew that this triumph through trial would be his and confidently he proclaimed: *"When He hath tried me, I shall come forth as gold."* In our lives too every adversity may be a glorious strengthening. Just as the purified gold comes out of the hissing, roaring, cracking furnace, so our faith may be purified by the refining fires of affliction. Just as every fruit tree is pruned, in the words of the Savior, *"that it may bring forth more fruit,"* so the unproductive elements of our life must be removed if we are to show forth the increasing fruits of faith. Just as the diamond must be cut into designs of many facets so that it may sparkle in its greatest beauty, so you and I need the friction of sorrow to add spiritual luster to our lives; and as the famous Kohinoor diamond flashed with more brilliance when it was recut and reduced by eighty carats, so deep material losses often help us gain in faith and lead us to join St. Paul in his cry of victory: *"I count all things but loss for the excellency of the knowledge of Christ Jesus, my Lord."*

Here, then, is gain through loss, strength through weakness, triumph through trial. Those who have listened to these broadcasts know that we have never held out to you any program of moneymaking, currency improvement, or financial profit. We leave that to those who promise the high hills of ease and comfort but always trap themselves in ravines of failure. Jesus never attracted His followers with the magnet of money, and neither do His disciples today. But He offered comfort for the soul, and so should we in His name. And because He promises: *"I will not leave you comfortless; I will come to you,"* I ask you to open your hearts and to gain that calm of Christian hope, that peace of purified faith, which Heaven itself has always poured into the troubled souls that answer the plea of the compassionate Christ: *"Come unto Me, all ye that labor and are heavy laden, and I will give you rest."*

You can take your hymnal and find practical evidence of the refining, purifying power by which we *"come forth as gold"* from the fires of affliction. Have you a sensitive, high-strung mind? Are you obsessed with fears and afflicted with melancholy doubts? Turn to William Cowper, who twice in one day tried to commit suicide, yet whose faith ultimately triumphed and inspired his immortal lines:

> God moves in a mysterious way
> His wonders to perform.

Are you out of work? Cross-burdened Paul Gerhardt paid for his loyalty to Christ by persecution and loss of his position; in addition he was bereaved of his wife and several children; nevertheless his faith broke forth in jubilant thanksgiving as he exulted:

> I will sing my Maker's praises.

Are you on relief? Are you down to your last dollar? Remember George Neumark, who lived at a time when there was no dole, during the Thirty Years' War, a long-drawn religious butchery, and who, on the verge of starvation, had to pawn his viola; yet his victorious faith gave the church the hymn of Christian resignation and courage:

> If thou but suffer God to guide thee.

Are you one of the unfortunate businessmen to whom the last six years have brought collapse and ruin? There is a lesson for you in the life of Thomas Moore, who overnight found himself liable for the sum of $30,000. Yet he soared on the golden wings of sacred song to the heights of faith that we should reach when we repeat his lines of loyalty to Chirst:

> Come, ye disconsolate, where'er ye languish,
>   Come to the mercy-seat, fervently kneel;
> Here bring your wounded hearts, here tell your anguish;
>   Earth has no sorrow that Heaven cannot heal.

But lay your hymnal aside, and let me ask whether in the midst of your sorrows you are singing songs of praise. I know men and women, brave, triumphant souls, whose sickrooms have become chapels of God's grace through their trust and confidence. I know weak and quavering voices of invalids that preach Gospel sermons as powerful as those of the most eloquent pulpit orators. They have turned pain into joy, affliction into devotion, trials into triumph. What better can you do than *"casting all your care upon Him"* *("for*

161

He careth for you"), to find this purifying power of pain, through your own suffering to deepen your sympathy for the sorrows of others, to be reminded through your grief of the immeasurably greater anguish by which the Savior paid the ransom price for all sin and for every sinner?

When our faith has been refined in the crucibles of sorrow, we have been granted the blessed assurance *"that the sufferings of this present time are not worthy to be compared with the glory which shall be revealed in us";* the eternal triumph, which, rising above hunger and poverty, sickness and pain, hatred and persecution, fear and doubt, crashed hopes and crushed ambitions, shattered promises and broken hearts, shouts the Christian's hymn of victory: *"All things work together for good to them that love God."*[56]

The outbreak of World War II in Europe serves as the background for the next address, which focuses on prayer and national defense. It was delivered in 1940, one year before Pearl Harbor, and shows how W.A.M. could speak to both the country at large and individual hearers in the same sermon.

On Your Knees, America!

"If My people, which are called by My name, shall humble themselves and pray and seek My face and turn from their wicked ways, then will I hear from heaven and will forgive their sin and will heal their land."—2 Chronicles 7:14

Conflicting cries reecho across our country in these problem-weighted days. "Protect yourself, America!" This plea demands increased armaments, more powerful airplanes, swifter cruisers, heavier cannon, bigger bombs, as the most stupendous defense program in our national history gets under way. With all our hearts we hope that these titanic efforts will remove the danger of foreign invasion; but we need more protection than even this gigantic rearming project. It took hundreds of thousands of men hundreds of years to build the Chinese Wall, the largest defense structure known to man; but even that barrier—it would stretch halfway across the United States—could not save China from devastation. The French boasted that the Maginot Line was impregnable, yet it fell without having its strength tested. In 1914 the Germans assembled the greatest war machine known to military science, yet

162

their well-equipped armies surrendered, and their navy was scuttled.

Others cry, "Remove your hidden enemies, America!" Martin Dies, chairman of the committee investigating un-American activities, has just issued a challenging volume in which he shows the fifth-column activities of Nazi, Fascist, and particularly of Communist forces. Again we agree that secret agents of Communists and totalitarians, as treacherous foes of our God and country, should be removed. Yet if every fifth columnist were exiled, other heavy problems would still burden us.

Again, this cry is heard, "Watch your financial structure, America!" Debates on currency and inflation, charges that wealth is being concentrated in fewer hands, fears produced by mounting national indebtedness, fill the air as money experts warn of impending danger. We realize too that the nation is living beyond its means, that all the gold safely stored in the Fort Knox vaults may not be sufficient to save us from monetary collapse; but if other nations have regained economic stability after the chaos of wild inflation, we can too.

Yet as Christians we have another cry, incomparably more vital in these question-marked years—not a new plea nor a slogan from our economists, intellectual leaders, Government officials, but an ancient appeal from God Himself. Here it is, the summons which can help bring peace and promise to every one of us and to our whole country, the Lord's demand:

On Your Knees, America!

A defenseless nation with prayer is better protected than a heavily armed nation without prayer. America on its knees can accomplish more than America with its head high in proud self-confidence. This is not human theory; it is rather God's truth, recorded in His words to King Solomon, Second Chronicles, chapter seven, verse fourteen: *"If My people, which are called by My name, shall humble themselves and pray and seek My face and turn from their wicked ways, then will I hear from heaven and will forgive their sin and will heal their land."*

Prayer Promises National Blessing

This glorious promise of healing for our country's ills is based on the condition that we approach the one true God. The Almighty says, *"Seek MY face!"* Too many have the loose idea that any plea, no matter to whom it is addressed, is an effective prayer. So they call upon the "Mighty Spirit," the "Supreme Architect," the "Great Unknown," the "Creative Force," either without actually knowing to whom they are speaking or, what is worse, deliberately directing their petitions to substitutes for the only Lord of heaven and earth. Because there is but one God, not a dozen gods, and only He can answer prayer; because He is revealed unmistakably in the Bible as the Father, His Son, the Lord Jesus Christ, and the purifying Spirit, your petitions must be addressed to that blessed Trinity. If you are praying in any other way, stop now! The true God, beside whom all other objects of men's worship are crude idols, declares, *"Seek MY face!"* *"Thou shalt have no other gods before Me."* If you are worshiping saints or angels, hear God say, *"Seek MY face!"* *"Put not your trust in men!"* If you utter vague, uncertain supplications without knowing that personal triune God of power, love, and glory; if you moan through the darkness of your sorrows, *"Oh, that I knew where I might find Him!"* stop now! Your search is ended. For here God the Creator, God the Redeemer, God the Purifier solemnly proclaims: *"Seek MY face!"* *"Call upon ME in the day of trouble!"* Therefore, when the cry reechoes, "On your knees, America!" it is a summons not simply to prayer but to the worship of almighty God, the Father of our Lord Jesus Christ; and one of the basic needs in this country today is that millions learn who the one true Lord really is.

Only God's people can pray acceptably. In the text our heavenly Father says: To have your prayers answered you must be one of *"My people, which are called by My name."* Now, to be God's, we must be free from sin, for no man burdened with the wrong inherited by every one of us at birth and acquired by everyone during life can approach Him.

No human agent or intermediary can bring your prayers before the heavenly throne. No church in itself, no minister or priest, possesses the power to make your prayers acceptable. No saint of old, no self-sacrificing mother, no godly husband or wife, can take your place in praying. In the Middle Ages forgiveness of sins was "sold" at specified rates, and today, with similar folly, people are urged to approach the Almighty by their character, their good intentions, and their good resolutions. You must have your sin forgiven before you can draw near to God.

164

Here it is that Jesus, the Savior of mankind, comes into our prayer life with His unfathomable, undeserved mercy. He broke down the barriers that separate us from God by taking away our sins, every one of them, transferring the guilt that rested on us to Himself, paying completely the penalty we should have suffered. All this Jesus did for us when at Calvary He hung on the cross between heaven and earth; and because as our Substitute He served the sentence that sin pronounced on every one of us; because the anguish and death of God's own Son was the required ransom price He paid to free us, the promise of His holy Gospel is the good news that *"there is therefore now no condemnation to them which are in Christ Jesus."* Through Christ we have no more unforgiven sin; and since faith in His reconciling, restoring love makes us the sons of God, nothing can keep us from approaching Him as trusting children petition their loving father.

Prayers, to be answered, must come from Christ-dedicated hearts. The Lord Jesus says, *"Whatsoever ye shall ask the Father in My name, He will give it to you."* Yet that holy name, above all other names, is systematically avoided today, when, more than ever, men should acclaim our Lord. Many, including some nominal Christians, do not like to mention Jesus Christ for fear they may displease those who reject Him. In this spirit certain churches have deleted "Jesus" from their prayers. In many lodges to which, inconsistently, some of you Christian men belong, all reference to Christ has been banned from the ritual. In politics prayers are spoken which drop His holy name so they will be wide enough to embrace those who deny the Savior's deity and atonement. During the recent presidential campaign one speaker closed his address with a petition for our country taken word for word from *The Book of Common Prayer* except—and I hope sincerely it was an oversight—that the concluding words of the prayer, "all which we ask through Jesus Christ, our Lord," were completely omitted.

May God give you the loyalty to Christ shown by Samuel F.B. Morse, internationally acclaimed inventor of the electric telegraph. He testified that in the darkest hours, when everything seemed hopeless, prayer to Jesus brought him light and the assurance of his salvation. He wrote: "To Him, indeed, belongs all the glory. I have evidence enough that without Christ I could do nothing. All my strength is there, and I fervently desire to ascribe to Him all the praise. If I am to have influence, I desire to have it for Christ, to use it for His cause; if wealth, for Christ; if more knowledge, for Christ."

If this cry, "On your knees, America!" is to help bring the divine answer to your problems, millions in this country must pray with contrite sincerity. The text reminds us that God requires His people to *"humble themselves . . . and turn from their wicked ways. Then,"* He promises, *"will I hear from heaven."* Common reason, not to mention the Bible warning, ought to make this fact clear: we cannot expect the national benefits which Thanksgiving week again recalls, to bless our land automatically and indefinitely if the rebellion against the Almighty and the bold breaking of His Ten Commandments continues unchecked. We cannot always be the most richly blessed and at the same time the most crime-ridden nation on earth. The call therefore is for a repentant, prayerful spirit throughout the land: Back to God, back to the Bible, back to Christ in humility and contrition!

Penitent prayer in Christ's name helped this nation in the past. George Washington on his knees at Valley Forge, his voice solemnly raised to God; Abraham Lincoln, who during the crucial years of the Civil War started the custom of an annual Thanksgiving Day—these men and millions of humble Christians joined with them in prayers mightily answered knew God's ancient promise, which also assures the American people today that, if they *"humble themselves and pray and seek My face and turn from their wicked ways, then will I hear from heaven and will forgive their sin and will heal their land."* Put confident prayer into the hearts of the nation's youth instead of the un-American drivel with which some of your sons and daughters are being filled today, and we shall have real patriotism. Nathan Hale, a young man of twenty-one, was sentenced to die for his country. During his last moments, instead of surrendering to fear, he turned his face heavenward and was in such complete communion with his heavenly Father that he did not even hear the harsh commands of the British hangman. Strengthened by prayer, he cried out from the gallows: "If I had ten thousand lives, I would lay them down for my injured, bleeding country. I regret that I have but one life to lose for my country." Let each of the quarter million churches in our forty-eight states intercede for the President, the Congress, and those in authority; teach all of us the power of Christ-exalting prayer—and with this obedience to the cry "On your knees, America!" we can, under God, bring America to its highest heights!

No matter how multiplied your difficulties, God tells you, *"I hear from heaven."* Take Him at His word today! Not long ago I read that a business concern employed a famous lawyer at a fee of $100,000 to draw up an unbreakable contract. Some time after the ironclad document was executed, however, the same concern found reason to change its policies and reengaged the same attorney, at another $100,000 fee, to break that unbreakable contract; and he did. A recognized insurance director claims: "There is scarcely a law governing business which cannot be broken with impunity if the breaker has any brains at all." But there is a law that God Himself can never repeal, His promise *"I hear from heaven,"* if you approach Him in Christ-grounded faith.

Pray confidently, believing that no problem you face is too great for the Almighty, with whom *"nothing shall be impossible."* Henry Ward Beecher tells of a poor Indian Christian woman on Long Island who faced a Thanksgiving without food. A day or two before the holiday, while standing on a hill overlooking the beach, she saw a large flock of wild geese and prayed, "Oh, that the Lord would give me one of those for Thanksgiving!" She had hardly uttered the words when a hawk flew into the flock and killed one of the geese, which fell to the ground not far away. Thus did God provide a Thanksgiving feast for an impoverished Indian.

Recall the prayer of Hudson Taylor, consecrated missionary to China. Once the sailing ship in which he traveled was becalmed close to a cannibal island. To the horror of those aboard, the ship drifted slowly shoreward, and nothing could stop its course toward the savages on the beach, who eagerly prepared for a great feast of human flesh. In that emergency the captain asked Hudson Taylor to beseech God for help. "I will pray," the missionary replied, "provided you set your sails to catch the breeze." At first the captain refused, but Taylor warned, "I will not pray unless you prepare the sails." That request carried out, the heroic man of God knelt in confident pleading. Before long the captain returned to say joyfully, "You had better stop praying now, for we have more wind than we can manage." With the ship a hundred yards from the shore, God had answered by sending a strong wind to save the passengers and the crew.

I can almost hear some of you object, however, "I have prayed, but God has not answered me." Perhaps you have not persevered enough, for our heavenly Father knows far better than we do the best time for answering. Most of us pray far too little, and to teach us the blessing of protracted pleading, God may let us wait. Sometimes Jesus was so busy that He would not eat; but He never was so preoccupied that He could not pray. Regularly He devoted hours to communion with His heavenly Father, and sometimes He spent the whole night in prayer. Yet we—may God forgive us!—are often too engrossed with our petty worries and trivial joys to find time for the Savior, who gave His lifetime for us. Pray continually and courageously!

If even our Savior in the agonies of Gethsemane prayed: *"Not My will but Thine be done,"* how much more should we, because of our selfishness and blindness, raise our prayers *"according to His will."* How tragic and confused life would be if every prayer were answered! No normal parent would be guilty of the folly of granting every impulsive wish of his children. If your boy wants a Thompson submachine gun for Christmas or an assortment of hand grenades, would you buy them? Only too often we are similarly childish in our prayers, so that, if it were not for the mercy of God, we should be "ruined by our request." We pray for money, for advancement, for success; but God loves us too much to heed our entreaty if the fulfillment of our wishes would mislead us.[57]

Again, some of you will object, "I have prayed incessantly. I have pleaded humbly and in Jesus' name; and yet God has done just the opposite of what I requested." Some of you clutch a baby's shoe or fondle a little pink garment to recall that you once implored the Almighty with persistent pleas to save an infant life; but the child died. Some of you think of the long nights of prayerful waking and watching with a beloved one, during which you literally wore yourself out; yet God took your dear one home. Some of you have continually prayed for health and happiness, but your bodies are broken beyond repair, your joy of life crushed into a thousand irreparable fragments, and you demand, "How can you say that God hears prayer?"

Human reason offers no answer, but faith does. Because you are Christ's, every time it seems such prayers are not heard and God, far from being the Lord of love, has dealt cruelly with you, He has in reality given far more than you have asked. Above our poor powers of understanding, Jesus, who loved us unto the bitter, bleeding end at Calvary, loves us even when it seems He hurts us. That child, snatched away all too young in your opinion, is far better off in the heavenly life than it would be were it to live longer on earth; and because you are the Lord's, you too will say in the joyful reunion of eternity, *"He hath done all things well."* The Christian husband or wife, called home against your wishes, was taken by God's mercy and not His cruelty, hard as it is to understand this. And in the fuller knowledge of the hereafter you will realize His blessed truth *"What I do thou knowest not now; but thou shalt know hereafter."* Would you not prefer heaven through Jesus, after broken health and heaped miseries, to hell without Christ, after the fleeting pleasures of this life?

I know of a man who graduated from a theological seminary and was privileged to serve his Savior three years as a missionary. Then his afflictions began. In the tropics he lost the sight of one eye. A few years later, without a moment's warning, the other eye failed to function. His little girl was smitten by infantile paralysis. His wife, on whom he leaned because of his blindness, was called home after severe suffering. Three years later his second child died. In the midst of these difficulties his shepherd dog, trained by the Seeing Eye Foundation, was killed in an accident; but as blow followed blow, did this twentieth-century Job rise up to curse God? No! Triumphant over these successive afflictions, he declares faith and the power of prayer have taught him that God's Word never fails. He has found the joy and peace which make him tell you in St. Paul's assurance, *"My God shall supply all your need according to His riches in glory by Christ Jesus."*

Will not you, my fellow redeemed, turn to our God in prayer and answer the appeal directed personally to every one of you: "On your knees, America! On your knees in penitent, humble prayer! On your knees in trusting, confident prayer! On your knees in the name of Jesus Christ"? God grant that you will for the Savior's sake! Amen.[58]

In 1941 all network radio stations carried *The Lutheran Hour* on a "live" basis, unlike today, when transcription discs are more appropriate. The advantage of live programming, of course, was instant response to national and international events, and Dr. Maier always tried to keep his references and illustrations "up to the minute." This proved to be the case also on the "Day of Infamy." About 2 p.m. (CST) on Sunday,

December 7, news reached St. Louis that Pearl Harbor had been attacked. An hour and a half later, W.A.M. offered an entirely new prayer to introduce his 3:30 p.m. broadcast, and for countless Americans this was the first news that America was now embroiled in war. (All sermons had such prayers preceding them, but space permits listing only this one.)

Heavenly Father, Lord of the nations, a crucial moment has come for our country with the reports of enemy bombardment; and we flee to Thee for refuge, strength, and the hope of victory. Humbly we bow before Thee to beseech Thy guidance during the heavy days before us. Direct the President, the Congress, and all responsible for the nation's future course along paths pleasing to Thee! Teach us individually to understand that we may be called to sacrifice life's most precious possessions for the defense of America and for the defeat of those who threaten to bring destruction within our borders! O God, who canst still break the bow and cut the enemies' spear asunder, we commit our cause to Thee as we humble ourselves to confess our sins and for Jesus' sake beseech Thy pardon. Help us in this crisis hour to declare, "If God be for us, who can be against us?" Therefore, O Lord of hosts, be with us now as Thou wast with our fathers! We ask it contritely because we pray in Jesus' blessed name. Amen.[59]

A week later W.A.M. made formal response to World War II in his famous sermon, which follows. His original address had been keyed, seasonally, to the Sunday in Advent heralding Christ's Second Coming, and he found this theme uniquely appropriate in 1941 also for the wartime crisis.

America, Embattled, Turn to Christ!

"When ye shall hear of wars and rumors of wars, be ye not troubled; for such things must needs be."—Mark 13:7

"If God be for us, who can be against us?" May this divine truth strengthen the souls of millions throughout America as our beloved nation finds itself treacherously attacked in the first week of a destructive war. We dare not make the fatal mistake of assuming that we can succeed without God or be victorious against Him! Our enemies are numerous, powerful, prepared; they will wage a long-drawn, hard-fought contest. Those who only a few days ago

170

predicted that the Japanese Empire would be smashed within six weeks will be forced to revise their opinion. This struggle may last six years or more. Before us, my countrymen, is a heavily weighted future, the end of which can be foreseen by no scientist, however learned, no statesman, however experienced, no economic expert, however renowned. Earnest appeals are made to patriotism; and may the love for America now ring clear and true in every heart! But patriotism will not be enough. We will be called upon to practice self-denial, and because of the rich blessings the United States has granted each one of us, we should be eager to forgo luxuries and nonessentials; but self-denial will not be enough. As the struggle continues, we will be asked to sacrifice time, energies, money, perhaps even our lives; and who, reflecting on the privileges and freedoms which are ours, will shrink from doing whatever is possible to transmit the heritage of liberty, received from our fathers, to our children? But even sacrifice will not be enough. We need the Almighty. Spiritual defense is as vital as military defense. We must turn to the Lord and exult, "A mighty Fortress is our God, a trusty Shield and Weapon!" Millions from coast to coast will require redoubled soul comfort and guidance during the heavy sieges of this conflict. As the Old Testament prophets during periods of national visitation were commanded, *"Comfort ye, comfort ye My people,"* so the consolation and strengthening which comes from faith in the redemption purchased by Jesus Christ, not the message of any counterfeit gospel, must be the keynote of wartime preaching.

Today, then, on National Bible Sunday and the first Lord's day in radio history on which a vast coast-to-coast broadcasting system can be employed in bringing the Savior's promise to the people of the United States at war, may God's Spirit mightily bless this appeal:

America, Embattled, Turn to Christ!

Accept His divine instruction and comfort given in our Scripture for today (St. Mark, chapter thirteen, verse seven), which says, *"When ye shall hear of wars and rumors of wars, be ye not troubled; for such things must needs be."*

Jesus Instructs Us in the Reason for War
Reviewing the events of the past several days we are startled by

171

the suddenness with which war began. A weekly confidential bulletin issued by financial advisers in Washington, dated December 6, expressed the opinion that conflict with Japan might be avoided; at worst, it was some distance away. Yet on December 7 Japanese planes attacked our island outposts. A magazine dated December 12 and purporting to give the last word in national affairs likewise predicted that hostilities, if they were declared, would be postponed for some time. Before that magazine reached its readers enemy bombs had taken their toll of American lives. On the very morning, just a week ago, when the struggle broke, a feature writer for New York's largest newspaper voiced this opinion, "Japan does not want war." But even as people were reading these wishful thoughts, American youth was being killed on our Pacific islands.

While human predictions—and there were many other similar mistakes—have collapsed notoriously, God's prophecies have never failed. Every one among the hundreds of Scriptural predictions referring to history, past or present, has been literally, exactly fulfilled. With all the mockery evil-minded men heap on Holy Writ, they have failed to produce a single volume which has foretold future events with only a fraction of the accuracy and detail found in Bible prophecies. It has always seemed to me that if men would use good, common, unbiased sense, they would come to the conclusion, on this basis of prophecy and fulfillment, that the Old and New Testaments must be, as no other book ever written or read, divine revelation. The basic trouble, however, is this: Usually the enemies of the Bible do not take time to read the writings they condemn. If they did and thus gave the Spirit a chance to work in their hearts, they could come to the conclusion reached by the famous British poet Cowper when he wrote, "If the prophecies have been fulfilled (of which there is abundant demonstration), the Scriptures must be the Word of God; and if the Scripture is the Word of God, Christianity must be true."

Thus when Jesus tells us in our text, *"Ye shall hear of wars and rumors of wars,"* that prediction, now 1900 years old, has never been realized as forcefully as now in the most widespread of all wars. For years unbelieving men sought to discount this forecast of *"wars and rumors of wars."* In opposition they taught that the race was constantly on the upgrade, steadily elevating itself by its own bootstraps. As the "human animals"—for so are people called by this delusion—steadfastly lifted themselves from the lower beast

172

level, crime would be checked, lusts restricted, greed controlled, hatreds removed, and, this is the repeated promise, bloodshed completely banished.

I submit to you that no other generation in American history should be more ready than ours to cast aside completely these rosy promises, because they contradict divine truth. At a time when culture, education, science, and invention have reached their height, international morals are at their lowest, international strife at its widest. Twenty-three years ago the first world conflict was concluded, the war that was to end all wars; but while that struggle involved sixteen nations, the present list of belligerents already numbers thirty-six, and many more may still be added before the victory is ours. Thus, while men, wise in their own conceit, have prophesied, *"Peace, peace!"* Christ has predicted, *"Wars and rumors of wars."* His Word alone is the immovable, unalterable, unbreakable Truth. Therefore believe with all your hearts that the thunderous denunciations of God's Law: *"The soul that sinneth, it shall die," "The wages of sin is death,"* are not theory, guesswork, speculation. *"Heaven and earth shall pass away"* before *"one jot or one tittle"* of these utterances is proved false. By the same heavenly power every promise of grace that Jesus, God's Son and the world's Savior, offers you—assurances like these beloved passages: *"God so loved the world that He gave His only-begotten Son that whosoever believeth in Him should not perish but have everlasting life"; "I am the Resurrection and the Life"*—these pledges are the sure, eternal, triumphant truth.

The Savior also declares in our text that wars *"must needs be."* In explanation the Bible, honored throughout America today, asks pointedly, *"From whence come wars and fighting among you?"* and answers, *"Come they not . . . of your lusts?"* In other words, Scripture teaches that bloodshed is provoked by sin. Examine every conflict since the cradle days of humanity, and behind each struggle you will find overreaching greed, the desire for more territory, more natural resources, more profit, more power, and with it envy, jealousy, race prejudice, hatred, oppression, conquest.

Besides, God often uses war as a chastening and a visitation of His outraged justice. If people live in the unbroken peace and the carnal security that forgets the Almighty; if atheism flourishes in universities; if pulpits are polluted with the denial of God and His Christ; if the Scriptures fall into neglect within buildings once dedicated to their teaching; if even homes are marked by irreligion, families forsake the faith—then He whose justice and righteousness prevent the sins of an individual, as of a nation, from remaining unrebuked often intervenes, and the horror of war begins its devastation.

"Such things must needs be," the Scriptures echo, also in the United States. This is not the hour, with American shore cities darkened by blackout, American defense seriously threatened, and American lives at stake, to speak in boastful, boisterous tones as though this nation did not need the Almighty. But it is the time, high time, for masses in America to approach God, to fall on their knees before Him in full confession of their sins, to find pardon and power through Christ. Over the clamor of this disturbed hour, at the beginning of a war that will cost us more in men and money, toil and tears than we now can measure, the momentous call resounds across the land, "America, get right with God!" Instead of shouting, whistling, screaming as many did last Monday when war was declared, Christians in this country know that for them the cry of this crisis is: "On your knees, America!" "Pray, America, pray!"

In another sense this conflict *"must needs be,"* for in the chapter from which our text has been chosen Jesus reveals that *"wars and rumors of wars"* are to foreshadow the beginning of the end for mankind. Indeed, the Scriptures foretell in scores of clear passages that this entire globe, with everything on and in it, will be destroyed when Christ at His second coming appears to judge the quick and the dead.

In order that believers, instead of being caught unawares when Jesus comes, may be fully prepared to meet Him, the Scriptures present a long list of signs, describing in detail church and world conditions which are to precede Christ's return in glory. Particularly prominent is Jesus' warning of *"wars and rumors of wars"* with His explanation that *"nation shall rise against nation and kingdom against kingdom"*—a prophecy now more clearly fulfilled than ever in past ages. We witness other evidences of this approaching end. Famines are predicted, and impoverished people by the millions in the small occupied countries of Europe, not to mention multitudes more in China, will not have enough to eat during the coming winter. Pestilences are foretold; physicians are forecasting epidemics which will sweep across nations after this conflict just as the dread influenza scourge accompanied World War I. Earthquakes are to

174

come; and it is on record that recent years have witnessed the most disastrous of such upheavals. In these last times, we are warned, *"false prophets shall rise."* Have they ever been as numerous before? *"Iniquity shall abound."*—Our crime records are at their highest figure. *"The love of many shall wax cold."*—How true, when we see the worldliness in many churches or survey the number of those who have turned from Christ! How readily we should conclude that if the primitive Christian church proclaimed, *"The Lord is at hand,"* then assuredly today, after 1900 years, His Second Advent may be upon us. He could come at any time.

May He not find us unprepared! The lessons of last week's attack at Pearl Harbor showed us how destructive it is to imagine danger far off. Therefore, as God's Word calls out: "America, turn to Jesus! He is coming soon!" let us keep ourselves in constant readiness for that hour which will bring terrifying rejection to those who have spurned Jesus, but a homecoming in joy and unspeakable glory for all who sincerely, trustingly acclaim Christ their Savior! If we could only realize what indescribably radiant blessings Christ's return will bring those who are His, every heart throughout this broad land would constantly repeat the prayer of the early church: *"Even so, come, Lord Jesus!"*

Jesus Gives Us Comfort in Time of War

Until this glorious Advent we must work and hope, watch and pray amid life's sorrows and joys. If this conflict continues to rage, year after year, we must be ready to give up many comforts and luxuries, to adopt a lower standard of living. Who knows whether that will be the end? Grave questions of inflation, serious problems of postwar reconstruction, the whole readjustment of our American life—all this puts everyone before the most deep-rooted difficulties we as a nation have ever faced. More penetrating will be the personal grief when war demands the limb or the life of a son, a father, a brother. The first days of fighting have made many gold-star mothers and brought bereavement into hundreds of American homes. While we pay tribute to the devotion and heroism of those who have died fighting our battles and resolve that, God helping us, their sacrifice will not have been made in vain, we must expect that as the war progresses casualty lists will be far longer and more of the sons to whom you parents waved a brave farewell will never return.

Now, where can we find unfailing solace, unchanging conso-

175

lation, unfaltering assurance? Where, if not in Him who is the Hope of the ages, the Help in every need, the Comforter for every distressed soul—Jesus, our Christ, who today tells us, *"When ye shall hear of wars and rumors of wars, be ye not troubled"*?

Had anyone else written this, *"Be ye not troubled!"*, were this the claim of a mortal leader, the wishful thinking of a social expert, we would shake our heads and turn away, unconvinced. Too often we have been tortured by the glib promises and false predictions which abound in our age. But take heart! Remember who spoke these words! This is the pledge of Jesus Christ, who is the very God together with the Father and the Spirit, the ever-blessed Trinity in ever-holy Unity, the words of One who never spoke an empty promise nor raised an unfulfilled hope.

The truth of this *"Be ye not troubled,"* is also assured us because Jesus, as approaching Christmas reminds us, is our Savior. He grants real assurance, unfailing strength, true courage, even for the worst that may confront us, because He, blessed Redeemer of our souls, has removed completely the evil responsible for fear, doubt, and dismay. Particularly let every soldier or sailor who may be summoned to fight the life-and-death struggles of this war accept Jesus now, before facing the brunt of battle, so that in the midst of tumult and strife faith in His constant companionship will bestow this assurance, *"Being justified by faith, we have peace with God"*—the inner peace *"which passeth all understanding"*!

"When ye shall hear of wars and rumors of wars, be ye not troubled!" because a Christian never need be troubled. If everything else crashes about him, with increasing power he feels the Savior's closeness. We who acclaim Jesus our only Redeemer know that the Lord, without whose will not a sparrow falls to the ground, has numbered the very hairs on our head. Therefore I said at the beginning, *"If God be for us, who can be against us?"* When Jesus rules your heart in a personal, pulsating faith, you can stand confidently in stormed trenches as the din of hell itself appears to loose its fury around you. You can crouch securely in blacked-out cities while bombs seem to blast away the earth beneath you. You can face hidden perils above and below the murky ocean with a bravery that is highest when true Christian faith is strongest. This is not fatalism nor irresponsible recklessness. It is rather the blessing which comes from the assurance that the Redeemer who died for us now lives for us and with us, constantly ready to protect us.

Sometimes, of course, it may be God's inscrutable will that we fall in life's battle. Rather than accuse our Father of cruelty, question His ways, drop into unbelief or snarling blasphemy, we need the faith which guarantees that *"whether we live . . . or die, we are the Lord's"* and which assures us that *"all things,"* even the most terrifying disasters the war may produce, *"work together for good to them that love God."* Deep-rooted reliance is required to believe that the losses this war may bring will become spiritual gain for those who are Christ's. But the Almighty has compassion on us in this respect too. He assures us, *"What I do thou knowest not now; but thou shalt know hereafter."* In heaven's hallowed bliss when we come to claim our prepared place in the many mansions—and all that we need for a title to our portion in the Father's house is this personal trust in the Lord Jesus— we will be able to survey God's marvelous dealings with us. The mists will clear, and as we see the harmony in the design of life He has helped us weave, there will be no more tears nor sorrows. We will exult, *"He hath done all things well!"*

It is to this faith in the redeeming, comforting, sustaining Christ that we pledge these broadcasts anew in an hour of crisis for the American nation. With God's help we will continue to preach nothing but His Word and to apply it to our multiplied needs. We are planning to bring these Gospel messages to the military youth in ever-widening range. Our transcriptions are being heard on certain battleships and at land stations.

We must send out the message of salvation, life, hope, and a blessed eternity in the Lord Jesus Christ with greater force and penetration. Stand beside us, then, as we begin our wartime broadcasting with the plea· "America, turn to Christ!" and the prayer "Christ, turn Thy mercies to America!" For in Jesus, our God and Redeemer, there is pardon, peace, and power—for the nation, for the church, for every believing heart.—God grant you this saving faith, for the Savior's sake. Amen.![60]

In the next address, which gave the title to one of his books, W.A.M. covered both a Good Friday theme, as well as the supportive and patriotic relationship between church and state. Many of his sermons in the early '40s, as might be expected, drew illustrations from World War II, and the following opener in 1942 would be typical.

For Christ and Country

"If thou let this Man go, thou art not Caesar's friend."—John 19:12

"Render . . . unto Caesar the things which are Caesar's and unto God the things that are God's!"—Matthew 22:21

During the past few days many of you have read newspaper dispatches which told how Japanese troops, landing on New Guinea, were guided on their march across the island by American missionaries. I for one simply do not believe such reports! To start with, these cables were based only on second- and third-hand sources. Besides, no modern invasion army needs missionary guides; long before the war started, the Japanese undoubtedly had accurate maps of this territory. Above all, true ministers of Jesus Christ are uncompromisingly loyal to the government under which they work. They have but one consuming purpose: to serve their fellow-men by bringing them the Gospel. They want to keep out of war and follow the pathway of peace. Yet they do not hesitate to withstand enemies when the souls and bodies of their charges are at stake. A Lutheran worker in China, for example, a young man who only a few years ago studied at our theological seminary in St. Louis, had to take charge of our divinity school in Hankow after the Japanese occupied the city. When the victorious Nipponese troops started to manhandle villagers near Hankow, five hundred women and girls fled to the enclosed seminary compound for refuge. By day and by night the wily invaders sought to scale the walls and capture the women. But our young missionary faced enemy bayonets and the threat of bombardment to protect these refugees. By God's blessing and his bravery the five hundred women not only escaped rape and ruin, but during the weeks of siege many of them learned to know the Lord Jesus.

Protesting against every slanderous claim that Christians are unpatriotic, that the Gospel is a creed of disloyalty, I want to show you today with the Spirit's help that the Christian's resolution always is:

For Christ and Country!

To this end we shall study the practical, present-day lessons contained in these two passages, St. John, chapter nineteen, verse twelve: *"If thou let this Man go, thou art not Caesar's friend";* and

St. Matthew, chapter twenty-two, verse twenty-one: *"Render unto Caesar the things which are Caesar's and unto God the things that are God's!"*

Christians Have Been Loyal to Their Country

Through the trial and conviction of our Lord men who previously had despised each other became friends and dropped their enmity as they united in crucifying Christ. Herod and Pontius Pilate had long been political rivals; yet on that first Good Friday, as each played his role in condemning Jesus, their mutual dislike vanished. Although two opposing factions, the Pharisees and the Sadducees, clashed in the religious life of Jerusalem, the desire to spill the Savior's blood made them forget their deep-rooted differences. Various cliques could be found in the Sanhedrin, the council of Christ's own countrymen; nevertheless, when Caiaphas asked them for their verdict concerning Jesus, without a single dissenting vote they cried, *"He is worthy of death!"*

More than satanic agreement, however, can be found in these actions. After Pilate had repeatedly pronounced Jesus innocent and the Roman governor seemed on the verge of setting the Savior free, the priests' diabolical craftiness became evident. They began to pose as patriots, and knowing Pilate's weakest spot, bluntly warned him, *"If thou let this Man go, thou art not Caesar's friend."* The mention of Caesar, the mighty Tiberius, was a threat that could bring fear into anyone's heart, particularly to the soul of a cheap politican like Pilate. With a record none too clean, he realized that if the citizens of Jerusalem ever formulated charges against him, the days of his official power would probably be at an end. Besides, one of his influential friends at Tiberius' court had just been convicted of treason, and even now the emperor's secret agents might be mingling in disguise among the crowd before Pilate's palace to investigate his loyalty. It was partly to protect himself, then, that against his own conscience, against all the evidence, against his wife's warning, Pilate listened attentively to these prearranged charges advanced in sham patriotism by the hypocrite temple officials.

No fair and honest judge could have found in the suffering Christ a foe of Caesar. Jesus was no one's enemy; He loved those who spurned Him and was ready to lay down His life for the heartless mob that was screaming: *"Crucify Him! Crucify Him!"* He was actually to give Himself into death for the leprous souls of those priests, for Pilate, even for Emperor Tiberius, a ruthless wretch, guilty of indescribable debauch. The false testimony, the malicious perjury, the scheming malice had not been able to prove that Jesus was anyone's adversary. On the contrary, Pilate, the rabbis, and the rabble should have recognized Christ as the greatest Benefactor of humanity ever to walk the pathways of Palestine. This Christ an enemy, Caesar's rival, a competitor with the Roman dominion? He did not have enough physical strength left to oppose even a child; for only a few moments before He had been tortured by scourging. The Gospel writers pass hurriedly over the horror of that suffering, a punishment so terrifying that often as the leather lashes, pointed with lead or spikes, lacerated the back, chest, sometimes even the face, the victim collapsed, a bleeding mass of torn flesh. No wonder Pilate, with open contempt for the Savior's accusers, twice placed the pale, staggering Christ before the bloodthirsty mob crying, first, *"Behold the Man!"* and then, *"Behold your King!"* He must have felt that His abject misery could soften even their granite hearts with the feeling of compassion that jungle savages sometimes seem to show.

When the Savior's persecutors told Pilate that he could not be a friend of Caesar if he refused to sentence their prisoner to the cross, they implied that Christ was a public enemy of the Roman state. They lied, of course. They knew well enough, these priestly hypocrites, that only three days before they had tried to trap Jesus with the question *"Is it lawful to give tribute unto Caesar?"* and He had answered uncompromisingly, *"Render . . . unto Caesar the things which are Caesar's!"* They lied because they must have recalled how when popular opinion, swollen to high-pitch enthusiasm, sought to crown Christ king, He had declined such honor and immediately escaped this fanatical homage. So in mock patriotism they screamed out their malicious charges against Jesus, whose record was completely flawless, and almost in the same breath demanded the release of Barabbas, convicted by the courts of open revolt against the authorities.

The same falsehood, in principle, branding Christ and His followers as opponents of the state, has been repeated through the ages. Soon after St. Paul was beheaded as hostile to the empire, not only the Roman rabble but also the upper classes accused the Christians of hating the human race. Nero blamed the first believers

180

in the capital for setting Rome on fire; and although even Latin writers expressed their doubt that the odious Christians were really guilty, yet the despised disciples were covered with pitch or saturated in oil, nailed to pine-wood pillars, then lighted and burned alive. Such persecutions continued until the beginning of the fourth century, the rule of Diocletian and his coregent Galerius, a second Nero. These two tyrants, who called themselves gods and claimed divine honors, tortured and killed aged men, nursing mothers, tender children—all on the false charge that these Christians were enemies of the state. Either reject Christ and worship the emperor, or forfeit your Roman citizenship, your property, your life—that was the choice placed before these early believers. To the honor of their faith let it be said that many of them, innocent of every crime against their government, accepted the pains of martyrdom rather than deny their Lord.

Even after the Christian faith was securely enthroned in Europe, the same vicious calumny continued. No more hideous records exist in the annals of the human race than the black chapters dealing with the destruction of the Waldensians and the Albigensians. These industrious, thrifty people in northern Italy and southern France were savagely assaulted by heavily armed regiments of soldiers, killed by the thousands. Why? They were accused of treason. On what count? The Waldensians wanted to read the Bible in their own language and serve Christ in the light of Scriptural doctrine. Nor has the human race dropped to deeper depravity than in the massacre of the Huguenots. Their leader, Admiral Coligny, was a man of notable loyalty to France; they themselves were God-fearing, thrifty, industrious people. However, because they insisted on reading the Bible in their own language, worshiping God according to its truth, they were branded as foes of the French king. It was maliciously claimed that in their church services they secretly plotted to overthrow the state. This was a lie, of course, but its falsity did not save tens of thousands from being cut down in one of the cruelest carnages men have ever witnessed.

Not only in bygone generations but also today, when the power and blessing of the Christian faith should be clearly manifest, the same groundless accusation persists that the Old and New Testament oppose national interests. In Germany Nazi critics of the church berate the Gospel not merely as weak and effeminate but also as directly contrary to their country's welfare. They continue the blasphemy of Friedrich Nietzsche, who wrote: "I call Christianity the one great curse . . . the one indelible blot upon the achievement of man." Don't try to laugh away statements like this by claiming that Nietzsche was insane or that the United States is not concerned with him! A Kansas publisher recently reissued the German philosopher's attack on the church in a cheap fifty-cent edition, glorified as "a great liberating work," and asked the masses in our own country to study it, asserting, "All culture, all scholarship, all progressive thought goes to support the indictment of Christianity which Nietzsche made."

Similar slander is being taught in certain American colleges and universities. Bertrand Russell, whose lectures are compulsory for some public schoolteachers in New York City, declared, "I say quite deliberately that the Christian religion as organized in its churches has been and still is the principal enemy of moral progress in the world." One shudders to think what the future will bring if tomorrow's leaders, the college men and young women of today, turn these destructive theories into practice.

More dangerous, however, is the unmistakable spread of atheistic Communism. Well known is Karl Marx's slogan: "Religion is the opiate of the people." He held that no nation can be really happy until religion has been abolished. Frederick Engels, co-founder of Communism, asserted, "There is no room for either God or a ruler," and he urged a thoroughgoing campaign to root out every creed. Lenin cried: "We must fight religion! . . . Religion must be abolished! The best country is a godless country." Lunatcharsky, educational expert of the Communists, admitted: "We hate Christianity and Christians. Even the best of them must be regarded among our worst enemies." A conservative scholar estimates that 1,860,000 Christians, regarded as enemies of their government, were slaughtered in a single year, 1918. American church members cannot close their eyes to the growing specter of Communism and collectivism. To my mind it constitutes one of the major menaces of tomorrow; we should use every means at our disposal to counteract its growth within our boundaries.

As the Savior's accusers lied when they told Pilate, *"If thou let this Man go, thou art not Caesar's friend,"* so Communists lie when they label our faith a national foe. Wherever Christ's Gospel reigns, the power of idolatry and paganism has been broken, tyranny and brutality checked, polygamy and divorce restricted, women and children elevated, the home and family firmly established, slavery and oppression abolished, labor and industry exalted, ignorance and superstition banished, schools and colleges multiplied, the sick and the needy supplied, hospitals and orphanages fostered, and a thousand more blessings otherwise impossible systematically promoted. Without the influence of the Gospel there would be no permanently free nation on the face of the earth today. The faith Christ gave the world is truly *"the salt of the earth,"* a preservative against internal decay.

You do not have to look for proof. Right here in our own country there is a vast demonstration of the building power exercised by faith. The United States was settled, not by Communists, freethinkers, atheists, but by Christians. The charters of our colonies were not sealed in the name of Buddha, Zoroaster, Moses, Lao Tse, but in the name of the Lord Jesus. Each of the thirteen colonies had a Biblical foundation, and each revered the Scriptures as divine authority. The Supreme Court of the United States has officially stated, "This is a Christian nation," not in the sense, of course, that we have an official religion or that the country does not tolerate all creeds, but because, as the highest court explains, the founding fathers, the original charters, the early practice throughout the country were distinctly Christian. Our blessings come from the Bible, from the Savior, from His Gospel. The reverses of the last years stem from the neglect of Christianity and the rejection of its truth.

The loyalty of the church and its deep-rooted patriotism are not loud and boisterous but sincere and effective. True pastors do not preach politics or engage in impressive demonstrations to attract public attention. In a quiet, unassuming way they occupy themselves with strengthening men's souls and thus build our spiritual defenses. The Christian workman who goes about his daily task in a quiet, unnoticed manner, who puts in a full day's honest labor, lives frugally, can mean more for the welfare of the United States than many a limelight orator who makes his own money by shrewdness and does not care how he spends other people's. A God-fearing mother who sacrifices herself to bring up her sons and daughters *"in the nurture and admomition of the Lord"* gives more to America in God's sight than some of the career women who do not want children, so that they can live public, applauded lives, unrestricted by families. The church member who saves defense stamps until he can buy an $18.75 bond may be a better patriot than the godless millionaire who buys the maximum quota simply for an investment.

Even by measurable standards, however, the Christians' support of their government is outstanding. The largest single group in the present United States Army, Navy, Marine and Air Corps is made up of church members. The first soldier in the AEF to step on European soil was an active Lutheran from Hutchinson, Minnesota. This loyalty, of course, is of the highest type because it is not a blind, unconditional allegiance. Our cry is not: "My country, right or wrong!" (for no follower of the Savior can ever be in favor of anything wrong), but: "My country, may she always be right! But if she is ever wrong, God help me make her right!"

Christians Must Also Be Loyal to Their God

Now, because no religion except the Gospel, no God other than the Trinity revealed by Christ can help in the emergency before us, we can fulfill our highest responsibility to the nation and ourselves by pledging allegiance to Christ and country. If during the storm and trial of the Civil War Abraham Lincoln could say, "Intelligence, patriotism, Christianity, and a firm reliance on Him who has never forsaken this favored land are still competent to adjust in the best way all our present difficulty," how eager we should be to follow the Savior's pointed direction: *"Render . . . unto God the things that are God's"* and to accompany devotion to our country with complete dedication to our heavenly Father! Fellow citizens and friends beyond our borders, our greatest need and yours, in Canada, in Mexico, wherever you may be, is the faith which enthrones our Lord in the hearts of the multitudes. Wherever Christ disappears, forces hostile to true Americanism always rise. When the flowers of Gospel faith are permitted to wilt and die, the poisonous weeds of godlessness and tyranny begin to flourish.

Therefore my appeal asks first of all that you accept Jesus as the Son of God whose atoning death on the cross grants you, without any charge, the assurance that even your scarlet transgressions have been removed forever; the pledge that life after death, heaven's joys after earth's sorrows are granted by His divine promise and power. Whatever may have kept you from Christ up till this moment, whether it be personal pride, the destructive self-righteousness which makes you thank God you are better than most people; or whether it be love of sin, greed for money, lust of the flesh, be fair enough to hear what Jesus offers and to ask yourself if there is any real reason why you dare refuse His matchless mercy.

Now, through Jesus we have not only this complete forgiveness, joy of life instead of depressing worry, spiritual strength to withstand temptation and overcome evil, eagerness to turn from self and serve one's fellow-men, power to triumph over all trials but also—and this is the thought I would emphasize—the power to be good citizens, to build the moral and spiritual defense of our country, to help increase that righteousness which exalts any nation.

When the Lord Jesus is securely enthroned within your heart, you will be able to apply the divine power Christian faith offers for helping this country. You will understand why in this emergency the cry must be: "Back to God! Back to Christ! Back to the Bible! Back to the Christian Church!"; why our heavenly Father wants a contrite, repentant, sin-hating people in the United States. You, on your knees in penitence and humility before the Almighty, can invoke Heaven's strength. Don't ever lose sight of the divine mercy that if the Lord was ready to spare even Sodom and Gomorrah, those indescribably vile cities, had there been only ten in their midst who did seek Him, then, if it be His purpose, His favor can be extended to any land in which masses of Christians implore His mercy. Blessed by the Lord Jesus, as a true American citizen, you have the promise of answered prayer for yourself and your penitent nation; but always remember that the Almighty answers our pleas in His own way and at His appointed hour.

Let the worst come, here is the cry for this crisis, the resolution for every American, the pledge for every Christian, the declaration by which true victory is ours. For Christ and country! God give every one of you in full measure the faith and courage to speak that double dedication to our glorious Savior and our God-blessed homeland! Amen.[61]

The thrust of the next address from 1942 is evangelism and Christian witness. It also focuses on the personality whom W.A.M. revered next after Jesus Himself: St. Paul.

Almost Persuaded

"Agrippa said unto Paul, Almost thou persuadest me to be a Christian."—Acts 26:28

In the early part of the sixteenth century two men, in different countries of Europe, each named Martin, came to the same glorious knowledge that they were saved not by their good works but by grace through faith in the Lord Jesus Christ. With the same marvelous opportunity of making that message of mercy known to their fellow-men, what did they do? The one Martin, fearing public disfavor, wrote these words on parchment: "Oh, most merciful Christ, I know that I am saved only by the merit of Thy blood. Holy Jesus, I love Thee!" The he secretly hid the parchment behind a stone in the wall of his chamber. Hardly one of ten thousand has ever heard of him and one in a million may know the details of his life. He was Martin of Basel, and it was only accidentally that, several hundred years after his death, his hidden testimony to Christ was discovered. Meanwhile the victorious promise of full justification by faith, which he in fear had concealed, was heard through the civilized world. Why? The other Martin, as soon as the light of saving grace illumined the night of his despair over sin, threw caution to the winds. He cried, "My Lord has confessed me before men; I will not shrink from confessing my Lord before princes and kings." Impelled by the love of his Savior, he used every means within his grasp—pulpit, lecture hall, printing press, schools, universities, churches, music—to spread the Gospel of salvation. That second Martin, I hardly need tell you, was Luther, the mighty Reformer, from whose world-moving testimony to Christ we date our modern era.—Martin of Basel was *almost* a mighty man of God. Few men in all history have even been offered the opportunity within his grasp. Yet he failed, as some of you have failed, because of fear and weak faith.

Yet a tragedy still more grievous than such refusal to exalt Jesus is the unwillingness even to accept Him, though the Spirit of God testifies that He is the Atonement and Redemption of our souls. Modern Chinese history knows two men who illustrate this truth. Both were officers serving their country. Both were well educated. Both had become interested in Christianity. When one was invited to make a decision for Christ, he told the missionary: "I'll see you tomorrow morning at eleven o'clock." Before that same day closed, he was assassinated. This man, apparently only a few hours distant from Christ, yet in reality an eternity from him, was Admiral Chen. The other national leader was urged by his mother-in-law to read the Bible and pray God for enlightenment. He followed her advice, and his private, early morning devotions brought the Holy Spirit into his heart and finally led him all the way to the Lord. That convert to Christ for whom *"almost"* was not enough is Generalissimo Chiang Kai-Shek, leader of 400,000,000 Chinese.

Because indecision, the refusal to accept salvation now, this coming close to the Kingdom but stopping short of the final step, is a soul peril which hangs heavy over many, I want to show you the folly and tragedy of being

Almost Persuaded

–*"almost"* but not completely convinced—that Christ is your atoning Lord. To learn this vital lesson, read in the Book of Acts (chapter twenty-six, verse twenty-eight), *"Agrippa said unto Paul, Almost thou persuadest me to be a Christian"!*

The Folly of "Almost" and Its Cause

Few scenes even in the swift-moving New Testament history are more powerful than the account from which this text has been chosen. St. Paul, mightiest of Christ's missionaries, had been imprisoned at Caesarea for two long years, guilty—O blessed guilt!—of preaching the reconciling Gospel and of showing his countrymen how the Old Testament prophecies were fulfilled in Christ. The governor at Caesarea must have believed his prisoner innocent of the fraudulent charges; but shrewd, graft-loving politican that he was, he thought he could demand a price for a release. After two years he was succeeded by the new governor, Festus. Paul's case was brought before him, and convinced of the apostle's innocence, Fetsus arranged for King Herod Agrippa, who ruled a section of Palestine through the favor of the Roman conquerors and was visiting Caesarea, to hear Paul.

What a striking spectacle ensued! With royal pomp and elaborate ceremonies King Agrippa, his sister Bernice, Festus, the governor, Caesarea's military and civic leaders, royalty and officialdom were assembled amid the display of palace luxury to hear Paul's defense. Not often have enthroned kings thus faced Christ's ambassadors. Throughout the centuries men who have wielded immense might have often satanically misused this control because they have spurned the Christian faith and utterly rejected our Lord. Oh, that in today's world, leaders of human affairs would take time to consider and apply the Savior's teaching!

God give you who know the Savior's love the same desire to testify to His grace which moved St. Paul before that impressive assembly! You may never have the apostle's opportunity of speaking to kings, but you can bear witness to others. If you are a maid in a non-Christian home, you may be able to speak of Christ to your employers, courteously but courageously, as Paul did. An unnamed Hebrew servant girl, as the fifth chapter of Second Kings tells her story, directed mighty Naaman, the commander-in-chief of the Syrian armies, to God's prophet for healing and salvation. If you work in an office, factory, store, you can tactfully but determinedly acknowledge your faith in Christ before those in higher positions.

Even more impressive than the fact that St. Paul addressed this royal assembly is the way in which he brought his message. We can almost see him there, erect, majestic, as he looks into Herod Agrippa's face or turns his penetrating gaze to the others seated before him. His eyes flash. His hands move in emphatic gestures. Words roll from his lips. Conviction speaks in his sentences. God's Spirit fires him with startling eloquence. Festus, the governor, unable to explain the power blazing from the apostle's words, interrupts him to cry out loudly, *"Paul, thou art beside thyself; much learning doth make thee mad."* But no one has ever been saner than Paul in that moment. He *knew* whereof he spoke. No "perhaps" or "maybe," no theories, guesses, or wishful thinking mark his defense. His words were uttered with personal conviction.

Paul went back to Moses and the prophets. He delivered a Scripture-grounded, Scripture-supported, Scripture-exalting sermon. In this respect, as has well been said, Paul, the preacher for kings, remains the king of preachers. God give us men in American pulpits who draw their sermons from the Bible, the whole Bible, and nothing but the Bible; who speak with authority because they declare, *"Thus saith the Lord!"* During this emergency help us keep our churches *churches,* that is, houses of the Lord, where God's Word is explained and applied! We have public forums at which political views may be aired; legislative chambers for the discussion of new laws and social codes; libraries where the latest books are reviewed; places of amusement for dispensing humor; college classrooms for expounding new theories; but for soul guidance and the spiritual defense of millions in this nation today we should guard our churches as God's sanctuaries where His Word, not man's, rules.

Note especially, however, that throughout the whole discourse Paul's purpose was to win Agrippa and the others in that palace for Christ! The Savior's suffering, redemptive death, and resurrection, reconciling the whole world to God, formed the climax of his entire plea, the startling truth that made Festus, the governor, charge him with madness. Today too, every local evangelist must expect to be denounced if he preaches the full, free message of the Savior's redemption. Let him be denounced! On the great day of His appearing Christ will bring those who have been faithful unto the end to His Father with the declaration: *"Well done, thou good and faithful servant!"* St. Paul could not deliver a sermon without asking a decision for Christ, and neither should you and I in any way neglect or ignore Him, the blessed Foundation of our faith. A hundred other activities can crowd into our religious work, but the one purpose of every truly Christian church is to tell all men that without Christ they are hopelessly lost in their sins, but with faith in the same Jesus they are eternally redeemed from their transgressions.

Nor should we overlook the personal, direct force of the apostle's plea to the whole assembly. Six times he speaks straight to King Agrippa, and though it is not given to me now to look into the face of everyone in this audience who has not received Christ, I want you to accept these words as directed to you individually. Your heavenly Father wants *you* to be saved. As St. Paul put this pointed question before his royal judge, *"King Agrippa, believest thou the prophets?"* and hoped the ruler would answer, "Yes, I believe the prophets and the Messiah of whom they have prophesied," so I ask you: "Do you believe the Bible and the Savior of whom the Scripture testifies? Do you acclaim this Christ as your own Redeemer?"

God grant that you give a better answer than Agrippa's reply: *"Almost thou persuadest me to be a Christian"!* Although this remark has been variously interpreted, his words certainly imply that a man has to be persuaded to become a believer, and yet, as a matter of fact, discipleship with Jesus Christ is the most marvelous blessing we can ever experience. You do not have to convince a drowning sailor to grasp a life line. You do not need a long, elaborate discussion to show a man that he ought to step from the path of an onrushing automobile, argue a starving man into accepting food, a lost traveler into following a forest ranger to safety. Why, then, must people be persuaded to accept that which is incomparably greater than the mightiest benefits man can ever give his fellow-man?

If people today would only take time to study our Christian faith and recognize the help it imparts, our churches would be overcrowded, the Bible universally read, the name of Jesus not abused in profanity but spoken with reverence. For He answers all questions disturbing to the mind and lifts every burden weighing heavy on our souls. Christian trust acknowledges that we are not accidental atoms of humanity, changed by chance from a lower brute stage, but creatures of God, the masterpiece of His almighty wisdom. Christian truth reveals whither we are bound. It assures us that we have been freed from the consequences of our sins by the suffering and dying of the Lord Jesus as our Substitute.

When we are Christ's and He is ours, we can rejoice in affliction. If all else seems dark and hopeless, we have light and assurance in the victorious truth that *"with God nothing shall be impossible."* His limitless love overnight can change tears into gladness. You ought to accept Jesus without any lengthy appeal and repeated plea, for He alone solves the mystery of the grave and answers your question, "What becomes of me after death?" While other creeds refuse to reply or offer vague, deceptive theories, Jesus declares with His divine authority: *"I am the Resurrection and the Life; he that believeth in Me, though he were dead, yet shall he live. And whosoever liveth and believeth in Me shall never die."* He promises world-weary believers, *"I go to prepare a place for you,"* and His holy Word reveals, as far as the mortal mind can grasp, the glory in a heaven of unspeakable bliss, a celestial radiance beyond compare; eternal companionship with the redeemed before the throne of the living God; heaven without tears and toil, without agony and grief, without pain and loss. You should be willing to give up everything you possess, sell everything you own to make these blessings of Christian faith yours. But when I tell you once more that His love is granted you freely by the magnificence of His mercy; that this redemption is yours, wholly, unconditionally, assuredly, by faith, why does every one of you not agree that instead of arguing whether or not you will accept Christ, you should fall on your knees and cry out, "O Jesus, by the promise of Thy love, as by Thy bitter suffering and death on the cross, receive me, wash me, cleanse me, make me Thine forever"?

Why was it, then, that Agrippa came close to confessing Christ yet failed to take the last, decisive step? The Book of Acts gives no explanation for Agrippa's action, but his motives were doubtless the same as those now influencing many people. Perhaps he feared the consequences of confessing Christ. It meant that he would be scorned by his royal friends. He would have to substitute faith for reason, and this he was unwilling to do. Becoming a Christian meant changing his life; and because he was living in sin, because he condoned immorality, he would not pay the price. Accepting Christianity might have involved the loss of his royal office, being stripped of gold, silver, precious stones; and he was too selfish to take up that cross, as Jesus commanded.

Are not these the very stumbling blocks which keep people from turning to Christ today? They feel inwardly that the Bible is the truth. They cannot deny or disprove its statements. They have a good word and a kind thought for Jesus. No one else who ever trod the face of the earth was His equal, they admit. They see that Christianity works. Yet in the decisive moment, when they are to declare Jesus their Savior and say without reservation, "I am a believer," it is either the dread of ridicule, the fear of loss, the love of sin, the refusal to live as Christians, or the reluctance to take reason captive—which helps make them deny Christ, forfeit their hope of salvation, close the gates of heaven against themselves.

The Sorrow of "Almost" and How to Avoid It

For, to be only *"almost"* persuaded really means to be lost. *"Almost"* is never enough. The airplane that *"almost"* clears the mountaintop is destroyed. The city that has *"almost"* enough defenses will be captured. The reprieve from the death sentence which comes *"almost"* in time, only a minute late, will not save the prisoner. "Dereliction of duty," neglect of watchfulness, such as reported at Pearl Harbor, has a spiritual counterpart when modern men and women are only *"almost"* prepared to resist the onslaughts of treacherous enemies.

It is not enough to call the Lord Jesus the most outstanding Person of the ages, the most unselfish Hero men have ever known, the greatest Benefactor our race has ever had. You must go all the way and, pointing to the Crucified, say, "He is my God and my Savior!" It is not enough to hear the story of His atoning love and then wonder whether or not there is forgiveness for your transgressions. You must take the final step and believe that you too are

191

saved, since no iniquities are too abhorrent to be removed by the compassionate Redeemer. It is not enough to think you can be saved provided you earn your entrance into heaven by a long list of penances, good works, and self-denials; you are *"justified by faith, without the deeds of the Law."* Jesus paid your entire ransom from sin, hell, and death's despair.

Herod Agrippa missed the opportunity of becoming a Christian, and never, as far as we know, did he embrace the faith. And finally he faded from the historical records of his day—an insignificant failure. Had he been fully persuaded to acclaim Jesus his Savior, his name would have been honored by hundreds of millions throughout succeeding centuries. What is of far greater importance, Jesus would have acknowledged him before His throne. Unknowingly he missed the greatest moment in his life.

Some years ago a young man of prominent social standing in Philadelphia killed a friend. He was arrested, tried, convicted, and sentenced to death. Powerful influences soon sought to have Governor Pollock commute the sentence, but he refused. Finally the mother of the condemned murderer journeyed to Harrisburg to plead with a mother's devotion for her wayward child. Governor Pollock told her that he could not change the sentence, then turned to his secretary and said, "One thing I can do; I will see the boy and prepare him for death." So he went to the cell and without revealing his identity spoke to the young man of God's promises in Christ to every penitent sinner, prayed with him, heard the condemned youth say that he was not afraid to die, and then left. A few moments later the prisoner called the warden to ask, "Who was that man who just now left my cell?" In surprise the warden exclaimed, "Why, he was Governor Pollock." "O warden," the prisoner cried, "the governor in my cell—and I didn't know it! If only you had told me he was the governor, I would have thrown my arms about him and never let him leave the cell until he had given me my pardon!" One incomparably greater than any governor now stands before you with full pardon for all your transgressions, offering you the commutation of that terrifying sentence which Scripture places on every unforgiven wrong when it warns: *"The soul that sinneth, it shall die."* God grant that you will not permit Jesus to pass out of your lives without receiving the joy of your salvation!

This may be the last broadcast you will hear, the final appeal for Christ ever directed to you. Don't make the fatal error of remaining an *"almost"* persuaded man or woman until death makes it impossible for you to be altogether persuaded! You need Christ for this life, particularly in view of the uncertainties of the conflict years now upon us. Most urgently, however, you need Christ for the next world, since His own words insist: *"I am the Way, the Truth, and the Life. No man cometh unto the Father but by Me!"*

Come to Him in His Word, you who have neglected or despised the Gospel! Take the sacred Book, read it without prejudice, and let God's Spirit work in your hearts! His divine Volume has turned many a skeptic into a saint, removed the *"almost"* and made it an "altogether"! M.L. Bautain, a French professor of philosophy, was an unbeliever until he studied the Scriptures. And then he wrote this remarkable confession: "A single Book has saved me, but that Book is not of human origin. Long had I despised it, long had I deemed it a classbook for the credulous and ignorant, until, having investigated the Gospel of Christ with an ardent desire to ascertain its truth or falsity, I found that its pages proffered to my inquiries the sublimest knowledge. Faith, hope, and love were enkindled in my bosom; and every advancing step strengthened me in the conviction that the morals of this book are superior to human morals as its oracles are superior to human opinions." In the same way the study of your Bible, the preaching of God's Word in true churches, the help of a real Christian pastor, your prayers in Jesus' name can take you, the *"almost"* persuaded, and by the outpouring of Heaven's highest grace help you join the mighty apostle in declaring: *"I am persuaded that neither death nor life nor angels nor principalities nor powers nor things present nor things to come nor height nor depth nor any other creature shall be able to separate us from the love of God, which is in Christ Jesus our Lord."* God grant that today many of you will come all the way to Christ! Amen.[62]

Finally W.A.M. took Psalm 23—most famous of them all—and related it to John 10 in this 1943 address, which is cross-sectional rather than seasonal or expressing a particular thrust. In expounding the pastoral theme he easily mixed theology with veterinary science.

The Lord Jesus Is My Shepherd

"I am the Good Shepherd; the Good Shepherd giveth His life for the sheep."—John 10:11

Some time ago a Swarthmore College professor told a religious conference that the Bible has outlived much of its usefulness, that it must be modernized, rewritten. "Take the Twenty-third Psalm, for example," he said, selecting the most frequently memorized verses of Scripture. "People who live in the city simply do not know the meaning of *'The Lord is my Shepherd!'* We must therefore scrap the Twenty-third Psalm and put its thought into modern language: 'The Lord is my automobile's low gear to help me in climbing hard hills. The Lord is my antiseptic in times of dangerous epidemics. The Lord is sunlight in my room, bringing me the health of ultraviolet rays.'" I shall not bother you with his other emendations.

Remarkably, however, this radical changing of the Twenty-third Psalm has boomeranged and been utterly discredited only a dozen years later by the agonies of war. A few days ago newspapers told the story of Vern Haugland, noted Associated Press foreign correspondent, who was forced to bail out of a crippled bomber over the New Guinea jungles. During forty-three days of groping through the trackless wilderness, over steep, jagged cliffs, through foodless weeks, in which he lost half his weight and developed arm sores and leg ulcers, what sustained him with unshakable courage? No atheistic boasting that *he* was the master of his fate, that, though his head was bloody, it was unbowed! The intrepid reporter, after receiving the Silver Star from General MacArthur, wrote his family: "I'd never have made it but for God's care and the prayers I know were being said for me. I often repeated the passage, *'The Lord is my Shepherd; I shall not want.'* It was marvelous how it worked; I would be unable to go one step further, and then I would remember, *'I shall not want,'* and sure enough, there would be some berries or chewable grass or a creek with good water just ahead."

About the same time, the daily press also reported, Secretary of the Navy Knox was so concerned about the secret movements of our troops to North Africa that for several nights he could hardly sleep. What finally gave him rest and assurance? Not a detective story—apparently the favorite reading material of many public figures—but, as Secretary Knox told an American Legion audience, the Twenty-third Psalm read to him by his wife. He said, "I finally dozed off with the words . . . echoing in my ears, *'The Lord is my Shepherd; I shall not want.'*"

Again, President Roosevelt has just issued a proclamation calling for two days of prayer to God, and in the climax of his appeal industrialists who profiteer by the shedding of human blood, dictators who play fast and loose with human lives have repeatedly incited the masses to hurl themselves into brutal conflict. Lying he asks the American people to keep a certain passage in mind. What is it—a quotation from the Atlantic Charter? A new promise of victory? No! Instead the President proclaims, "I recommend that all of us bear in mind this great psalm, *'The Lord is my Shepherd; I shall not want.'*" Thus a war correspondent, the man entrusted with the destiny of hundred thousands of American men at sea, and the chief executive of the nation found rest despite the present-day crisis in the very psalm rejected a dozen years ago by a modernist professor.

No matter who you are, this glorious Shepherd Psalm can similarly bring you guiding strength and send you out into a world of war and woe with peace in your heart, provided—and this is often overlooked—you understand its deathless words as they have been explained by that perfect, sinless Teacher of all teachers, Jesus Christ. In the tenth chapter of St. John's Gospel and its eleventh verse that blessed Savior, referring to the words, *"The Lord is my Shepherd,"* assures us in our text, *"I am the Good Shepherd; the Good Shepherd giveth His life for the sheep."* May we (every one of us, O Holy Spirit) look to our royal Redeemer, and as we declare in firm faith,

"The Lord Jesus Is My Shepherd,"

find eternal blessings in this promise of grace and glory!

Every One of Us Needs Divine Guidance

To measure fully the meaning and comfort of Scripture's many shepherd passages, we must understand how clearly the weaknesses of sheep suggest people's frailties. First of all, sheep are easily misguided. Many stockyards employ a ram or goat—in East St. Louis they call him "Judas"—which stands at the foot of the runway whenever a shipment of sheep arrives. These new animals, fresh from prairie farms, accept his leadership and follow him into the killing pens. But as soon as the gates of the pens are closed, "Judas" is not to be found among those assembled for slaughter. Is this not a striking picture of humanity as it is often misled? Every century of history is marked by deep sorrows which have come from blind obedience to selfish leaders. War lords who delight in slaughter, teachers of religion have directed multitudes from heaven to hell. False prophets and false Christs have repeatedly made their victims suffer anguish, despair, excruciating death.

Many of you are following destructive direction. In swift, blind affection you married someone whose heart was estranged from God, and as a consequence your own faith is weakening. Some of you trusted associates in financial matters, only to be cheated; you shared your confidences with friends, only to be betrayed. You have been lured by the lust of the flesh and are now distressed in your conscience to find yourselves on the road to moral ruin. Others, once firm in the faith, listened to enemies of the Bible who have coaxed you away from church (perhaps because it was no longer large and fashionable enough) into Christless creeds that have no confession of sin and therefore no room for the Redeemer from sin. Every one of us has too often followed Satan instead of the Savior, practiced folly instead of faith. This is Humiliation and Prayer Sunday, the day on which, according to ancient custom, Christians should bow penitently before the Almighty to admit their guilt. Let us make this a nationwide humiliation-and-prayer service, as everyone—and I make no exceptions—kneels in spirit before the just God to confess with the ancient prophet: "'All we like sheep have gone astray,' away from our heavenly Father and the Word of His truth, away from the cross of His Christ and the promise of His pardon. O God, have mercy upon us! O Christ, have mercy upon us! O Holy Spirit, have mercy upon us!"

Not only do sheep readily accept false leadership, but of all domesticated animals they have the poorest sense of direction. In heavy snowstorms they have been known to hurl themselves blindly over cliffs. Most of our world today has also lost its way. God, who has spoken twice to this generation in the sorrow of history's bloodiest wars, is still not recognized and obeyed. We have more atheists in the United States than ever before. Even some who have pledged their loyalty to Christ and His church have been caught in the carnal carousal of these trying times, when they ought to stop and ask themselves: "Where am I? Am I on the pathway to God or on the highway to hell?" As we confess that, like wandering sheep, we have repeatedly lost the way, what better can we do than turn to God and, begging for pardon, plead: "O heavenly Father, have mercy upon us! Guide us aright and teach us to walk in Thy ways!"

Sheep are pitiful creatures also because they often deliberately return to the very dangers from which they have been saved. If the barn in which they are kept catches fire, the flock can be led out to safety only with the utmost difficulty; and usually the sheep try to run back into the flames. Hard as it is to explain this, it is a hundred times harder to account for the fact that human beings, gifted with reason and intelligence, are guilty of a far more serious folly. Recall what has happened within twenty-one years! One war was concluded that cost 37,000,000 lives in slaughter, starvation, and disease—not to mention the financial loss of $350,000,000,000. Yet before another generation arose, humanity with all its culture and scientific achievement led itself back into even more destructive flames of fiery conflict. The principle of this world tragedy is reenacted in individual lives. Christ's Gospel is preached to multitudes who contemptuously turn from His outstretched arms and wilfully reject the message of His surpassing love. Why? Simply because they insist on continuing in their transgressions. They do not want to be rescued from the flames of their passions, their illicit affairs, their hatreds, their evil ways. After they have confessed and renounced their sins, after they have known the grace of Christ, they deliberately hurl themselves back into the ruin of their old, death-dealing vices!

Again, sheep are easily frightened. A clap of thunder can throw a flock into terror. Even a fluttering piece of paper may produce panic among them. How similarly people are agonized into unfounded fright! Beneath the glamor of this pleasure-seeking age, fears gnaw at our peace and composure. For masses these are the years of deep worry and disquieting uncertainty. Nervous breakdowns, mental disorders, suicides, all poisonous fruits of fear, have cursed our age. While Jesus repeatedly seeks to sustain us with His comforting promises: *"Be not afraid"; "My peace I give unto you"; "Let not your heart be troubled,"* too many, spurning His mercy, are endangering their souls, injuring their bodies, reducing the power of their minds by vicious fear.

Besides, we, like sheep, are powerless to defend ourselves, too weak properly to direct our own lives. With all our colleges and universities, our resources and material advances, we are still unable to secure the simplest and most basic of life's blessings. How, for example, can we establish peace on earth and stop men from killing one another by the millions as they have in recent years? By diplomacy? In 1939 Edouard Daladier, French statesman, asserted that his country and Great Britain were "inseparably united even beyond victory." Less than three years later, however, France is at virtual war with England. Can we establish peace by international law if this is completely cast aside whenever selfish interests wish? By a League of Nations when its headquarters are closed and barred during a world conflict? By peace movements when we realize that every endeavor of this kind has failed in the past? By Esperanto, or a universal language? No; it takes more than a common speech to make people live and act in harmony. By education? The world's worst war is being fought when culture has reached its highest level. Now, if people of and by themselves are too weak and powerless to maintain outward peace, how can they establish the inner harmony with God and their consciences, for which we yearn with unsatisfied longing? If some of you cannot get right with your fellow-men, how can you get right with the Almighty?

No, in this age of unparalleled pride and boasting, people are like wandering sheep, deprived of their sense of direction, lost in their own trespasses and sins. It ought not be hard to convince people, with danger and death lurking on all sides for millions of the nation's young men, that our insistent prayer should be: "O God, give me the guidance of a divine Shepherd, who will lead me along the right path and accompany me especially when I *walk through the valley of the shadow of death*!"

Every One of Us Can Have Christ as "The Good Shepherd"

That plea has been marvelously answered by God's grace in Christ. Jesus is not only *a* shepherd for wandering mankind, He is *the* Shepherd, the *"Good Shepherd,"* as He calls Himself in our text for today.

What a wealth of reassuring love in this statement that He, our great and glorious God, is *"the Good Shepherd"!* There was nothing in our sin-stained lives that could deserve His consideration, nothing that could make Him leave His heavenly glory to live for thirty-three years in this selfish, greed-cursed world. Yet all this and much more Jesus, *"the Good Shepherd,"* did for every one of us.

See how the Scriptures repeatedly stress His good and gracious shepherding! He leaves the flock of ninety and nine to go and seek the one stray lamb until He finds it. May that merciful pledge strengthen many who are wandering and lost! We all rejoiced when, after a long search, the United States Navy found Captain

198

Rickenbacker and his companions afloat on a raft in the South Pacific. However, the newspapers make no comment on the far greater rescue by which the Lord Jesus constantly saves those who without Him are eternally lost. For years He has invited you: Come back to God! Be reconciled with your heavenly Father! He sought you while you tried to avoid Him. He found you and pleaded with you when you would have hidden from Him. Today through this broadcast He continues to seek you. How much longer must He plead: *"Come unto Me!" "Follow Me!" "Believe . . . in Me!"*?

Again, Jesus is *"the Good Shepherd"* because He leads us aright. What marvelous assurance to know that in a world of falsehood and error there is an unfailing source of true direction for prosperity and pain, joy and sorrow, life and death itself! No one has ever made a mistake in following Christ; for while the road along which He conducts us may often be hard and steep and stony, it is always the right path. Though it starts with the cross, it always ends with the crown. If you want to rise above the disappointments and failures of a selfish existence, if you want your home to radiate joy and calm, then make His Word your guide! Take time to study His Gospel and apply its saving truth to yourself!

Jesus is *"the Good Shepherd"* also because He knows our weaknesses and is ready to help bear our burdens. If Old Testament prophecy could foresee Him as One who carried the sick sheep and the little lambs in His arms, then how much more should we, who have seen the New Testament fulfillment of His promised support, believe that in every moment of affliction He is at our side to uphold us! Make the most of this heavenly comfort, you to whom life has been a rough pathway through a wilderness of sorrows! Some of you, as you write me, have been languishing on sickbeds for ten, twenty, thirty years! Not a few are weighted down with the heaviness of unfaithfulness, cruelty, abuse, murder in your own households. Still others suffer from a hundred additional sorrows. Though your burdens are crushing, they are never too heavy for Him; though your afflictions are many, they can never be too numerous for His divine help.

Jesus likewise is *"the Good Shepherd"* because He knows His sheep; and, as the text chapter reveals, *"He calleth"* them *"by name."* In the regimentation and mass production of our age, men often lose their identity and become mere numbers. In armies including millions and in countries populated by many tens of millions the individual may count for little or nothing. Do you complain that nobody pays friendly attention or shows real regard for you? Jesus does! He knew you before you were born. He calls all this world to repentance and to faith, but when you hear that invitation, He is summoning you especially, you individually.

Some years ago three American travelers went to the top of Mount Calvary, cut a small piece of wood there and had it made into a walking stick. This they presented to Governor George Briggs of Massachusetts with the words: "We wanted you to know that, when we stood there at Calvary, we thought of you." The Governor thanked them for the gift but added, "I am still more thankful, gentlemen, that there was Another who thought of me there." As Thanksgiving week dawns, have you raised your heart in similar gratitude to Christ? He thought of you when the agonies of Gethsemane almost crushed His soul into death. He thought of you when on that cross He died your death. You can take every promise of God in Christ and write your full name into its pledge. He tells you, *"Fear not . . . I have called thee by thy name; thou art Mine."*

There at Calvary we learn fully that Jesus is *"the Good Shepherd"* because, as He assures us today, He *"giveth His life for the sheep."* His flock will be attacked by ravenous bears, hungry lions, treacherous wolves—foes so powerful that the sheep would be destroyed, were it not for His willingness to protect them. You too are beset by enemies of your soul which seek your destruction. Sin and hell are mobilized against you in a death struggle. You yourself can never overcome them. You are doomed to defeat. But Jesus enters the battle in your behalf, crushes this opposition completely and forever, though He pays for that triumph with His lifeblood. All this happened when at Calvary the Son of God became our all-embracing Sacrifice for sin, the ever-valid Atonement for every sinner. He died that you might be saved. He was crucified for your victory.

Don't be impressed, then, when they tell you that it is out of date and out of fashion to say, *"The Lord is my Shepherd!"* This Shepherd Psalm has been the refuge and strength of God's children in every hour of trial. It was prayed by the martyrs in the first Christian church before they stepped into the Roman arenas to be torn to pieces by wild beasts. It was studied by Bishop John Hooper before he was burned to death in the cruel persecutions under Bloody Mary. It was intoned by Isabel Allison and Marion Narvie, two young girls hanged in 1681 at Edinburgh because of their religion. "Come, Isabel," said Marion, only twenty years old, as they stood on the scaffold, "let us sing the Twenty-third Psalm!" and with *"The Lord is my Shepherd"* on their lips they went to a blessed eternity. Now, this year, you too can have every want supplied, *"green pastures"* for rest and refreshment, *"still waters"* after every hot conflict, guidance for the right path from earth to heaven, if with contrite hearts and confident spirit you say, *"'The Lord'* Jesus *'is my Shepherd.'"*

If you are a sheep in the Savior's flock, you will also remember His words: *"Other sheep I have, which are not of this fold; them also I must bring."* That missionary motif was carved into the gravestone which marks the earthly resting place of David Livingstone, mighty messenger of God. Does your life show a love for souls, a sacred passion for the redemption of your fellow-men? Oh, work and pray that many more from all corners of the earth be brought into Christ's fold! Help us in this far-flung mission of the air as we dedicate our efforts especially to bringing Christ to the nation's armed forces, to gather the Savior's redeemed into the one eternal flock, the church of Christ in earth and heaven! O Jesus, Shepherd of our souls, bring us all to Thee, and keep us in Thy fold forever! Amen.[63]

10
VOICE

Walter A. Maier's postwar sermon themes in the late '40s returned to more traditional motifs, although his concern for the cold war was indicated in such sermon titles as "Must We Fight World War III?" A broadcasting milestone was realized in 1947 with the address, "A Thousand Voices for Our Redeemer's Praise," indicating that the *Lutheran Hour* network had passed the thousand radio station mark. His Jeremiah-like concern for national ills continued too and was reflected in sermons like "The Moral State of the Union," delivered in January 1949.

This year would also be his last. Yet even after his death on January 11, 1950, W.A.M.'s ministry would continue through both pen and voice. Three of his books were published posthumously, and his voice carried on an independent ministry of its own. Already recorded on large transcription discs, his sermons were transferred to 33 r.p.m. records as well as cassette tapes and distributed widely. From time to time these have also been broadcast, sometimes in a regular series. On Sunday mornings KFUO in St. Louis airs a program called *Yesterday's Lutheran Hour,* featuring the Maier sermons from the 1940s.

The last *Lutheran Hour* sermon he personally delivered was on Sunday, December 25, 1949. Typically, it was preceded by a prayer that employed the reverential King James English still used for such petitions at that time.

Blessed Babe of Bethlehem's manger, Thou didst truly bring joy to the world when on the first Christmas Thou wast born for us. Even more, in giving Thyself to us, Thou didst enrich all of us, the poorest, the plainest, the most pain-ridden, with Heaven's highest treasure, pardon for our sins and the promise of Paradise. Oh, grant that above the earthly glitter and glamour, through which many forget Thee on Thy birthday, we may believe the angel message: *"Unto you is born this day in the city of David, a Savior, which is Christ, the Lord,"* and receive Thee in our hearts and homes, ere this day closes, as our Redeemer from eternal ruin, who didst come to cleanse us with Thy blood, our divine Deliverer, incarnate to fulfill the Bible's promise, and our God, with all power in heaven and on earth Thine! Oh, give Thyself now to every searching, sorrow-filled heart, every darkened, unbelieving soul in this mission of the air, so that each of us can join the heavenly host in praising Thee and proclaiming, *"Glory to God in the highest, and on earth peace, goodwill to men!"*

Heaven's Love Lies in the Manger

"If God so loved us, we ought also to love one another."—1 John 4:11

As this broadcast wishes all of you, above everything else, a Christmas filled with the Christ Child's blessing, we ask you to listen to the story of the frontiersman, Hugh Glass. It will do you good, especially if today on Christmas you have hatred in your heart for those who have harmed you!

Hugh Glass was a scout in Major Henry's fur-trapping expedition which set out from St. Louis in the summer of 1823. One day in the northwestern part of South Dakota a huge grizzly attacked Glass, a giant of a man. Though sixty years old and armed with nothing more than a knife, he killed the bear—after one side of Glass' face has been scraped away and other injuries in his mangled body brought him to death's door.

Because the expedition of eighty men could not linger, two

experienced plainsmen were chosen to remain with him until he died. Somehow the man lived, though often unconscious. After five days of waiting, his companions found the delay too tedious and dangerous. They took Glass' few possessions, heartlessly deserted him, and a week later overtook the expedition, reporting that they had given him "a decent burial."

However, Glass had not died. A few mornings after the two men left, his mind cleared, and he began a heroic struggle. His first thoughts centered on his faithless companions. They had not only abandoned him, they had also robbed him of his gun, his knife, his flint and steel for making fire. The burning desire to take bloody revenge helped keep him alive. He headed toward the Missouri River, a hundred miles to the east. At first he had barely enough strength to crawl, and all the painful way he lived on berries, grass, roots, or, frightening the wolves away from a buffalo carcass, on raw meat.

Finally at the Missouri, Glass met two trappers who took him northwest to the mouth of the Yellowstone. Now he was well on the way to recovery; besides, he had secured a rifle, a pistol, and a knife. He had it all planned. One bullet from his rifle, one from his pistol, and his false friends would be no more. He found the fort where the expedition was to have wintered deserted, and he had to push on, 250 miles more to the Big Horn River. By this time the northwest winter had set in; but through blizzard and subzero cold Glass plodded on, goaded by the mania for revenge. Finally, near Custer, Montana, he came to the Henry expedition's winter fort.

Quietly he entered the lighted room and without a word of greeting demanded of the awe-stricken men who first thought him a ghost, "Where are the two curs who deserted me when I was dying, stole my rifle, my knife, and everything I had?" No one answered; instead all eyes centered on two men, and Glass caught the meaning of their glances. This was the moment for which he had dragged his aching, mutilated body across almost endless miles of prairie, through foodless days and freezing nights. In a flash the score would be settled! Just one shot from his gun and one from his pistol! So he pulled the pistol from its holster. As he did, he noticed for the first time a rough, evergreen cradle with a homemade figure of the Christ Child placed in the straw. Then his eyes swept the room to see decorations of pine boughs and red calico strips. After an amazed moment he paused to ask: "What's all this? Why all the pretty things?" The answer came from several men, but they all gave the same reply, "Christmas!"

A single word! As Glass looked once more at the hand-carved Christ Child, the Savior's love it recalled proved itself stronger than the avenging desire to kill which had goaded him on through those mad months. Dropping his rifle, he stared in bewilderment and cried: "Christmas! And I'm here to take my revenge! But I can't kill a dog on this day!" He glanced again at the Christ Child in the bark and pine-cone manger, and his voice softened and broke as he cried, "The hellish misery they've put me through—I forgive them."

Today some of you have greeted Christmas, as Hugh Glass did, without the love of Christ in your hearts. It may be sorrow, worry, or sordid sin that has robbed your life of the peace and joy which you should have at all times but in double measure on this happy anniversary of your Savior's birth. To you we wish not so much a Merry Christmas as a Christ-centered Christmas on which you will join us in a soul pilgrimage to Bethlehem, there to learn this supremely sacred lesson:

Heaven's Love Lies in the Manger

and to exclaim in these twelve words of triumphant faith (First Letter of John, chapter four, verse eleven): *"If God so loved us, we ought also to love one another."*

In the Cradled Christ Child We Find the Love That Has Saved Our Souls

There can be only few people in the United States like Hugh Glass who do not realize that today is Christmas. Fifty million dollars was spent this year, in a new high, for Christmas trees alone. If you add to this the cost of lights and trimmings for the 20,000,000 trees, the expenses for other forms of holiday decoration, you realize that the inhabitants of our country have thus paid more for evergreens and adornments than they give back to God this Sunday for His unspeakable Gift, His saving Son, the Lord Jesus Christ.

Our magazines are larger and more attractively printed than ever before; but who can tell from their pages that this is the anniversary of the day when the angel announced: *"Unto you is born this day in the city of David a Savior, which is Christ the Lord"?* Three of our national magazines last year printed 898 pages of liquor advertisements which paid them almost $13,000,000; and at Christmastime they devoted three times the average space to alcohol.

Even some of the books which bear the word "Christmas" in their title do not reveal the significance of this day nor its blessing for you. For years Charles Dickens wrote special Christmas articles for the December number of several magazines. These have been printed in two large volumes called *Christmas Stories*, but you search them in vain for any explanation of the real heart and center of this happy day.

How many of our boys and girls know the true meaning of Christmas? A recent investigation questioned 1,000 Protestant and Catholic children in 21 American cities. Thirty-two percent of them did not know the town where Jesus was born, 33 percent did not know the country, 55 percent did not know whose Son Christ is, and 76 percent did not know who ruled Palestine when our Savior was born. These were Sunday school children too! The 14,000,000 youngsters under the age of thirteen who have absolutely no religious training believe far more of the commercialized fiction of Christmas than they do of the Christ Child.

To understand just what Christmas is and what God Almighty wants it to mean to us, our text emphasizes the depth of our heavenly Father's love for us in Christ when it says: *"If God so loved us"*; and this *"so"* stresses the extent, the height, the depth, the breadth of God's love for you, its intensity, its unfailing power, its unselfish sacrifice—all for you.

Believe first that this Child cradled in the manger is the eternal Son of God, yes, the Almighty Himself. Of course, you cannot grasp this miracle which Scripture itself calls a mystery. If you could survey the sky through the 200-inch telescope of the California Institute of Technology, you would find that our solar system, a vast conglomeration of several billion stars, is only a small part of a gigantic cluster of such systems and that, at present, astronomers have found about 500 clusters of such universes distributed rather regularly throughout space. Your human mental powers are altogether too small to grasp this immensity or to understand the system, power, and purpose of these titanic heavenly bodies, but there they are! You can see them through the telescope. Similarly, now you cannot analyze and explain the incarnation of Christ nor use logic, science, or philosophy to prove that He is your God; but you can believe it once you accept the testimony of the Holy Spirit.

Whatever men may say of the Child in Bethlehem's manger, here is the verdict of God's Word: St. Paul, pointing to the Miracle Child, cries out: *"God was manifest in the flesh."*

Dr. Charles M. Stine, for many years director of research for the Dupont Industries, writes: "It is the doctrine of the incarnation and the atonement at which men of worldly wisdom stumble. We will accept the statements of the astronomers, the physicist, the biologist, the research worker in a dozen sciences, but when we turn to the statements of a Book that claims no less an authority than God, a Book that two thousand years of reading and study by countless generations of men have not discredited, then we hesitate and stumble and question this and reject that. . . . For forty years I have been reading my Bible and thinking of its wonderful truths in the light of college and university studies. . . . All this has engendered in my mind a constantly increasing appreciation of the wisdom stored in the God-inspired pages of the old Book. . . . Science— or man's wisdom—is a fluid and changing body of opinion as compared with the ineffable perfection of the wisdom of that Majesty who sits enthroned on high." If this scientist, for many years research director for one of the nation's largest corporations, finds no difficulty in acclaiming the Christ Child his God and Savior, what right have unbelievers, skeptics, and atheists to claim, as they do, that the Christmas story is unscientific?

Believe the divine message the holy angels of God caroled over Bethlehem's fields that the Christ born in the manger is *"the Lord."* For you God's Son left heaven and came to earth. We sometimes read of epidemics so terrifying and contagious that even doctors deal with patients only from a distance; but Christ, the holy, stainless God, so loved you that He came right into the midst of this madhouse, into the closest possible contact with sin and crime, disease and death. Russian Czar Peter the Great used to disguise himself and travel incognito among his people, remembering and rewarding their kindnesses to him; but he, high though his position, was a mere imperfect man, like all of his people, and he stayed with them a relatively short time; but Christ was pure, perfect, and He lived in this sin-saturated world for a third of a century.

He to whom the cherubim and seraphim sang their sacred songs was destitute, friendless, and forsaken, so that you, trusting Him, would never be alone but constantly experience the truth of His promise: *"Lo, I am with you alway, even unto the end of the world."* Bethlehem had no room for its Redeemer; and the Son of God was pushed out into a barn, made the companion of cattle, to show you that He knows the heavy sorrows of loneliness and rejection which weight some of you down because you are alone, divorced, deserted, disappointed in love, self-exiled far from your family who want you with them, or burdened by the solitude of bereavement. Rejoice, for Christmas, with its joy in Jesus, has come to replace sadness with gladness!

Christina Rossetti, the daughter of a language professor at King's College, London, was preparing for marriage, but the engagement was broken for religious reasons. In her heartache she began to study the Bible more intensely than ever before. She wrote eight different books glorifying Christ; and one Christmas season, as she taught a Sunday school class of the very poor, she composed this Christmas carol for them:

> In the bleak midwinter
> A stable place sufficed
> The Lord God Almighty,
> Jesus Christ.

The acceptance of the Savior's love took her loneliness away, just as personal, trusting faith in the miracle of the manger will grant you His constant companionship.

Heaven's love lies in the manger, because all earthly devotion, at its highest and noblest, cannot even approach Christ's affection for you. He loved you with such a desire to save you from the curse of your own sins that for you He knew hunger and thirst, loneliness and grief; for you He was slandered and falsely accused, forsaken even by His Father and made to feel the terror of divine wrath on sin; for you He was in darkness and agony; for you He wore the crown of thorns and bore the cross of shame; and—O heavenly love beyond our deserving, understanding, and describing!—He cherished you more than His own life, dying to make His own holy body the substitutionary sacrifice for your sins. Yet because He is your God, He rose again to give you the assurance of your redemption.

My brothers and sisters, this is the real Christmas message: *"The Father sent the Son to be the Savior of the world."* This is Jesus' Christmas greeting to you: *"The Son of Man is come to seek and to save that which was lost."* This is Christ's Christmas gift to you: your full, free salvation and with it the new, reborn life; the power to resist and repel temptation, to follow the paths of purity, to break destructive habits, to accept your hardships as divine helps, and to welcome death, because it assures you of a heavenly place, prepared by Christ Himself.

Now if the Christ Child today holds out to you these glorious birthday blessings, will you who began this Christmas still without faith in God's atoning Son end it in unbelief? God forbid! Few people can be happier than we are this Christmas, for listen to these gifts of grace which have come to us in recent days:

From Antwerp, Belgium: "I am a listener to your Gospel broadcasts, and through them I have found my Savior again."

From Sioux City, Iowa: "My sister and I were baptized and confirmed this morning. We are very happy and know that Jesus Christ is truly our Savior. Through your broadcasts we came to know Him."

A Cleveland pastor telephones to tell us that he takes into his church, right before Christmas, the family of a newspaperman who had heard the broadcast in Scotland.

From New York: "I am glad that I am able to receive your Bible lessons. It took a prison sentence to bring me close to Jesus. I was once carefree and a worshiper of Satan, in more than one way. I could tell the good from the cheap whiskey and had little or no care for tomorrow—then 'Bang!' into prison I went. Having been here five years, I realize that God was knocking at the door."

From Pennsylvania comes a Christmas card written by a mother whose son, an evangelist, feeling that he was forsaken by God, tried to commit suicide. It happened here in St. Louis, and in the depth of his agony God led him to recall the one name he knew in our city—ours—which he had learned from listening to the broadcast. The poison he had taken was enough to kill a dozen people, but the Lord helped us bring him back to Christ. His mother writes: "I want to thank you this Christmas for what you did for my son last spring."

You can understand that with letters like these pouring in, we thank the Almighty that He uses us, unworthy as we are, in offering the gift of salvation to many who thankfully receive it and keep it. Today, however, on the Savior's birthday, we want *you* to be born again into a new life through Him who at Bethlehem was born for you. God help you break down every barrier which would keep you from Jesus and bring you, in spirit, on your knees before the manger. God lead you to Christ this Christmas Day!

In the Cradled Christ Child We Find the Love
That Can Save Our World

To you who know the Lord Jesus as your Savior, this Christmas Day brings the pointed appeal of our text: *"If God so loved us, we ought also to love one another."* A lonely ranger in Idaho writes: "You talk to unbelievers, atheists, and infidels, and I know that is the main purpose of your broadcast; but don't forget that the rest of us need to be told what God expects of us." We will not forget, especially on this day.

Therefore we tell you believers: the greatest need in our world today is faith in Christ. Second only to that is the need of putting the Savior's love into practice. Instead of the love which should bind nations together in harmony, jointly to meet the issues of this critical day, we meet selfish, violent opposition. Red writers openly boast of their hatred for Christianity. A book that turned up in Germany and was widely read by our GI's eighteen months ago told the American soldiers and civilians there not to pity the little German child they might see standing in the rubble, poorly dressed, cold and hungry; for, this book warned, "Don't forget, in twenty-five years this little boy may be killing your son!" Our men were not moved by such appeals. This Christmas season again, recalling the Savior's words, *"Love your enemies,"* our soldiers have remembered the undernourished and underprivileged children in the defeated countries.

We need the love of the Christ Child throughout our own land where, despite all efforts to conquer prejudice and selfishness, class hatred still thrives. Praise God that the Christmas tidings of good cheer are for *"all people,"* that the cradled Child in Bethlehem was worshiped by lowly shepherds and exalted scientists, by Jews and Gentiles, that He has no preferred group but came for all, lived for all, and died for all! If His spirit could rule our nation, the all too frequent clashes between white and black, rich and poor—and may God forgive us, between creed and creed—could be avoided.

Even churches sometimes need a new reemphasis on the Redeemer's love. When the pastor of a Georgia congregation can address and encourage the Ku Klux Klan; when some congregations forbid blacks to cross their threshold; when certain exquisitely decorated sanctuaries in fashionable suburbs today have no real room and welcome for the laborer and his family, we must pray and work with redoubled fervor to have Christ's all-inclusive love crowd

210

out the pride and the arrogance which narrow lives and make selfish men look down on those whom the Son of God loved and delivered from the curse of eternal death.

We praise God that as another welcome gift, during the days before Christmas, clergymen of every denomination have written to us to say, in effect, as an Ohio pastor of the Evangelical United Brethren Church wrote: "Keep preaching Christ Crucified as the lost world's only Hope of salvation. I pray daily for you and your entire radio staff. Although I am not a member of your church, I am for your broadcast and your preaching 100 percent."

Standing at the manger, we realize, too, how sorely many need the reflection of the divine Love which lies in the manger in their own homes. One out of every six marriages, a recent survey reports, is truly happy. Is yours among the five of the six families which have either only an occasional glimpse of joy or are altogether steeped in strife and misery? Are you suffering from family quarrels which somehow are heavier in these sacred holidays than otherwise? Are you lonely because your husband or your wife has deserted you, because you are separated and plan a divorce? Do you feel as an Ohio listener writes me: "My husband and I are parted. I have sued for divorce, and now he is begging for a chance to show me that he can do right. I have lost all respect and affection for him and have nothing left but pity. Under these conditions do you think it is God's will that I return to him? I don't want to, but if you think it is my duty, I will"? Then Christmas has come for you with the appeal that you follow Heaven's love manifest in the manger. Always ask yourself, "What would Christ do?" and you will find the answer which tells that Ohio woman: Give your husband another chance. But don't be satisfied simply with taking him back. Put Christ and keep Christ in your family life! Take him back under the condition that you will both daily read the Bible and pray together; that you will attend a true church together; that you will make Jesus the Head of your home and have Him who promises, *"Behold, I make all things new,"* give you the riches of His renewing grace!

If your Christmas joy is not complete; if you have no peace in your hearts but only fear and worry; if you have not yet learned to know what true, unselfish love is, don't let the day close without having God bless you with the gift of this grace. When Handel wrote *The Messiah,* which every Christmas season brings joy into millions of hearts, he locked himself in his room in London for twenty-four

211

days, with no other printed material than the passages of Holy Scripture dealing with Christ to form the text of his masterpiece. He let everything else fade away. At mealtime a servant brought him food, but the tray often remained untouched. It is recorded that the servant stood by in silence as Handel's tears dropped on page after page to mingle with his sacred score. A visitor found the composer convulsed in sorrow as he wrote the music for *"He is despised."* When he finished the "Hallelujah Chorus" and wrote at the end, above his signature, *"S. D. G.,"* a common abbreviation for the Latin "To God alone all glory," he later confessed, "I did see all heaven before me and the great God Himself." You can have similar joy this Christmas. Even though you cannot take twenty-four days, before this Sunday has ended you can take twenty-four mintues apart from the rush, the feasting, the merrymaking and dedicate these to the Christ Child. As you read aloud, either alone or preferably with your friends and family, the record of the Savior's birth in St. Luke's simple story; as you pray for the Christ Child's presence and blessing in your heart and in your life, His love will warm your soul with its divine glow, and loving Jesus who first loved you, you will learn the high and holy lessons of self-sacrificing love. With that love the Christ Child would enrich each of you this day. God grant that you will now receive it and ever after glorify God for it! Amen.[64]

The "Amen" was Walter A. Maier's final broadcast word. Four days later he was felled by a coronary but not before he had composed his New Year's Day address, which follows. While he lay in the hospital, his veteran associate, Dr. E. R. ("Rudy") Bertermann, delivered this sermon in his place over *The Lutheran Hour* on January 1, 1950. This is the last material W.A.M. wrote, and it clearly shows him ready for the second half of the 20th century. In dealing with the folly of atheism it also shows him coming full circle to thoughts expressed in his very first *Hour* address a score of years earlier.

Don't Be a 1950 Fool!

"Christ shall give thee light. See then that ye walk circumspectly, not as fools but as wise, redeeming the time, because the days are evil."—Ephesians 5:14-16

212

This Lord's day, by the grace of God, brings us to the middle of the twentieth century; and it is well that New Year's Day comes on Sunday, giving us time and opportunity to reflect on the momentous meaning of 1950.

When this twentieth century began, many things were entirely different in our country and our world. In 1900 Secretary of State Hay announced the "Open Door Policy" in China. Today we have a closed door there, with Communism gradually taking over control of almost 500,000,000 people and giving Christian missions in China one of the heaviest setbacks they have ever sustained.

In 1900 predictions of peace were so strong and optimistic that our government signed a treaty declaring that the Panama Canal would never be fortified. Today the canal has strong military protection, and after two World Wars the prospects of a third global struggle are so terrifying that next week the President will ask Congress to make the largest peacetime military appropriation any country has ever known.

In 1900, under Queen Victoria, Great Britain, at the pinnacle of its prosperity, was building its empire by annexing the Orange Free State and the Transvaal; today, as its own spokesmen admit, England is almost impoverished and its empire ties have loosened.

Even greater has been the change in the realm of religion and the spiritual life of the masses. When the twentieth century began, most of the churches in our land stood on the Bible as the inspired, infallible Word of God; preachers who denied that Jesus Christ, the Son of God and the Savior of the world, had shed His cleansing blood to rescue mankind from eternal ruin were few and far between. Today all this is changed. Within fifty short years entire denominations, the great majority of their leaders, and in some cases most of their preachers refuse to receive the Bible as the Almighty's inspired Word and to exalt the divine Christ as their Redeemer.

In 1900 few people took the Communists seriously, but in 1950 their program calls for the conquest of the world. Never during any previous half century has the change in human affairs been as drastic, far-reaching, and destructive as between 1900 and this year of our Lord.

On New Year's Day we are inclined to look to the future; and while some of you may accuse me of pessimism, I still declare that unless there is a deep-rooted change in the hearts and lives of our

213

people during the coming twelve months, 1950 will continue the away-from-God march which has marked our age and is speeding mankind to disaster. Scripture asks: *"When the Son of Man cometh, shall He find faith on the earth?"* The Bible makes it clear that in the latter times unbelief will run riot over the surface of the globe; and as if in fulfillment, Carl von Weigand, dean of American foreign correspondents, writes from Italy: "The Christian era is nearing its end. . . . Unless the torch of true freedom can be relighted and the true Christian spirit rekindled, much of Western civilization and culture will pass with the Christian era."

Before you think of national and international issues on New Year's Day, think of yourself! What can the new year bring you? About a million people in the United States will leave the church this year. Will you be one of them? About 3,000,000 will lie in hospital beds. Will you be one of them? Almost a million and a half will die in the United States during 1950—almost half of them without Christ and without hope. Will you be one of them? Are you for Christ or against Him? There is no middle ground. You will either help crucify Him anew with your sins or glorify Him with your Christian life. Which will it be for you? God's Word calls out to you:

Don't Be a 1950 Fool!

Rather be wise in Christ! As we wish you a God-blessed New Year in the Savior, we take our first text for 1950, as always from God's unbreakable Word, where we read (St. Paul's Letter to the Ephesians, chapter five, verses fourteen to sixteen): *"Christ shall give thee light. See then that ye walk circumspectly, not as fools but as wise, redeeming the time, because the days are evil."*

The Folly of Living in Sin, Without Christ

When St. Paul declares that *"the days are evil,"* some of you may be ready to object: "No, the world has steadily become better. The cruelty and the brutality which ruled the world in the apostle's time have disappeared." Have they? Roman General Sulla, who lived shortly before Christ, cut down 5,000 of the people's leaders in cold blood and made himself "perpetual dictator." Yet he could boast that never in his campaign did he wage war on women and children. Sulla was a crude pagan; but on August 9, 1945, a

Christian leader could thank God over the radio for the atomic bomb which had killed almost 200,000 Japanese, more than 40,000 of them women and children, in the deadliest massacre history knows; and the same broadcast could ask the Lord to use the atomic bomb for "His purpose," as though the God of love could ever be pleased with a mass destruction of mothers and their babies!

We say that our marriage standards are higher now than they were when the apostle wrote, *"The days are evil";* and thanks to the Holy Spirit's enlightening power, millions who love Christ do enjoy history's highest standards of mutual love and family happiness. But Christians are in the minority. On November 19 the *Los Angeles Examiner* published the notice of 189 marriage licenses and 164 applications for divorce on the same day—almost as many requests for divorce as for marriage!

St. Paul lived under the madman, Nero, whose name has become one of the blackest of all times, particularly for his brutal persecution of believers. Nobody knows how many martyrs died in Rome under his rule; but everybody should know that their total, tragic as it is, is only a small fraction of the number of martyrs satanically slaughtered in our generation by Communist criminals.

Julius Caesar and Emperor Augustus, renowned Roman rulers before and after the Savior's birth, waged heavy warfare; but they were amateurs in military affairs when compared with modern warlords who in thirty-five years have produced two global conflicts with 100,000,000 casualities.

Thank God we have truly Christian churches to proclaim the Gospel by which every sinful, selfish man can be *"a new creature" "in Christ";* yet unbelief has increased more rapidly than the church has, with the result that today, nineteen centuries since the Savior was born in Bethlehem, more hundreds of millions of infidels, skeptics, heathen enemies of the Redeemer populate the globe than at any previous time. We have more congregations but less genuine faith; larger organizations for peace but bloodier wars; more colleges and universities but more spiritual ignorance; more crying for humanity and justice but wider practice of inhumanity and injustice; more giving away billions of public funds but more thanklessness and ingratitude for this generosity; more experts on the home but more shattered families; more laws but more crime; more millions spent for youthful recreation but more juvenile delinquency; more millions in government service but more waste

215

and more practice of statism; more products from our farms and orchards but more forgetfulness of the Creator and more starvation in the world's hunger centers; more money made than in any previous generation but more lost by high prices and high taxes.

It is no pleasant task to apply these four words of the apostle: *"The days are evil,"* to our times and to tell you that unless our country sees the greatest wave of repentance, return to the triune God, revival in the faith once given, and rededication to the Savior, we are headed for the end of our Christian age. If Holy Writ says, *"The days are evil,"* of an age in which the rejection of the Savior had not spread around the world as it has today, how can anyone spray the decadence of our day with rose water or paint over the putrid places in the body politic of our country and claim, as many do, that our world is getting better?

In this age of atheism's greatest advance, God's Word warns you on the first day of this new year: *"Walk circumspectly, not as fools."* Many of you resent a statement like this. You have attended college and received the bachelor of arts degree. You do not want anyone, even God and His Bible, to warn you against living in 1950 as a fool. Yet Scripture speaks plainly of the follies which destroy men's souls, and you will do well to ask yourselves whether you belong in any of these classifications of fools:

When the Bible says: *"The fool hath said in his heart, There is no God,"* it presents the atheist fool. Do you belong in this group? Almost 4 percent of the American people deny that God exists. Do you claim that during 1950 the world will go on with no higher power to direct it and that you need no God for the unmarked pathways ahead in your life? If you do, the Almighty have mercy on your soul and show you what a perfect fool you are, contradicting the evidence of your own senses! Look at the Christmas tree in your home or still standing in the stores and public places. Did you ever hear of a person so bereft of common sense that he maintained, "All these Christmas trees have come into existence accidentally, with no one to place the decorations and string the lights"? How, then, can anyone be inconsistent enough to deny that "only God can make a tree," a living, growing, beauty-filled monument to His power? Who would reject his own reason and claim that the trillions of trees all over the world fortuitously sprang into existence; that the globe made itself; that our solar system, with its tremendous distances and overwhelming sizes, merged into being by itself; that the entire universe, which has hundreds of solar systems like ours, came about through sheer chance?

Listen to these seven devastating reasons for rejecting atheism: First, this folly contradicts God's Word. Second, it contradicts human reason. Third, it robs its followers of divine protection. Fourth, it takes away the hope of heaven. Fifth, it produces cruel brutality. Sixth, it leads mankind to low immorality. Seventh, in the hour of death it leaves its victims in despair.—Think this over, and if you have lived without God, stop being a fool! Begin the new year and finish it, if God lets you live that long, with faith in His almighty power!

The Bible says that those who deny that Christ suffered and died for men's sins, then rose again to seal their redemption, are guilty of heavy folly. Jesus Himself told His two disciples on the Emmaus road, *"O fools and slow of heart to believe! . . . Ought not Christ to have suffered these things and entered into His glory?"* If you are starting the new year without a personal, penitent faith in the Lord Jesus as your own Savior; if, as you hear these words, you do not believe that the Son of God took your sins, placed their guilt, their curse, their punishment on Himself, served the death sentence they imposed by shedding His blood on Calvary's cross, and died amid unspeakable anguish, only to be resurrected from the grave, and now lives, enthroned in the eternal heavens, let me tell you what you miss! You are without the forgiveness of sins, without the promise of heaven, without the companionship of Christ which you need for the untrodden pathways of the future, without the Savior's blessing, guidance, strength, and comfort, without the victory over evil, fear, temptation, without the power to lead clean, godly lives, without the peace, courage, and joy of divine blessing. Won't you be sensible enough to consider the evidence, to read the Gospel record? Don't be a fool and spurn your Redeemer! Come, start the new year right by starting it with Jesus!

The Bible lists many other follies. Plainly it says: *"Fools make a mock at sin";* and how many fools there are in our nation today who love sin and serve sin! Now if some of you who hear these words are recovering from an alcoholic dusk-to-dawn New Year's celebration, with a bitter taste in your mouth, and an even more bitter impress of guilt on your lives because you have disregarded God's decency commandment, forgotten His directive: *"Keep thyself pure,"* cheated your husband or your wife, brought disease and sorrow on yourself by the vicious sins of lust, then, no matter how smart and sophisticated you may think yourself, God cries out to you, "You are a fool." Someday, unless you repent, you will pay and pay and pay the prohibitive price which divine justice demands of all who rebel against God. Don't be a fool! Get right with God and with your own conscience, while you can, through faith in Christ!

The Bible warns: *"A fool despiseth his father's instruction."* Are you young folks guilty of this folly? Stop right on the threshold of the new year, and realize that your parents who gave you life love you more than anyone else can; that when in God's truth they warn you, or in God's Word plead with you, they are speaking for the Almighty. Don't enter the new year disobedient to your parents! Write or phone your father or mother this day if you are separated from them because of your refusal to follow their instruction!

Again, God's Word says: *"He that trusteth in his own heart is a fool,"* and if you have made resolutions for the new year without invoking the help of the Lord Jesus, you are under this condemnation. For the battle against sin, the devil, and your all-too-human flesh you need divine strength, just as for the tremendous issues before our nation and our world we need God on our side. The tragedy of it all is that men are trying to create a new world in such utter disregard of the Almighty that His name cannot even be mentioned in prayer at their international deliberations. Is it any wonder, then, that we have met one worldwide tragedy after the other and that at a time when men have boasted most blatantly of their own strength, they have shown themselves the weakest in preventing bloodshed? Therefore don't be a 1950 fool! Don't continue to forget your God, neglect His Word, rebel against His Law, crucify Christ anew by godless living! Don't exalt yourself above Him and begin the year in unbelief.

The Wisdom of Living in Grace, with Christ

Rather be wise! Start 1950 in the Savior's name! Follow our text when on January 1 it tells you: *"See . . . that ye walk circumspectly . . . as wise."* Some predict that 1950 will be a holy year; old Moore's Almanac in England foresees this as a quiet year; but for many of you it will be a hard, trying year. How necessary, then, to be truly *"wise"!* The Bible tells us: *"The fear of the Lord is the beginning of wisdom";* and it is only when you recognize God as your divine Creator, Protector, Provider, that you can find the

218

support and guidance you need for the uncertain pathways before you.

A few days ago Dr. Einstein published his "generalized theory of gravitation," which sets forth the laws governing gravitation and electromagnetism, two basic forces of nature. The newspapers declare that his formula, if it can be proved, will stand as the highest scientific achievement of all times and will help to solve the mystery of life. The difficulty is this: Dr. Einstein cannot think of a physical test by which he can prove his theory; and some of the leading scientists, to whom his twenty-page theory was submitted, have not been able even to read the formula, let alone understand it. How different the sacred wisdom which God wants you to follow during the new year when His Word pledges you: *"The Lord God . . . will be with thee; He will not fail thee nor forsake thee"!*

The question before you now is this: "Will I be wise and recognize God as my greatest Need? Will I admit my own weaknesses, mistakes and repeated sins, the follies and failures with which I filled the last twelve months? Then as evidence of supreme wisdom, will I accept and confess Jesus Christ as my Savior, the Son of God who, moved by His immeasurable love for me, transferred all my transgressions to Himself?"

The first to seek the infant Savior after Christmas were the Wise Men, whose Epiphany visit the church commemorates this week. They made the hard, dangerous journey over hundreds of miles to kneel at the Christ Child's manger and to give Him gifts of gold, frankincense, and myrrh. Since their day mighty minds of all ages have humbly worshiped the Savior. Be wise! Begin 1950 with Jesus, and you will have His promise for every day of joy or sorrow: *"I will never leave thee nor forsake thee."*

When Christ controls your heart and directs your life, you will fulfill the second requirement for a truly happy year. You will follow the plea of our text and *"walk circumspectly,"* carefully surveying your surroundings, thoughtfully watching each step you take. Nineteen hundred and fifty will bring most of you face to face with alluring evil, the opportunity to make money in dishonest ways, the urge to have the kind of "good" time which later becomes a ghastly nightmare, the appeal to forget Christ and follow your flesh as you heap ruin on yourself and on your loved ones. Every year you live in this unbelieving and adulterous age your faith is attacked as the devil works overtime to keep you from Christ. Therefore *"walk circumspectly,"* by following the Savior's footsteps. Keep away from sin. Don't pray: *"Lead us not into temptation,"* and then proceed to lead yourself into evil!

For the Christ-like life you need divine help. Our text tells us to be *"wise, redeeming the time,"* using every moment to the fullest in a life consecrated to Christ. The passing of another year reminds us to number our days and consider personally how swift and fleeting the relentless flow of time is. If you will not live until New Year's Day in 1951, begin today, on January 1, 1950, to redeem the time, to get the most for your soul from every moment. The science editor of the *New York Times* discusses the greatest discoveries of 1949, and he lists these outstanding scientific achievements of the last year: radio astronomy, which enables us to hear stars too far away to be seen; the blood test of cancer patients; the new antibiotics; the giant cyclotron of Berkeley, California, which will reveal new secrets of atomic structure; cortisone for the relief of arthritis and rheumatic fever; the fertility hormone which, it is hoped, will help childless couples become fathers and mothers; vitamin B-12 with the relief it offers for pernicious anemia; the 200-inch Palomar telescope, through which scientists can see twice as far as heretofore. These are stupendous discoveries; but as Sir William Simpson, one of Britain's foremost scientists, stated that his greatest discovery came on Christmas 1868, when he learned that he was a sinner and that Jesus Christ was his Savior, so we broadcast to every one of you that your most blessed discovery for 1950 is this: that Jesus Christ, the Son of God, came into this world and died to save you. To learn this truth, to grow in this grace, *"redeem . . . the time"!* Start now, in this very moment, and receive Jesus as your Redeemer! He wants you to begin the new year with a new life which He gives all those who receive Him as their divine Deliverer.

"Redeem . . . the time" during the new year by a life of prayer. What divine help, comfort, strength, and guidance we can secure through the faith which speaks in our petitions to the Almighty! During the last year some of you did not pray regularly, fervently, in Jesus' name, as you should have; but you paid for that neglect, and the longer you set aside these petitions to your heavenly Father, the heavier will be the price you pay. Resolve now that you will begin and end each day of the new year with humble, trusting intercessions of request and thanksgiving; that you will pray in your household, in the moments of family worship, at work, while traveling, and in

many quiet moments which present themselves! Pray humbly, confessing your sins! Pray confidently, trusting Heaven's promises to hear! Pray fervently, in the hope of triumphant faith!

"Redeem . . . the time" by joining a true church of Christ to enjoy spiritual instructions, fellowship with believers, and the other blessings God attaches to public worship! Resolve now in the second new year's resolution, which the Holy Spirit will help you keep, that your entire household will unite with the church; that your children, if possible, will be enrolled in a Christian day school; that your home will henceforth be a house of God!

"Redeem . . . the time" by working for Christ and helping to lead others to the blessings of faith with which your life has been enriched! You have 365 days in which you can tell others of Him who loved you and gave Himself for you! If you know what it cost God's Son to save you and if you realize that without faith in Him there is no hope of salvation, you certainly will want to use the best of the time that you have hitherto wasted senselessly, sometimes sinfully, to help win souls for Him. Resolve, then, in the third resolution, that this year you will stand up for Jesus in stalwart testimony to His grace!

Who, we repeat, can tell what the moments ahead may bring? You, the bedridden and crippled, may be called upon to endure even longer hours of heavier pain. You, the disappointed, who have met opposition or suffered serious loss during the past year, may find that sudden disaster and darkness sweep down unannounced upon you. Now in bleak sorrow, which will drive thousands to despair, insanity, even suicide, where, should this year bring reverse to you, can you find light to vanquish gloom, light to trace the path before you? Not in fortunetellers, who each January 1 make predictions for the new year and each December 31 have to admit that their forecasts were false. Not in spiritist mediums who fraudulently claim to communicate with departed souls. Not in psychiatrists who contradict Scripture and tell their patients to forget the Bible. All these can only help make the darkness deeper.

For every heartache which the twelve months ahead can bring, hear on January 1 God's promise in our text: *"Christ shall give thee light"!* Repeat these five words every day this year in trusting faith, and you will have the divine power to make this a year of new joy in Jesus. According to the Savior's own promise: *"I am the Light of the world,"* He will dispel every darkness which may enshroud your life, once you give yourself fully to Him. Nineteen hundred and fifty may burden you heavily, but the compassionate Christ will help you carry whatever His wisdom permits to be laid upon you. He will also turn your grief into blessings according to the promise of this passage which offers you God's guarantee of unfailing grace: *"All things work together for good to them that love God."*

Christ, and He alone, *"shall give thee light"* by showing you that all your sorrows are part of Heaven's merciful plan for your spiritual growth, the strengthening of your faith, the deepening of your dependence on God, the increase of your sympathy for others. This pledge: *"Christ shall give thee light,"* has been so marvelously fulfilled in those who completely trust Jesus that their faith has banished all darkness, that even lifelong invalids have thanked the Lord for the affliction which has helped bring them to the Cross.

Dedicate 1950 to Jesus, the Savior of your soul! Resolve with the Spirit's help to walk in the radiance of His redeeming love! Then, but only then, will you have a right, bright new year. The Holy Spirit help every one of you decide now, in this moment, for Christ, your Guide, your God, your gracious Savior, throughout 1950 and into eternity! Amen.[65]

In the fall of 1949 the ABC radio network was added to the Mutual and transcription chain broadcasting *The Lutheran Hour,* and W.A.M.—but for his final Christmas address—had prepared an entirely *different* set of sermons for the ABC broadcasts. Accordingly he had much of the manuscript dictated also for his January 1, 1950, New Year's message for ABC, which sounded an entirely different theme from the Mutual address above. With poignant irony—the author dictated it just a day or two before his own fatal illness—it concerned the spiritual basis for good health. Following are several excerpts from this unfinished and unpublished manuscript—the *very* last thing Walter A. Maier ever authored.

We Wish You Good Health!

St. John writes to his friend Gaius: *"I wish . . . that thou mayest be in health"* [3 John 1:2]. We repeat this as a New Year's wish for you; for certainly good health is one of the greatest of God Almighty's gifts. For many it is beyond the possibility of purchase since the New Year finds them infected with a humanly incurable disease; but all the rest of you, by the will and blessing of God, can enjoy good health during 1950.

After discussing the wonders of the human body as evidence of God's creation and providence, W.A.M. offered very practical advice on how to maintain one's health. At the close of his list is an illuminating paragraph on psychosomatic relationships, which was probably intended as the closing paragraph of the address itself.

Finally, stop worrying. Fight despair and despondency by reassuring yourself that God loves you. Diseases like stomach ulcers seem to stem from the fears and phobias which restrict the body's power to assimilate food and receive the blessings of rest. In one of the greatest medical advances made during the past half a century, experts in somatic diseases understand the connection between human emotions and human health. If you have the peace of God in your heart and trusting Him at whose birth the angels announced: *"Fear not!"* and whose resurrection greetings reechoed: *"Fear not!"* you can overcome the tyranny of fright and with the Spirit's help triumphantly trust God, who can help you back to health in 1950. We repeat John's ancient wish as our New Year's greeting to every one of you: *"I wish . . . that thou mayest be in health."* To have this wish become a reality, resolve to walk in God's ways during the new year, to keep the temple of your body pure, to get sufficient sleep, not to overeat or overdrink, and to live in total abstinence of everything that can injure your body and soul. Have a physical checkup of your body, and live a Christ-centered faith to receive the guarantee of grace with which the Divine Healer will bless both your body and your soul.[66]

A prophetic foreboding of his own illness, or poignant coincidence? The latter, emphatically. W.A.M. maintained a *joi de vivre* up to the very night of his illness. Evidently, though, the man who "kept his pulse on human affairs" in order to have a message as applicable to as many people as possible was also keeping pulse on himself better than he ever knew.

11
PROFESSOR

Throughout his years as *Lutheran Hour* speaker, there was another Walter A. Maier—W.A.M., the professor and scholar. This had been his original calling, and, indeed, he had achieved his Doctor of Philosophy degree in Semitics at Harvard University with extraordinary honors, for which he had had to master almost a dozen Near Eastern and research languages. But it was not for lack of interest that later in life he spent less time in library stacks or the classroom than in the studio or on the dais. Perhaps his seminary colleague, Greek lexicographer William F. Arndt, expressed it best in his address at Dr. Maier's funeral:

> It was on account of his truly astounding gifts as a writer, together with his wide acquaintance with his chosen field, that his friends often discussed the question whether he should not be induced to give his time and efforts to the production of scholarly, learned commentaries on books of the Bible and other strictly theological works rather than to the radio ministry to which during the last years he more and more devoted his whole energy. He replied that, while works of this nature are needed, there are millions of

souls who are famished for want of the Gospel, and that the question is not what is needed, but what is needed most urgently.[67]

Still, W.A.M. relished the world of scholarship, and some of his contributions have been discussed in Chapter 4. One of his favorite scholarly thrusts was to demonstrate how archaeology and history corroborate the Old and New Testaments. In 1933 he published a three-part series of articles on this theme in the *Concordia Theological Monthly.* Because the articles are highly technical, only the briefest excerpts are listed here.

Archaeology—the Nemesis

When at the middle of the last century the epoch-making excavations in the Mesopotamian Valley lengthened the historical perspective and pushed back the horizon of the ancient Orient, these archaeological discoveries were hailed with mixed feelings. An attitude of doubt and suspicion clashed with an exaggerated credulity. . . .

Notable in the former group were critical minds that in spite of their characteristic inclination to explore new avenues of departure remained anchored on their old critical basis. The great Noeldeke, prince of Semitists, as late as 1871 declared that the results of Assyriology both in matters of linguistics and history were characterized by "a highly suspicious air." The school of Wellhausen, with its dominant emphasis on the history of religion, paid scant attention to archaeology and dallied with it as a toy of sophisticated Semitism. A perusal of Julius Wellhausen's *History of Israel* shows the pronounced indifference with which he regarded Assyriology.

This neglect has proved fatal to many of the theories which have been set up as canons of criticism. Archaeology has convincingly demonstrated its capacities as a nemesis of higher criticism. Scores of hasty judgments and other scores of intricate theories, spun out of critical fancy, now appear as entirely fallacious in the light of archaeological research. And while it is a thankless task to enumerate negatives and to collate errors, the cumulative force of the archaeological rejection of higher critical extravagances must react very decidedly in emphasizing the truth of the Scriptures.

Since higher criticism has particularly three methods of attack by which the authenticity and the veracity of the Biblical books are assailed: the arguments based on language, situation, and theology, I have selected the following typical instances in which higher critical dicta have been nullified or reversed by subsequent archaeological data in the fields of philological research, historical investigation, and the comparative study of Semitic religions.

One example from the argument based on language—the *Sprachbeweis*—must suffice.

It is the claim of Max Mueller (*Encyclopedia Biblica,* col. 3687) in regard to the title "Pharaoh" that "the Hebrews could have received it only after 1000 B.C." He asserts that the term was unknown in Egypt, in the way in which the early Biblical writers know it, until that time. If this statement were true, it would of course wipe out with one stroke the entire Mosaic authorship of those Pentateuchal portions which employ the term. As a matter of fact, however, Mueller's contention was set aside by the archaeological light on this title, its meaning, and its abundant use long before 1000 B.C. The occurrence of the term in *The Tale of Two Brothers* shows its common employment several centuries before the time permitted by critical analysis. It is now definitely recognized on all sides that the term "Pharaoh" is the Hebraized "Per'o" (Herodotus: "Pheron"). As early as the fourth dynasty, centuries before Moses' time, several different hieroglyphics preceded the name of the Egyptian king as distinctive titles. Among these there was a drawing of a structure "representing the facade of a building, perhaps a palace." Now Alexandre Moret (*The Nile and Egyptian Civilization,* p. 130) summarizes the meaning of this symbol: "An old term for the royal palace establishment and estate, Per'o, 'the great house,' and this gradually became the personal designation. In the Memphite period this came to designate the king himself."[68]

A whole generation of Concordia Seminary students can testify to the lofty academic standards demanded by Professor of Old Testament Interpretation and History Walter A. Maier. His classroom notes were voluminous, and he set the same standards for his own scholarship, as witness the *Nahum* project. For years this pet hobby involved researching a commentary in depth on the thirty-fourth book of the Old Testament, written by one of the most significant minor prophets. The manuscript was nearly complete by the time of his death, and Concordia Publishing House printed *The Book of Nahum* posthumously in 1959.

What intrigued W.A.M. about the prophet-poet Nahum, who lived in Judea c. 650 B.C., was how accurately he foretold the fall of the Assyrian capital, Nineveh, and he cited twenty-two specific details that were fulfilled in 612 B.C., when the city was vanquished by the Babylonians and Medes. Liberal and critical scholarship, however, insisted that the book must have been written immediately before or, more likely, *after* the events it "predicted." So, was Nahum a true prophet or a mere war correspondent? Professor Maier decided to make this book a case history on the integrity of Old Testament prophecy. Since it is manifestly impossible to distill 386 pages into a few excerpts, the following samples at least show how the author could make scholarly argumentation agreeable reading.

On Dating Nahum's Prophecies

It is just as much out of place to picture Nahum directing his denunciations against Nineveh, the deceased overlord of Judah, in the period after 612 B.C., as it would be for a Northern poet, a few years subsequent to the defeat of the Southern States in the Civil War, to predict the collapse of the Confederacy.[69]

Another argument for a date at least several decades before 612 B.C. is the decisive fact that when the prophet pens his prediction, Judah is definitely under the Assyrian yoke, restrained by its bonds (1:13). Groaning under Ninevite tyranny, the Hebrews are in no mood to celebrate their festivals (2:1). Obviously Nahum must have written while Judah suffered the affliction of Assyrian rule. The entire purpose of the book demands this background, and its statements imply this dating. At what time, then, was Judah subjected to Assyrian exploitation? During the entire reign of Manasseh (698—642 B.C.) Judah was a vassal state. Both Esarhaddon (680—668 B.C.) and Ashurbanipal (668—626 B.C.) list Manasseh as among their tributary vassals. It was not until 626 B.C., the year of Ashurbanipal's death, that any hope of freedom from Nineveh's yoke crystallized. At that time Josiah (639—608 B.C.), the grandson of Manasseh, found the Assyrian Empire so weakened that he could omit paying tribute; and the great reform in 621 B.C., which cleansed the temple in Jerusalem also of Assyrian idols, became a symbol of Judah's complete political independence.

We are entitled to conclude, therefore, that Nahum, chafing under the Assyrian oppression, must have penned his prophecies no later than the early years of Josiah, who began his reign in 639 B.C. To place the prophet after 621 B.C. is to make his words an oracle against a nation which no longer harassed Judah and a people whose power had already been broken.[70]

On Textual Criticism of Nahum

In summary it may be stated that every verse in the entire three chapters has been assailed by some important critical writer as non-Nahumic. Most modern interpreters remove at least one third of the verses as spurious glosses. In the sections regarded as authentic every verse has been subjected to drastic alteration, emendation, addition, change of words or phrase order. In this way some recent exegetical works change at least two-thirds of the entire prophecy. These extremes mark the fatal weakness of such radical exegesis, showing both the arbitrary nature of its *modus operandi* and the unsatisfactory force of its conclusions. No other literature on earth has suffered from such arbitrary excisions and additions. Significantly enough—and this is one of the strongest defenses for the position taken in this commentary—the Book of Nahum, when read as preserved in the Masoretic Text, presents a poem, in the Hebrew sense, which for vividness of presentation, order of development, and force of prophetic forecast stands unexcelled in all literature.[71]

On Attempts to Pit Nahum Against Other Prophets

In all these attempts to establish contradiction between Nahum and other prophets, the obvious fact is overlooked that the ancient seers, as modern writers do, may view the same theme or concept from different angles and that variety of presentation does not presuppose mutually exclusive theological principles. It is just as unwarranted to place Nahum's short, specifically directed prophecy denouncing Nineveh in opposition to Jeremiah's or Isaiah's large and comprehensive oracles with their varied purposes, as it would be to infer that one sermon on the Nativity and another on Christ's substitutionary death are inconsistent, or to maintain that the short Letter to Philemon was written by an apostolic mind ignorant of the great issues in the Epistle to the Romans.[72]

Practical Lessons from Nahum

The book also abounds in stating and implying profound, practical lessons for our age. The warning against the pride of Assyrian haughtiness that insolently resists God (1:1) should be invoked to rebuke parallel tendencies in our times. The woe chanted against "the bloody city" (3:1) should be repeated in our day which, more than any other generation in modern history, has suffered from war's carnage. The destiny of Nineveh, the vampire queen of the nations, who had ruled with unchecked oppression, should deter those twentieth-century dictatorial empire builders who would stride ruthlessly over prostrate nations in adding conquest to conquest. The fortresses that fall like ripe figs, the hastily erected defenses, the fleeing armies, the heaped corpses—these symbols of a doomed, bloated militarism, bristling in its own might and then dying in its own blood, are replete with meaningful warnings for our world, which has seen the most widespread wars of aggression.[73]

Validity of Prophecy

The pages of Nahum are of extraordinary value in underscoring the validity of OT prophecy and the divine nature of these Scriptures. No human document of such restricted size has ever attempted to foretell in detail the march of future events; and none ever could. . . . Nineveh fell and in dramatic succession one prediction after another was literally fulfilled.[74]

Prediction No. 19 (of the 22)

19. Dispersion is likewise predicted. When the city [of Nineveh] falls, the *"people is scattered on the mountains, and no man gathereth them"* (3:18). Not all captured and devastated cities have suffered this fate. Babylon was laid completely waste by Sennacherib with a massacre regarded as bloody and horrifying even in those cruel days; but the citizens of Babylon returned, rebuilt their city. . . . The captive and dispersed citizens of Nineveh, however, never returned to restore the capital. Its inhabitants disappeared so completely that they have left no impress on subsequent ages. No people have lost their identity more completely and quickly than did the Ninevites, confirming Nahum's prediction. *Cambridge Ancient History,* III, 130, declares: "The disappearance of the Assyrian people will always remain an unique and striking phenomenon in ancient history."

This prediction becomes the more remarkable when the scope of its time is understood. Even those critics who maintain, against the internal evidence, that the prophecies are *post eventum* cannot explain, even on their own theories, how Nahum with its long-range view, covering all subsequent centuries, could declare that no man would gather the scattered remains of Nineveh; yet 2,500 years of history have strikingly corroborated this forecast made before the city collapsed.[75]

Some of the other predictions which W.A.M. culled out of Nahum include: a long siege of Nineveh, frantic defense efforts, stormed city gates, drunken Assyrian soldiers led by an effeminate king, destruction of the city also by flood and fire, the ensuing slaughter of the inhabitants or their precipitous flight, general pillaging and plundering, desecration of all temples in the city limits, utter extirpation of the Assyrians, and the enduring memory of the wickedness of the Ninevites. All these, the author shows, were fulfilled, as can be verified from literary or archaeological sources.

In summary

The harmony between prediction and fulfillment is so clear and startling that some recent writers have declared the book to be a *post eventum* record of the fall. Thus Humbert says that the passages describing the fall of Nineveh are so precise and vivid that they were written after rather than before the event. But Nahum's book, even according to a critical consensus, is a preview rather than review, and as such it constitutes one of the most dramatic and electrifying instances of divine prophecy in the OT.[76]

12
PASTOR

Walter A. Maier authored a voluminous amount of devotional literature. While he never served a regular congregation as pastor, he compensated for it, in a sense, by his lifelong effort to help erect "the family altar" in as many homes as he could reach. He urged domestic worship in a final chapter from *The Happiest Home.*

Build the Family Altar!

During the first two Christian centuries there were apparently no church buildings. The early believers, man-hunted and persecuted, had no temples as did their heathen neighbors, no synagogs as did their Jewish friends. They often gathered in a private home, and unnoticed by the pagan hatred, they read the Scriptures, united in prayer, and raised their hymns to God. Without ecclesiastical buildings these first Christians had a firmer faith than many of us today. Christianity began for them where it should begin for us, among our own beloved. The apostle urges that we *"learn first to show piety at home"* (1 Timothy 5:4). When we know what Christ has done for us, we should strive to follow the example of the early Christians, who bravely founded the church in their homes.

Some years ago the Rev. Joseph Dare of Australia gave a missionary convention this account of prevailing family prayer among the converts in the Fiji Islands: "I was taking tea with a missionary and his wife in the lone island of Kandavu, in the midst of 10,000 Fijians. As we were at tea, the bell rang. The missionary said, 'That is the signal for family worship. Now listen. You will hear the drums beat.' And immediately they began to echo to each other around the shores of that southern sea. The missionary said, 'There are 10,000 people on these islands, and I do not know of a single house in which there will not be family worship in the course of half an hour from this time.'"—Yet, with the many superior blessings that are ours, thousands of Christian homes begin and close each day without thanks to God and prayer for His guidance.

Frequently it is objected that in our crowded, modern life no time remains for the family altar. However, we must make time for Him who gave His whole lifetime for us. Leaders in human affairs have often been noted for the faithfulness with which they maintained family worship. Few men since the days of the apostles have had the varied responsibilities which confronted Martin Luther. With his preaching, his writing, his instructing, and the titanic task of reforming the church, he still had time to worship Christ in his home. He writes: "Let him who can read take up each morning a psalm or other chapter in the Scriptures and study it for a time. This I do: When I rise with the children, I pray the Ten Commandments, the Creed, and the Lord's Prayer, and some psalm besides."

In the present crisis we have encouraging examples like that of Generalissimo Chiang Kai-Shek. A Canadian visitor on official business in Chungking, the capital, who was invited to dine at the general's home, tells how soon after his arrival the air-raid warnings were sounded. The Japanese, evidently in search of the Chinese leader, who was worth more to them than the capture of an army, destroyed an entire city block within less than a quarter of a mile from General Chiang Kai-Shek's dwelling. After dinner, when the Canadian prepared to take his leave, the general asked, "Must you go immediately? We shall be happy if you will stay and join us in our evening devotion." The invitation was accepted, a Bible was brought, and a portion of Holy Scripture read. Then the general began to pray. His guest relates: "I never expect to hear such a prayer again in all my life. The general began with a simple expression of thanks for their personal safety. Then he added thanks for the courage of the nation under fire. Then he prayed for strength for the men in the field and along the firing lines; he prayed for guidance and wisdom that he should not fail the people. But the most amazing thing in his prayer was a plea that God would help him, and help China, not to hate the Japanese people. He prayed for the Japanese Christians and all the suffering multitudes of Japan whose impoverishment was making the war on China possible. He prayed for the people who were bombed and for forgiveness for those who dropped the bombs." The Scripture-reading and prayer took a half hour, and when the visitor departed, he said to himself, "At last I have found two Christians." Could a casual dinner guest leave our homes with a similar conviction?

Frequently people write: "We should like to start family devotions, but we do not know how. Please help us!" No exceptional ability or technical preparations are required. Practical suggestions for the maintenance of the family altar may be reduced to these three:

1. Each devotion should embrace at least a portion of Scripture, a prayer by one of the family, and a prayer in unison. If time and circumstances permit, a few stanzas should be sung from the hymnal.

2. Scripture reading should be taken from the Bible, while the devotional exercises and the prayers may be read from one of many good devotional books, calendars, or pamphlets. Basic in all prayers should be the petition for the forgiveness of sin and the gratitude for Christ's redeeming grace. The spontaneous prayer from the heart of father or mother, mentioning the special, individual needs of the household, emphasizing the requests that crowd themselves into the family life, are of course particularly beneficial, but for some the most difficult of all prayers.—Why is it that we so often hesitate to discuss with our nearest relative and kin those needs which are of indescribable importance for our soul's welfare?

3. The devotional exercises should meet the understanding and the requirements of the younger members of the household.

Much depends on regularity of worship. If the family altar is neglected one day, it is twice as easy to neglect it the second day. When the Savior is worshiped in any family circle, irrespective of financial or social rating; when His Word is read and reverenced,

His name invoked in personal prayer, His glories sung in family hymns, that home becomes a blessed sanctuary; that family, by His own promise, *"Where two or three are gathered together in My name, there I am in the midst of them"* (Matthew 18:20), becomes a church, a house of God.

A home built on Joshua's resolution *"As for me and my house, we will serve the Lord"* (Joshua 24:15), may be shaken by storms of unemployment, illness, suffering, and death; but it will have a peace which a self-indulgent world knows not, for it will have Christ. Its walls may witness some of the tragedies bred by survivals of selfishness, but self-sacrifice and forbearance will triumph, as Christ hallows the relation of husband to wife and of parents to children. For that family circle, that altar-building, Sripture-searching home is the home of highest happiness. (*THH*, 61 ff.)

Quite exuberantly Dr. Maier practiced what he preached. No evening meal at the Maier household was ever concluded without family devotion, and he went far out of his way to provide the devotional literature he had called for in point 2 above. In 1935 he penned 40 Lenten meditations in a booklet entitled *Beautiful Savior*, after the *Lutheran Hour* sign-off theme. One of these follows.

The Sovereign Question

"Art Thou, then, the Son of God?"—Luke 22:70

Church history repeats itself. This question hurled at Jesus by the high priest: *"Art Thou, then, the Son of God?"* is asked and answered in every attitude which people today take toward their Savior. With more books written about Him than any other figure in history, with His name and His fame known to friend and foe alike, modern man, consciously or unconsciously, is put before this question: Is Christ the Son of God?

Jesus' own decisive *"I am"* is too frequently rejected. Many are ready to concede a certain greatness to Him. Some indeed would not hesitate to acclaim Him the greatest of all men, the most influential personage in all human development.

But let us remember that, if the Christ who was born in Bethlehem and died on Calvary is merely an innocent victim of unfavorable circumstances, who lived many centuries before His time, merely a social revolutionist who had come to submit a new code of ethics to a hard, cold world; if He is, as an eminent historian has designated Him, "the most perfect being who ever trod the soil of this planet," but only this, we must sacrifice the very essence of Christian hope.

But when we confess in the warm, pulsating words of Luther: "I believe that Jesus Christ, true God, begotten of the Father from eternity, and also true Man, born of the Virgin Mary, is my Lord," we have been granted the basic premise on which the great Reformer builds this conclusion: "who has redeemed me, a lost and condemned creature, purchased and won me from all sins, from death, and from the power of the devil."

Then we realize that Christ had to be God to achieve the superhuman task of appeasing the wrath of His Father, of accomplishing that which is humanly impossible: the vanquishing of sin, death, and hell. We know that He is God because the witness of His Spirit to the salvation of our souls remains as the peerless, priceless blessing of the faith and gives us the unshakable confidence that *"neither death nor life nor angels nor principalities nor powers nor things present nor things to come nor height nor depth nor any other creature shall be able to separate us from the love of God which is in Christ Jesus, our Lord."*[77]

A similar booklet followed in 1946, entitled *My Suffering Redeemer,* from which this excerpt is selected.

Jesus, Our King of Grace

"My kingdom is not of this world."—John 18:36

Earthly rulers use force. They maintain armies and navies. They wage war—offensive and defensive. But our Savior-King whom we behold persecuted before Pilate, as He says, "My kingdom is not of this world," reigns with grace, love and mercy. One day in exile on the lonely island of Saint Helena, Napoleon told General Montholon, his attendant, "Alexander, Caesar, Charlemagne, I myself have established far-flung empires. Upon what did we build our power? We have built upon force and violence. Jesus Christ has built His kingdom upon love." Christ the King, with a realm far greater than this world, gave His own body, shed His own blood to save us for eternity. Not long ago a cable from Asia revealed that in the heart of ancient Mongolia a silver casket has been found which apparently contained the remains of Genghis

Khan. This dispatch was restricted to a short paragraph tucked away with inconsequential news on an inside page. Yet Genghis Khan was perhaps the mightiest militarist of all times. He ruled from China to Europe; in twenty-two years, it is said, he killed fifteen million people. While today Genghis Khan is unknown to most people, millions dedicate their lives to Christ, the Lord of love, the Prince of peace, who gave Himself for His enemies, for the cruel priests and churchmen, plotters of His destruction, the fanatics screaming for His blood, the Roman soldiers guilty of the most monstrous misdeed in history. He died personally for you and for me, even though our thanklessness and rejection of divine mercy had arrayed us against God and His Anointed. No one else can save us but Christ, and there is no cleansing power besides His blood. Where human effort fails, Christ our King comes with heaven's mercy.

All other rulers in the changing pageants of history have lived their life span and then disappeared forever. Christ alone is eternal and gives eternity. In the great climax of His conquering love He completely vanquished the last enemy, death. What seems to be the triumph of the grave is really a joyful victory when sinners, saved by grace, are brought to the waiting arms of their Father in heaven.

In one of the smaller islands of the Philippines there is a street of unusual name and character, "Victory Road," leading to a cemetery. It is the way along which the broken, ravaged bodies of dead lepers from a Christian colony are carried to their final resting place. To them, as to St. Paul and all heroes of the faith, death is a glorious release, the evidence of eternal triumph. When Christ is your King, He will so fortify your courage that you too can exult: *"O death, where is thy sting? O grave, where is thy victory? . . . Thanks be to God, which giveth us the victory through our Lord Jesus Christ!"*[78]

In *"Christ Died for Us"* (1948) W.A.M. again had the suffering in mind with his meditation for Easter Sunday.

Easter Triumph

"It is sown in corruption, it is raised in incorruption; it is sown in dishonor, it is raised in glory; it is sown in weakness, it is raised in power; it is sown a natural body, it is raised a spiritual body.— 1 Corinthians 15:42-44

We can triumph at the empty tomb this Easter Day because the

236

new and heavenly life Christ promised us brings a bodily resurrection in which, marvelously beyond our understanding, our corpses will be raised, purified, glorified, and made perfect, without spot or blemish, without missing members, without scars and wounds, without dimmed or destroyed senses. What comfort this gives you, the tens of thousands of God's children who have stumps instead of limbs, hooks instead of hands, whose eyes are shrouded in darkness, whose lips are sealed in silence, whose ears are deaf and dead to every sound. What an inexpressible consolation to you who have spent most of your years on sickbeds, to know that in heaven with Jesus all sickness and sorrow will vanish. On Easter Day, before the open grave, make sure of this victory over sorrow and sickness, as God's own Word calls out: *"It is sown in corruption, it is raised in incorruption;* it is sown in dishonor, it is raised in glory; it is sown in weakness, it is raised in power; it is sown a natural body, it is raised a spiritual body."* For there the eternal truth promises: *"We shall also bear the image of the heavenly."*

Triumph also at the open grave because the everlasting life which Easter pledges all believers includes a blessed reunion of those who have died in the Lord. When the Last Day comes and the trumpet of God summons the dead to rise, all over the earth graves will be opened, and by the Easter victory the dead in Christ shall arise to live face to face with Him. Wherever the remains of God's children are, at home or abroad, they will be gloriously resurrected and before the celestial throne presented to the true and triune God.

For those, however, who love the Lord and know that because their sins have all been washed away, their heavenly Father will welcome them home to heaven, the promise of this life after death is the most marvelous blessing of their Savior's grace. They are assured there is a glorious existence beyond the grave where all the wrongs of earth will be righted.[79]

My Daily Prayer Guide (1940), *Wartime Prayer Guide* (1942), and *Continue in Prayer* (1947) were among the prayer books authored by Walter A. Maier. One specialized petition from the *Wartime Prayer Guide* can serve as an example of this form of writing.

For Those Missing in Action

Lord Jesus, Thy Word promises us that Thou didst come *"to*

seek and to save that which was lost." Thou Thyself didst tell us of the true Shepherd, who left the ninety-and-nine to go into the wilderness after the one stray lamb until He found it. Many men who have fought in the battles of this war have been listed as missing. We thank Thee, however, that they are not unknown to Thee. If it be Thy will and these defenders of our nation are still alive, bring them back to us in Thy time, and by Thy mercy lead them to a saving knowledge of Thy grace! But if they are never to be found, if they lie buried in some unmarked grave, then comfort all their dear ones with the hope of a heavenly reunion and the assurance that all who died in Christ will be raised again by Him! Hear us, precious Savior, who didst find us in our sin and bring us to grace! Amen.[80]

One final devotional format lay very close to W.A.M.'s heart. *Day by Day with Jesus* was—and is—an annual series of calendar leaflets for each day of the year with a 200-word meditation on one side while the other contains a prayer, a "Thought for the Day" (a key illustration), and a hymn stanza. Walter A. Maier authored a dozen years of this series from 1940 through 1951, increasing its circulation to nearly 50,000 copies annually. The 1950 and 1951 editions were published posthumously, and this is the obverse and reverse of the *Day by Day* leaflet for January 11, 1950 (the date of his own death), which sounded an Epiphany theme:

JANUARY
11—354

1950

Wednesday

11

MORNING
1 Chronicles 11

EVENING
Psalm 100

First Indian School established,
New England Puritans, 1651

"When they were come into the house, they saw the young Child with Mary, His mother."
—Saint Matthew 2, 11

When the Magi arrived at Bethlehem, the Holy Babe no longer lay in the manger. No more was Mary huddled in the stable of the over-crowded inn. Our Scripture text for this Wednesday tells us that the Christ Child and His mother were within a *"house."* Someone had found room for Jesus. The Infant Rescuer of the race at last had a home fit for human beings. Perhaps some sympathetic souls in Bethlehem, moved by pity for a baby in a stable mercifully shared their dwelling with Joseph, Mary, and the Child. We, too, can help furnish shelter for the homeless. The Son of God has promised to bless us, when in His name we remember the destitute millions driven from place to place. Especially should we welcome the Christ Child into our own homes by beseeching His presence at the beginning and end of each day, at every meal, and at dozens of other times. Our thoughts should constantly revert to the marvelous mercy which led Him, the Son of God, to become the Son of Man for us, to die, crucified as a criminal, yet in truth as the sinless Savior, who laid down His life to rescue every one of us from eternal ruin.

THOUGHT FOR THE DAY

Old Russian peasantry clings to the legend of Baboushka. She was at work in her house when the wise men from the East passed to find Christ. "Come with us," they said; "we have seen His star in the East." She answered, "I have my house to set in order. When this is done, I will find Him." She still searches for Him. It is she who in Russian and Italian houses is believed to fill the stockings and dress the tree on Christmas morn. The children are awakened by the cry, "Behold the Baboushka!" She fancies, so the legend goes, that in each poor little one whom she warms and feeds she may find the Christ Child, whom she neglected ages ago.—Adapt.

PRAYER

Heavenly Father, our great and glorious God: Praise and glory be to Thine infinite goodness for innumerable blessings of food and shelter, work and happiness which Thou hast granted the nation's families, and for all the glorious bounties with which Thou hast enriched us and our homes! Particularly do we thank Thee for our Savior, and the full, free, final gift of salvation in Christ's atoning death. Forgive us for His sake the ingratitude of our cold hearts and sealed lips! Help us translate our thankful thoughts into grateful deeds! We plead in Jesus' blessed name! Amen!

SPECIAL PRAYER

Entreaty for the conversion of the natives in the Pacific islands.

HYMN

Holy Jesus, every day
Keep us in the narrow way;
And, when earthly things are past,
Bring our ransomed souls at last
Where they need no star to guide,
Where no clouds Thy glory hide.

Walter A. Maier was a youngish age 56 when he died, and many in his vast audience questioned the timing of Providence. But the very day after he was buried, W.A.M. had a message for all his mourners.

JANUARY

15—350

1950

Sunday

15

MORNING
1 Chronicles 15

EVENING
1 Samuel 1, 20-28

THE SECOND SUNDAY AFTER EPIPHANY

First American passenger railroad,
the Charleston and Hamburg, 1831

"The sufferings of this present time are not worthy to be compared with the glory which shall be revealed in us."
—**Romans 8, 18**

The Holy Spirit help us believe the comfort contained in the Scripture text for this Lord's day, *"The sufferings of this present time are not worthy to be compared with the glory which shall be revealed in us!"* We should not let sorrow over our departed dear ones blot out the vision of the cross, the resurrection grave, the open heavens! Rather should we hear the Son of God promise, *"What I do thou knowest not now; but thou shalt know hereafter,"* and then kneel before Him with the victorious resignation, "Whatever God ordains is good!" When we believe the Gospel of Christ's atoning death for our life; when we begin to realize that one moment in heaven is worth more than centuries on earth, we will understand that God let our Christ-dedicated dear ones meet death so that they could the longer enjoy the hallowed bliss and beauty with their Redeemer. Then, washed in the blood of the Lamb, resurrected in celestial radiance, we will know in higher knowledge that our hours of agony are *"not worthy to be compared with the glory which shall be revealed in us,"* when, face to face with Jesus, the unspeakable glories of Heaven are ours.

Within a week a mass of mail with that leaflet arrived at the Maier residence in St. Louis, expressing the hope that his own family would not miss the message in the turmoil.

The same triumphant eschatology is expressed in this final selection from a *Lutheran Hour* sermon in 1946. It shows that a versatile, Harvard-honed intellect, expressing itself with voice and pen in a dozen different roles, could still reflect a childlike faith.

240

Believers like to dwell on the happiness of meeting certain people in heaven. As for me, if I have time—provided there is time in eternity—after worshiping the glorious Trinity, I want to meet my Christ-exalting father and mother, who helped bring me into the Kingdom. I want to stand with my whole family, my wife and sons, before the throne to say, *"Behold I and the children which God hath given me."* I want to sit at the feet of the men who wrote the Bible, the people who built the church, the saints whom the Lord used to keep its truth for me. With Martin Luther I want to sing, in fulfillment of Scripture's promises, "A Mighty Fortress Is Our God." It is my heart's special desire, however, and I pray for this daily, that I will meet all of you there, my beloved. I want the joy of knowing that you to whom I have written, whom I have warned, with whom I have pleaded, whom I have pointed to Christ, have come all the way to Jesus. Will you be there? Will we meet before the throne? God grant that we will![81]

NOTES

1. *The American Lutheran,* XXXIII (February 1950), 4.
2. Paul L. Maier, *A Man Spoke, a World Listened* (New York: McGraw-Hill, 1963), p. 77.
3. *Ibid.,* p. 158.
4. Walter A. Maier, *Courage in Christ* (St. Louis: Concordia Publishing House, 1941), pp. 215 f.
5. Walter A. Maier, *The Jeffersonian Ideals of Religious Liberty* (St. Louis: Concordia Publishing House, 1930).
6. Walter A. Maier, *For Better, Not for Worse* (St. Louis: Concordia Publishing House, Second Edition, 1936), pp. v ff.
7. *Ibid.,* pp. 9 ff.
8. *Ibid.,* p. 49.
9. *Ibid.,* pp. 485 f.
10. From the original sermon manuscript, as preserved by Arthur Carl Piepkorn, a copy of which is at the Concordia Historical Institute in St. Louis. This sermon appeared under the title "The Folly of Atheism" with addenda in Walter A. Maier, *The Lutheran Hour* (St. Louis: Concordia Publishing House, 1931), pp. 45 ff.
11. Walter A. Maier, *Christ for the Nation* (St. Louis: Concordia Publishing House, 1936), pp. 11 ff.
12. Walter A. Maier, *The Cross from Coast to Coast* (St. Louis: Concordia Publishing House, 1938), p. 179.
13. Walter A. Maier, *Go Quickly and Tell* (St. Louis: Concordia Publishing House, 1950), pp. 345 ff.
14. Walter A. Maier, *For Christ and Country* (St. Louis: Concordia Publishing House, 1942), p. 173.

15. Walter A. Maier, *Christ for Every Crisis* (St. Louis: Concordia Publishing House, 1935), p. 49.
16. Maier, *The Lutheran Hour*, pp. 248 ff.
17. Walter A. Maier, *He Will Abundantly Pardon* (St. Louis: Concordia Publishing House, 1948), p. 87.
18. Maier, *Courage in Christ*, p. 226.
19. Maier, *For Christ and Country*, p. 14.
20. Walter A. Maier, *One Thousand Radio Voices for Christ* (St. Louis: Concordia Publishing House, 1950), p. 338.
21. Walter A. Maier, *Rebuilding with Christ* (St. Louis: Concordia Publishing House, 1946), pp. 109 ff.
22. Maier, *For Christ and Country*, pp. 358 f.
23. Walter A. Maier, *Fourth Lutheran Hour* (St. Louis: Concordia Publishing House, 1937), p. 239.
24. Maier, *Courage in Christ*, p. 227.
25. Maier, *The Cross from Coast to Coast*, p. 233.
26. Maier, *Go Quickly and Tell*, p. 16.
27. Maier, *The Cross from Coast to Coast*, p. 225.
28. Maier, *Christ for the Nation*, p. 63.
29. Maier, *Courage in Christ*, pp. 70 f.
30. Walter A. Maier, *Jesus Christ, Our Hope* (St. Louis: Concordia Publishing House, 1946), p. 176.
31. Maier, *Rebuilding with Christ*, p. 6.
32. *Ibid.*, p. 28.
33. Maier, *Fourth Lutheran Hour*, pp. 151—62. The date given for the sermon—here and subsequently—is the year the sermon was actually delivered on *The Lutheran Hour*, not when it appeared later in book form.
34. Walter A. Maier, *Global Broadcasts of His Grace* (St. Louis: Concordia Publishing House, 1949), pp. 173—194. Apparently this was also one of W.A.M.'s favorite sermons, since he provided the bulk of its thrust for a much shortened version in G. Paul Butler, ed., *Best Sermons, 1949—50 Edition* (New York: Harper & Brothers, 1949). pp. 105 ff.
35. Maier, *Fourth Lutheran Hour*, pp. 333—44.
36. Maier, *Rebuilding with Christ*, pp. 277—93.
37. Maier, *Christ for the Nation*, p. 77.
38. Maier, *Jesus Christ, Our Hope*, pp. 106 f.
39. Maier, *For Christ and Country*, p. 183.
40. Maier, *Courage in Christ*, pp. 31 f.
41. Maier, *Global Broadcasts of His Grace*, pp. 237 f.
42. Walter A. Maier, *America, Turn to Christ* (St. Louis: Concordia Publishing House, 1944), p. 300.
43. Maier, *The Cross from Coast to Coast*, p. 130.
44. Maier, *Rebuilding with Christ*, p. 166.
45. *Ibid.*, pp. 156 f.
46. Maier, *Go Quickly and Tell*, p. 330.
47. *Ibid.*, p. 332.
48. Maier, *Jesus Christ, Our Hope*, pp. 13 f.
49. Maier, *Christ for the Nation*, p. 210.
50. Maier, *Fourth Lutheran Hour*, pp. 121 ff.
51. *Ibid.*, pp. 135 f.

52. Walter A. Maier, *Let Us Return unto the Lord* (St. Louis: Concordia Publishing House, 1947), p. 149.
53. Walter A. Maier, *The Airwaves Proclaim Christ* (St. Louis: Concordia Publishing House, 1948), p. 170.
54. Maier, *Christ for the Nation,* pp. 269—71.
55. Maier, *America, Turn to Christ,* p. 14.
56. Maier, *Christ for the Nation,* pp. 182—92.
57. This paragraph only in this sermon derives from another address on prayer W.A.M. had written earlier, "God Answers Prayer," in *Christ for the Nation,* pp. 63 f. It is included here because it was a point W.A.M. usually made in his messages on prayer.
58. Maier, *Courage in Christ,* pp. 39—51.
59. The published version of this prayer appears in Maier, *For Christ and Country,* p. 102. It was aired, however, on December 7, whereas the sermon, "America, Embattled, Turn to Christ!" with which it is linked was broadcast on December 14, 1941.
60. Maier, *For Christ and Country,* pp. 102—15.
61. *Ibid.,* pp. 314—28.
62. *Ibid.,* pp. 204—17.
63. Walter A. Maier, *Victory Through Christ* (St. Louis: Concordia Publishing House, 1943), pp. 58—71.
64. *The Dr. Walter A. Maier Memorial Booklet* (St. Louis: Lutheran Laymen's League, 1950), pp. 6—19. This sermon was edited for this anthology, however, on the basis of the actual broadcast manuscript W.A.M. used for his final program and therefore incorporates nearly all the cuts entered on that document. This text, then, closely approximates what actually went out over the air.
65. *Ibid.,* pp. 20—34.
66. From unpublished ms. for the *Lutheran Hour* address for ABC on January 1, 1950. Only Part II apparently was dictated. This ms., along with others, is in the Maier Archives at the Concordia Historical Institute, Concordia Seminary, St. Louis.
67. *Maier Memorial Booklet,* pp. 44 f.
68. Walter A. Maier, "Archaeology—the Nemesis," *Concordia Theological Monthly,* IV (February 1933), 95—7. The other articles followed in the March and April issues.
69. Walter A. Maier, *The Book of Nahum* (St. Louis: Concordia Publishing House, 1959), p. 29.
70. *Ibid.,* pp. 30 f.
71. *Ibid.,* pp. 69 f.
72. *Ibid.,* p. 81.
73. *Ibid.,* p. 85.
74. *Ibid.,* p. 86.
75. *Ibid.,* p. 134.
76. *Ibid.,* p. 139.
77. Walter A. Maier, *Beautiful Savior* (St. Louis: Concordia Publishing House, 1935), p. 25. This booklet was reprinted with addenda by the Lutheran Laymen's League in 1945.
78. Walter A. Maier, *My Suffering Redeemer* (St. Louis: Lutheran Laymen's League, 1946), p. 38.
79. Walter A. Maier, *"Christ Died for Us"* (St. Louis: Lutheran Laymen's League, 1948), p. 84.

80. Walter A. Maier, *Wartime Prayer Guide* (St. Louis: The International Lutheran Hour, 1942), p. 15.
81. Maier, *He Will Abundantly Pardon,* pp. 12 f.

BIBLIOGRAPHY

Writings of Walter A. Maier

Books

(Listed in chronological order)

The Lutheran Hour. St. Louis: Concordia Publishing House, 1931. 324 pp.

Christ for Every Crisis. St. Louis: Concordia Publishing House, 1935. 174 pp.

For Better, Not for Worse. St. Louis: Concordia Publishing House, 1935. 557 pp.

Christ for the Nation. St. Louis: Concordia Publishing House, 1936. 272 pp.

Fourth Lutheran Hour. St. Louis: Concordia Publishing House, 1937. 357 pp.

The Cross from Coast to Coast. St. Louis: Concordia Publishing House, 1938, 403 pp.

The Radio for Christ. St. Louis: Concordia Publishing House, 1939. 417 pp.

Peace Through Christ. St. Louis: Concordia Publishing House, 1940. 364 pp.

Courage in Christ. St. Louis: Concordia Publishing House, 1941. 387 pp.

For Christ and Country. St. Louis: Concordia Publishing House, 1942. 392 pp.

Victory Through Christ. St. Louis: Concordia Publishing House, 1943. 411 pp.

America, Turn to Christ! St. Louis: Concordia Publishing House, 1944. 341 pp.

Christ, Set the World Aright! St. Louis: Concordia Publishing House, 1945. 377 pp.

Jesus Christ, Our Hope. St. Louis: Concordia Publishing House, 1946. 289 pp.

Rebuilding with Christ. St. Louis: Concordia Publishing House, 1946. 310 pp.

Let Us Return unto the Lord. St. Louis: Concordia Publishing House, 1947. 319 pp.

He Will Abundantly Pardon. St. Louis: Concordia Publishing House, 1948. 373 pp.

The Airwaves Proclaim Christ. St. Louis: Concordia Publishing House, 1948. 297 pp.

Global Broadcasts of His Grace. St. Louis: Concordia Publishing House, 1949. 308 pp. and succeeding editions.

One Thousand Radio Voices for Christ. St. Louis: Concordia Publishing House, 1950. 454 pp.

Go Quickly and Tell. St. Louis: Concordia Publishing House, 1950. 444 pp.

The Book of Nahum. A Commentary. St. Louis: Concordia Publishing House, 1959. 386 pp. and succeeding editions.

Three sermon book manuscripts for the 16th and 17th *Lutheran Hour* seasons are unpublished.

Booklets

The Jeffersonian Ideals of Religious Liberty. St. Louis: Concordia Publishing House, 1930. 22 pp.

Beautiful Savior. St. Louis: Concordia Publishing House, 1935. 48 pp. Reprinted with addenda by The Lutheran Laymen's League, 1945. 83 pp.

The Happiest Home. St. Louis: The Lutheran Laymen's League, 1941. 72 pp.

My Suffering Redeemer. St. Louis: The Lutheran Laymen's League, 1946. 83 pp.

Christ Crucified. St. Louis: The Lutheran Laymen's League, 1947. 83 pp.

"Christ Died for Us." St. Louis: The Lutheran Laymen's League, 1948. 85 pp.

"Behold the Lamb of God!" St. Louis: The Lutheran Laymen's League, 1949. 83 pp.

Prayer Booklets

My Daily Prayer Guide. St. Louis: The Lutheran Laymen's League, 1940. 48 pp.

Wartime Prayer Guide. St. Louis: The International Lutheran Hour, 1942. 65 pp.

"Continue in Prayer!" St. Louis: The Lutheran Laymen's League, 1947. 65 pp.

"Pray Without Ceasing!" St. Louis: The Lutheran Laymen's League, 1948. 65 pp.

"Lord, Teach Us to Pray!" St. Louis: The Lutheran Laymen's League, 1949. 65 pp.

Other Devotional Literature

Day by Day with Jesus—A Christian Devotional Calendar. New York: Ernst Kaufmann, Inc., 1940 through 1951. 365 or 366 pp. each.

KFUO Tracts—Addresses Broadcast over Station KFUO. Nos. 1—16. St. Louis: Concordia Publishing House, 1926—30. 13-15 pp. each.

Articles

Space prohibits a complete listing here of the hundreds of articles and editorials W.A.M. authored for *The Walther League Messenger,* Volumes XXIX (December 1920) through LIII (July 1945), as well as for other popular, professional, and scholarly journals. A complete collection of all his writings is available at the Maier Archives, Concordia Historical Institute, Concordia Seminary, St. Louis, Mo.

DATE
SEP 2
DEMCO 38-297